Masculinities in Joyce

To Terry,

with affection and
overwhelming gratitude. You know
better than anyone else how you
have made this book possible.
You are the indispensible person.

How can I adequately thank you?

Endlessly in your debt,

Cappen

EUROPEAN JOYCE STUDIES

10

General Editor: Fritz Senn
Associate Editor: Christine van Boheemen

POSTCOLONIAL CONSTRUCTIONS

Edited by

Christine van Boheemen-Saaf
and
Colleen Lamos

DEDICATED TO

TERRY MUNISTERI

Amsterdam - Atlanta, GA 2001

EJS gratefully acknowledges permission from the Poetry and Rare Books Room at SUNY-Buffalo to use Brancusi's profile of Joyce on the cover.

The paper on which this book is printed meets the requirements of "ISO 9706:1994, Information and documentation - Paper for documents - Requirements for permanence".

ISBN: 90-420-1276-5 (bound)
©Editions Rodopi B.V., Amsterdam - Atlanta, GA 2001
Printed in The Netherlands

CONTENTS

BIBLIOGRAPHICAL NOTE

In keeping with the previous volumes in the series we adopt the following conventions to refer to what we have treated as the standard editions of Joyce's works:

CW   Joyce, James. *The Critical Works of James Joyce*, ed. Ellsworth Mason and Richard Ellmann. New York: Viking Press, 1959.

D   Joyce, James. *Dubliners*, ed. Robert Scholes in consultation with Richard Ellmann. New York: Viking Press, 1967.

FW   Joyce, James. *Finnegans Wake*. New York: Viking Press, 1939; London: Faber and Faber, 1939. These two editions have identical pagination.

GJ   Joyce, James. *Giacomo Joyce*, ed. Richard Ellmann. New York: Viking Press, 1968.

JJII   Richard Ellmann, *James Joyce*, rev. ed. (New York: Oxford University Press, 1982).

Letters I, II, III Joyce, James. *Letters of James Joyce*. Vol. I, ed. Stuart Gilbert. New York: Viking Press, 1957; reissued with corrections 1966. Vols. II and III, ed. Richard Ellmann. New York: Viking Press, 1964.

P   Joyce, James. "*A Portrait of the Artist as a Young Man: Text, Criticism, and Notes*, ed. Chester G. Anderson. New York: Viking Press, 1958.

SH   Joyce, James. *Stephen Hero*, ed. John J. Slocum and Herbert Cahoon. New York: Viking Press, 1975.

U   +episode and line number. Joyce, James. *Ulysses*, ed. Hans Walter Gabler, et al. New York and London: Garland Publishing, 1984, 1986. In paperback by Garland, Random House, and Bodley Head and by Penguin between 1986 and 1992.

JOYCEAN MASCULINITIES
INTRODUCTION

COLLEEN LAMOS
and
CHRISTINE VAN BOHEEMEN-SAAF

Masculinities in Joyce: Postcolonial Constructions is the first volume to address the topic of masculinity in relation to Joyce's writings. The essays compiled here range in their discussion from *Dubliners* to *Finnegans Wake*, and they focus upon masculinity from a variety of angles and critical methodologies. Drawing upon historical research, and the intersecting insights of postcolonial, poststructuralist, feminist and queer theories, they examine the complexity, and the contradictions, of the construction of masculinity in Joyce's work in close detail. The premise of this book is that masculinity, like femininity, is an ideologically constructed parameter of human identity, and that understanding the principles and implications of that constructedness adds to one's insight in both literature and history.[1]

Although masculinity studies is fast establishing itself as a new and challenging subject of inquiry, hitherto the representation of masculinity in Joyce, the ideological and textual structures by which it is supported and defined, its cultural and political constraints, have not yet received

---

[1] For an introduction to masculinity studies see: J. Hearn and D. Morgan, eds., *Men: Masculinities and Social Theory* (London: Hyman and Unwin, 1990); or Mairtin Mac An Ghaill, *Understanding Masculinities* (Milton Keanes: Open University Press, 1996).

much critical attention.[2] One of the reasons for this hesitancy to broach this rich subject, which was taken up eagerly by both postcolonial and Irish studies almost a decade ago,[3] may be that Joyce studies has been marked by an unusually strong interest in feminism and Joyce's representation of women. While the cultural construction of femininity in Joyce, and Joyce's supposedly "feminine" style were the subject of intense critical debate, the realization that Joyce's depiction of masculinity in fiction is similarly constructed, and no less deeply (counter)ideological, was left to wait.

The most important conclusion of the essays in this volume is that masculinity, as Joyce portrays it, is characterized by a remarkable degree of internal contradiction. Masculinity seems a continual dilemma rather than a definitive state, or a sexual or social identity. Joyce's protagonists must labour to maintain a precarious sense of self-identity and self-respect, whether as young boys or fully mature profesional men. In its premises, effects, and implications, in Joyce, masculine gender proves an unstable construct that generates intense self-consciousness and doubt. Thus the following essays present an exploration of the specific constraints and demands placed upon Irish men in the early twentieth century, including men's traumas and shames, their fetishes and anxieties, their humiliating abjections and strategies of survival.

Moreover, the study of masculinity in Joyce's texts opens a wider critical perspective on the operations of

---

[2] The notable exception is Joseph Valente, ed. *Quare Joyce* (Ann Arbor: University of Michigan Press, 1998).

[3] See *Nationalisms and Sexualities*, ed. Andrew Parker, Mary Russo, Doris Sommer, and Patricia Yaeger (New York and London: Routledge, 1992).

gender   in   literary modernism in general. The analyses of our contributors of the functions of masculinity in Joyce's works provide numerous points of comparison and contrast with the treatment of masculinity in the works of other male modernist writers. A growing body of scholarship on T.S. Eliot, William Faulkner, Ernest Hemingway, F. Scott Fitzgerald and others indicates that masculinity is proving a challenging subject within the field of modernist studies, as well as within postcolonial and Irish studies. Because the essays in this volume show that Joyce's texts subvert contemporary gender and sexual norms (and collude with them), Joyce's works pose masculinity as a problem which challenges the more traditional representation of masculinity in modernist literature. Joyce's *oeuvre* also presents a problem to some forms of poststructuralist and queer theory.

Although not everywhere made explicit, the common perspective taken by these essays is that the particular construction of masculinity in Joyce's work cannot be divorced from the specific cultural and ideological conditions of the world in which his narratives are set. The consequences of Ireland's history as a colonized nation also pertain to gender identity. The English cherished a long-standing tradition of feminizing Ireland, most remarkably in the nineteenth century. As recent Joyce scholarship has often emphasized, writers such as Ernest Renan and, following him, Matthew Arnold, pontificated on the racial character of the Celts, rendering the difference with the English in terms of gender difference: "[I]f it be permitted us to assign sex to nations as to individuals we should have to say without hesitation that the Celtic race . . . is an essentially feminine race."[4] Arnold, in "On the Study of

---

[4] Ernest Renan, *The Poetry of the Celtic Races*, trans. W. G. Hutchison (London: Walter Scott, 1897), p. 8.

Celtic Literature," concludes that "the sensibility of the Celtic nature, its nervous exaltation, have something feminine in them, and the Celt is thus particularly disposed to feel the spell of the feminine idiosyncrasy; he has an affinity to it; he is not far from its secret."[5] Little attention has been given to the paradox this construction presents to the self-understanding of the Irish male: the complexities imposed on strategies of maintaining self-respect, of projecting masculine authority in social situations or exercising paternal control at home. These essays address the complexity of Irish masculinity in the context of the cultural contradiction inherent in the colonial situation. They do not present Joyce as a nationalist or even a political writer, however. Rather, they illustrate the ambivalence of Joyce's relationship to British imperialism, his collusion with as well as subversion of the masculine norms advanced by the Empire. Instead of outlining a clear and circumscribed profile of Joyce as either in resistance or in compliance, nationalist or cosmopolitan, these essays display the intricacies of Joyce's implication in the ambivalently gendered construction of subaltern masculine identity, which he makes visible in his art.

In presenting the essays in this volume, we hope to open up new and important avenues for future Joyce studies, and above all, to demonstrate the relevance of inquiries into the constructions of masculinity in the intersection of Joyce studies with scholarship in the fields of postcolonial studies, modernist studies, cultural studies, queer studies, psychoanalys and philosophy. In other words, this collection intends to be more than a series of readings of the ways in which Joyce's texts portray or stage

[5] Matthew Arnold, *On the Study of Celtic Literature and Other Essays* (1910; reprint, New York: Dutton, 1976), p. 86-87.

masculine roles. Our intention is to demonstrate the inescapable link between constructions of textuality, or personal, national or literary-historical identity, and configurations of gender.

In addition, we argue that the study of literary texts may be a means of retrieving the cultural unconscious. As Fredric Jameson argues, it is possible that we are unable to fully grasp historical forces by direct observation. He suggests that, like the Lacanian "Real," the forces of history elude consciousness. It is in textual form, as story and narrative, that the past may become accessible as representation reveals the interplay of repression, prohibition and proscription that constitutes cultural contradiction.[6] Since sexuality and gender are central in social and economic organization as well as in our sense of self, a study of masculinity in the works of Joyce may have wider implications than just literary ones. It may point to a history which consciousness has not been able to grasp as yet.

The essays in this volume may be roughly grouped into categories, clustering around the following concerns: 1) Masculinity and the effects of colonialism. 2) The subversion of stereotyped gender roles. 3) Masculinity and homosociality or homosexuality. 4) Masculinity and literary authority. 5) Joycean masculinities and theory. These categories overlap, of course, so that one essay may contribute to more than one of the perspectives offered above; but outlining them in this way offers an overview of the book's recurring and central themes and perspectives. By contrast, the order of the essays in *Masculinities in Joyce: Postcolonial Constructions* roughly tracks the chronology of

---

6 *The Political Unconscious: Narrative as a Socially Symbolic Act* (Ithaca: Cornell University Press, 1981).

the publication of Joyce's works from *Dubliners* to *Finnegans Wake*. Our reason for presenting them in this more or less sequential order is that there may have been an internal dialectic at work in Joyce's thinking about masculinity. As we get closer to *Finnegans Wake*, the intellectual dilemma which masculinity and identity present seems to become more acute. Whereas the stories of *Dubliners* sketch the complexities and pitfalls of maintaining masculine and authorial self-presence in Dublin around the turn of the nineteenth century in painful detail, *Finnegans Wake* seems to ridicule the claim to self-presence of the Shaun figure, and to reduce Shem's writerly authority to joyful wallowing in the filth of anal creativity. Thus the final work ironizes the preoccupation with masculinity which is the central concern of the earlier works.

The essays collected in *Masculinities in Joyce: Postcolonial Constructions* demonstrate the fruitfulness of masculinity as a subject as well as a variety of modes of addressing it. By examining masculinity in Joyce's works we have attempted to explore its historical and cultural contingencies, and to open up masculinity as a problematic construction in need of scholarly attention.

Rice University.
University of Amsterdam.

MASCULINITY GAMES IN "AFTER THE RACE"

MARGOT NORRIS

Abstract. "After the Race" may be read as a story in which the social insecurity of the arriviste combines with homosocial desire to make a nouveau riche young Irishman vulnerable to predations whose object is financial, but whose tactics are homosocial and masculinist. If Jimmy Doyle's Continental Cambridge friends are construed as swindlers out to despoil Jimmy of the fortune he had planned to invest in their motor enterprise, their strategies become visible as a staging of the structure and devices of seduction and rape.

James Joyce's story "After the Race" exhibits a curious paradox. As the *Dubliners* story representing the most powerful figures--economically and socially--the story itself has emerged as perhaps the weakest in the collection and the one most vulnerable to critical disparagement. Emboldened by Joyce's own judgment--"The two worst stories are *After the Race* and *A Painful Case*" ("Letter to Stanislaus Joyce, 6 November 1906,[1]--Warren Beck virtually dismisses the story for being "labored" and "awkward" in narrative technique; and, in comparison to the other stories in the collection, he finds them "less penetrating," "sketchier," and "the least realized."[2] Whether or not one

---

[1] James Joyce to Stanislaus Joyce, 6 November 1906, *Selected Letters* 123. I am indebted to H. Riikkonen of the University of Helsinki for pointing this letter out to me. Tanja Vesala-Varttala's dissertation chapter on "After the Race" (entitled "Whose Folly? A Dialogic Evaluation of Jimmy Doyle") also gave my study of "After the Race" much inspiration. I thank them both.

[2] Warren Beck, *Joyce's "Dubliners": Substance, Vision, and Art* (Durham, N.C.: Duke University Press, 1969), p. 123.

concurs with these judgments, the story's vulnerability deserves to be explored through a somewhat less formalistic prism than Beck's. Like Beck, I am inclined to find the story's weakness linked to the class and status of its figures. But I am convinced that the story's vulnerability is less a symptom of Joyce's social inexperience with the upper-middle class -- "Possibly Joyce, in weighing such a segment of Dublin life, knew too little of it at first hand, and also shared, if anything, some of its naïvete"[3] -- than a strategy for staging the paradoxes of masculinity and masculinism.

R. B. Kershner puts his finger on one aspect of the story's vulnerability when he calls Jimmy Doyle a "helpful" animal (in contrast to Eveline's "helpless animal") "who assists in his own embarrassment."[4] Jimmy's embarrassment, of which the narrator is an agent and the reader an uncomfortable spectator, is dilated within a social space defined by the intersection of an arriviste class dimension and a homosocial gender dimension. The social insecurities of the Doyles are inscribed in the Victorian resonances of disparaged "trade" in Mr. Doyle's epithet of "merchant prince" (*D* 43), and the narrator is quick to remind us that the species of trade was of a particularly vulgar kind ("He had made his money as a butcher" [*D* 43]) with possible overtones of graft and betrayal shadowing its success ("He had also been fortunate enough to secure some of the police contracts" [*D* 43]).[5] But

---

[3] Beck, p. 124.

[4] R. B. Kershner, *Joyce, Bakhtin, and Popular Literature: Chronicles of Disorder* (Chapel Hill: University of North Carolina Press, 1989), p. 72.

[5] Joyce troubled to verify the plausibility of Mr. Doyle's police contract by asking his brother Stanislaus to check on the matter: "Dear Stannie Please send me the information I ask you for as follows: . . . *After the Race*--

maneuver in depicting the social world of "After the Race" as exclusively homosocial has the effect of generalizing the Doyles' specific social insecurities by complicating their symbolic order with the perils of gender. More specifically, I believe that Joyce has the volatile commercial economy in the story -- the thrill of fortunes rapidly gained and lost by the Doyles, *père* and *fils* -- function to trope the Doyles' equally labile symbolic economy of social regard and prestige. The thrill and anxiety that attends uncontrollable gain and loss -- figured also in the various forms of masculine sport and gaming in the story -- can be psychoanalytically grounded in the constitutive effects produced by the castration complex in the assumption of gender. Jacques Lacan argues that the knot-like structure of the unconscious castration complex produces a paradox in that the very dynamism governing the terror of loss that produces pathological symptoms is inescapably necessary for the achievement of gender identity: "There is an antimony, here, that is internal to the assumption by man (*Mensch*) of his sex: why must he assume the attributes of that sex only through a threat -- the threat, indeed, of their privation."[6] Both male and female children unconsciously "experience" the perceptual error that elaborates the presence or absence of the penis into a narrative of violence and loss whose redemption is accomplished by the compensations and appeasements of the gender identification process. But the condition of apparent absence in the female creates a secondary

---

Are the police supplied with provisions by government or by private contracts?" (*Selected Letters* 75). Richard Ellmann's note to this query says that "[t]his detail does not appear in the published story," although it patently does.

[6] Jacques Lacan, *Écrits: A Selection*, trans. Alan Sheridan (New York: W. W. Norton, 1977), p. 281.

méconnaissance with consequences for the delineation of sexual, and gender, difference: the female "lack" is endowed with *temporal* significance in a translation that castration has already occurred and is behind her, while for the male it remains proleptic, a psychic sword of Damocles that constitutes masculinity as only provisionally unmutilated and perpetually imperilled. I invoke this speculative elaboration of the Lacanian theory of gender formation in order to suggest an etiology of primal anxiety to the febrile temper of the action in "After the Race" and to the provisionality of the narrative rhetoric. The ontological perils of masculinity are both represented and performed in the text.

Temporality is, of course, the donnée of the story's title -- taken from an interview with one of the French contenders for the 1903 Gordon Bennett Cup Race that Joyce published in the *Irish Times* in April 1903. "Will you remain any time in Ireland?" Joyce asked the racing champion and automotive tycoon Henri Fournier. Fournier replied with a question --"After the race?"[7] -- and answered that he would not. The temporal order of the interview and the story are reversed -- Joyce interviews Fournier *before* the race, but he sets the story *after* the race. Joyce then inverts the causality of Fournier's success--making his firm's fabulous prosperity merely proleptic in the story ("money to be made in the motor business, pots of money" [*D* 45]), and giving it a fictional genesis that sketches how an enterprise like "Paris Automobile" might have gotten started with the unscrupulous exploitation of a naïve rich young Irishman *after* the July 1903 Gordon Bennett Cup Race. Judging from Joyce's preface to the interview we could speculate that the young Joyce might have wished to

---

[7] James Joyce, "The Motor Derby," in *CW*, p. 108.

take revenge on the highly successful Fournier ("on great shelves extending from the floor to the roof are ranged motor-cars of all sizes, shapes, and colours" [*CW* 106]) who kept him waiting for hours on several occasions before granting a terse and unresponsive interview: "[It] is almost impossible to see M. Fournier unless one is prepared to wait two or three hours for one's turn. . . . The morning, however, is more favourable, and yesterday morning, after two failures, I succeeded in seeing M. Fournier" (*CW* 107). In "After the Race" Joyce inverts the psychological temper of the scenario -- if not its deep structure -- by making the blasé young Frenchman, who yielded only the dull and meager calculations of speed to Joyce in the interview, now eager to impress the young Irishman with his automotive knowledge:, "Rivière, not wholly ingenuously, undertook to explain to Jimmy the triumph of the French mechanicians"(*D* 46). Joyce sets the story at a liminal moment when the young Frenchman's fortune hangs in the balance of a fictional transaction whose tender is purely symbolic: the metaphysical desire of Jimmy Doyle, his thirst for prestige and recognition, for social status, that Garry Leonard formulates in the Hegelian dynamic of "Jimmy Doyle's slavish dependence on the Other to authenticate the myth of himself."[8] This Hegelian genealogy informs Lacan's coincidence of the genesis of desire with the genesis of gender, which identifies masculinity as the ongoing negotiation with the Other in the quest for significance, and as defense against its loss. One can speculate that the young Joyce -- stung by the young Frenchman's hauteur and disregard -- went on to undergird the founding of the modern French automotive industry with a fable of French

[8] Garry M. Leonard, *Reading "Dubliners" Again: A Lacanian Perspective* (Syracuse: Syracuse University Press, 1993), p. 116.

masculinism's exploitation of Irish social and cultural insecurity.[9]

Like many other *Dubliners* stories, "After the Race" hints at an embedded hidden narrative that can be inferred and hermeneutically constructed from the narrative account of the narrative events, but not verified.[10] The liminality of the story's moment -- the poising of the events on the evening after the race as a threshold for changing fortunes -- holds the key to a specific scenario of a young Irishman's exploitation by a group of sophisticated foreigners whose actions have the ethical significance of a seduction and rape, specifically, a species of homosocial date-rape or gang-rape. To construct this scenario, the issue of temporality needs to be clarified with respect to the timing of Jimmy Doyle's investment in Ségouin's company. The ambiguity of the language --"Ségouin, perhaps, would not think it a great sum" and "he was about to stake the greater part of his substance" (*D* 44)--leads Garry Leonard to assume that the investment has already taken place ("Doyle has invested a good deal of his father's money in

[9] James Fairhall, after researching a number of *Irish Times* articles and editorials on Dublin's hosting of the Gordon Bennett Cup Race in 1903, concludes, "We can see why Joyce chose the Gordon Bennett Cup auto race as the backdrop for this glimpse into the lives of Dublin's *nouveaux riches*. It provided an opportunity to show Ireland as the victim not just of England, but of the international imperialist and capitalist order, and a somewhat willing victim at that" ("Big Power Politics and Colonial Economics: The Gordon Bennett Cup Race and 'After the Race,'" *James Joyce Quarterly* (Winter 1991): 395).

[10] The story that follows "After the Race" is "Two Gallants," in which, I argue, there is a similar hidden transaction that requires Corley to extort money from the slavey, in return for romance, sex, and the implicit prospect of marriage, in order to repay a debt to Lenehan, who perhaps owes money to loansharks borrowed to bet on the Gold Cup Race. See my essay "Gambling with Gambles in 'Two Gallants,'" in *Novel* (Fall 1995): 32-44.

Ségouin's new motor establishment".[11] I will suggest that we can better account for the Continentals' blandishments of Jimmy and the Doyles by reading the temporal tense of the investment as proleptic, and by imputing the extravagance of the evening's arrangements and excitements to the grooming of a business deal that has been pledged but not yet consummated. One can speculate even further that the evening's events could be the outcome of a venture to secure Jimmy's promised investment without the legal encumbrance of the Doyles, by simply stripping the dazzled and overstimulated young Irishman of the money he is known to possess ("he really had a great sum under his control" [D 44]) in a drunken game of cards. "Jimmy did not know who was winning, but he knew that he was losing. But it was his own fault for he frequently mistook his cards and the other men had to calculate his I.O.U.'s for him" (D 48).

Although my scenario is difficult to prove, there is nothing in the story that precludes it, and it therefore remains available to our reading of the plot.[12] The notion of a conspiracy of young non-Irishmen to defraud the rich young Dubliner of his fortune, requires that we assume a deep level of hidden preparation that would make their plot a variant analogue to the common eighteenth- and nineteenth- century novelistic marriage swindle in which a young cad, feigning greater wealth and rank than he

---

[11] Leonard, p. 115.

[12] An alternate scenario of fraud is suggested by Harold Mosher, who suggests a far more sinister and professional confidence game in progress in the story. Mosher believes that the card game, and other games of the young Continentals, are intended to divert Jimmy's attention from the actual fraud, which is the bogus financial investment ("The Narrated and Its Negatives: The Nonnarrated and Disnarrated in Joyce's *Dubliners*," *Style* [Fall 1993]: 407-28).

possesses, courts a plain young woman of great fortune with the intent to deflower and defraud her. This plot, which can readily be read into gaps between the lines of the narrator's curious locutions, melds quite seamlessly with many small allusions to masquerade, including gender masquerade, throughout the story. Jimmy's mounting debts, we realize, began, not at Dublin University, but at Cambridge, where "he had met Ségouin" (*D* 43). Jimmy does not know Ségouin very well ("They were not much more than acquaintances" [*D* 43]), and neither does the narrator, who repeats -- but does not verify -- the rumour of Ségouin's fortune, that "he was reputed to own some of the biggest hotels in France"(*D* 43). Jimmy's father's approval of this friendship, and his urging of an investment of Jimmy's fortune in Ségouin's proposed automotive venture, take on the colorations of paternal support for an advantageous "match" for his son. Ségouin primes the Doyles by heightening the aura of his commercial eligibility -- "Ségouin had managed to give the impression that it was by a favour of friendship the mite of Irish money was to be included in the capital of the concern"(*D* 44-45) -- and the allure of his wealth, which the narrator nonetheless qualifies as an appearance rather than a fact: "Ségouin had the unmistakable air of wealth" (*D* 45). The young French motor mavens, aware of Jimmy's twin interests of music and cars ("he divided his time curiously between musical and motoring circles" [*D* 43]), are able to satisfy the latter, and they import a musical Hungarian ("Villona was entertaining also--a brilliant pianist" [*D* 44]) to appeal to the former. Jimmy's twin passions can be seen as indulged simultaneously during the triumphal ride back to Dublin after the race, when Jimmy gets to ride in their "lordly car" (*D* 45) while being serenaded by Villona's "deep bass hum of melody for miles of the road" (*D* 44).

The title of "After the Race" might reflect, like Joyce's

interview with Fournier, a moment in a discourse, perhaps the answer to the query "When?" if the discourse is construed as a conspiracy against Jimmy's money. The narrator himself supplies the "why" of this timing, when he explains that "[r]apid motion through space elates one; so does notoriety; so does the possession of money. These were three good reasons for Jimmy's excitement" (D 44). The liminality of the story's moment *after* the race exploits the ambient effects of elation and celebration after the successful race as atmospheric contributors to the bedazzlement and seduction of Jimmy Doyle, who is configured as the ingenue among his "friends." His vanity puffed up with the ride in a gorgeous car and the glow of reflected celebrity, Jimmy is introduced to a French racing champion who dazzles him with a brilliant smile: ("[The] swarthy face of the driver had disclosed a line of shining white teeth"[D 44]). The event is staged amid a crowd of racing spectators transformed into an admiring audience: "It was pleasant after that honour to return to the profane world of spectators amid nudges and significant looks" (D 44). An intimate, but gala, dinner is planned for that evening at Ségouin's hotel -- an event that even bedazzles Jimmy's family, who have pronounced it "an occasion"(D 45). The strange narrative interlude that depicts the family's pride as they stand in the hallway, approving their son's formal attire and ingratiating themselves with his companion, has the character of the launching of a debutante or the parental blessing of a young couple on prom night: "Jimmy, too, looked very well when he was dressed and, as he stood in the hall giving a last equation to the bows of his dress tie, his father may have felt even commercially satisfied at having secured for his son qualities often unpurchasable. His father, therefore, was unusually friendly with Villona" (D 45). But we are told that, as Jimmy goes off with Villona, a "certain pride mingled with his parents' trepidation" (*D* 45). The parents of this twenty-six-year-old man are portrayed as nervous--as though their offspring were a virginal girl going out with a strange foreigner.

The aura of romance that imbues the evening incorporates other figures who are unexpectedly interpolated into the scene. The dinner party is enlarged by the addition of an Englishman named Routh, "whom Jimmy had seen with Ségouin at Cambridge" (*D* 46) and therefore does not appear to know. But although it remains undecidable whether the late addition of Routh and the accidental meeting of the party with the American Farley are prearranged and part of a plot, the narrator seems to suggest that virtually nothing about the dinner party is casual or spontaneous. Even Jimmy detects Ségouin's deliberate orchestration of the social interactions: "He admired the dexterity with which their host directed the conversation"(*D* 46); and the reader can readily divine Ségouin's intentions. Rivière, who "not wholly ingenuously, undertook to explain to Jimmy the triumph of the French mechanicians"(*D* 46), and Villona, who holds forth on the English madrigal, are set up to appeal to Jimmy's twin passions for motor racing and music, respectively. The narrator's betrayal of Rivière's disingenuousness suggests that other aspects of the heady talk are contrived for Jimmy's benefit. Villona's disquisition on the madrigal sets up both the theme and the mood of the romance of the pastorale that eventually infects the narrator's own rhetoric: "The resonant voice of the Hungarian was about to prevail in ridicule of the spurious lutes of the romantic painters when Ségouin shepherded his party into politics"(*D* 46). Villona's specific inveighing against inauthentic music and contrived painting might have served as a self-reflexive warning to Jimmy to listen for the spurious in the lute of Villona's discursive music, and to question the authenticity of the tableau in which he takes part. Instead, Jimmy's ill-trained imagination is "kindled" at the outset to produce his own decadently artificial tableau, whose "grotesquerie" R. B. Kershner identifies as "parasitism and suppressed homoeroticism,[13] "Jimmy, whose imagination was kindling, conceived the lively youth of the Frenchmen twined elegantly upon the firm framework of the Englishman's manner. A graceful image of his, he thought, and a just one" (D 46). Jimmy, an incompetent judge of his own words, as we see in his later inability to assess the merits, or demerits, of his drunken speech, fails to recognize the potential truth his strange fantasy may embed, one of entwined and colluding snakes replacing the ivy of the pastorale.

Ségouin is a sinister shepherd in this pastorale under electric lights. As the young Frenchman leads an Irishman and an Englishman "into politics," the narrative comment-- "Here was congenial ground for all" (D 46)--is either stupid, cruel, or sarcastic. But the prevailing happy mood is such that Jimmy and Routh are difficult to egg on into open political conflict, with "the torpid Routh" slow to react to the Irishman's slow retrieval of anticolonial anger buried beneath two generations of Doyle prosperity and complacency. One could construe that Ségouin's intention was precisely to provoke the "danger of personal spite" (D 46) in order to give the proleptic card game, toward which all the various arrangements are tending, a personally and nationally rancorous edge that will insure that the betting will run very high and require the exchange of paper or the production of manipulable IOUs. The cosmopolitan toasts repeatedly needed to tamp down the liminal national animosities--"The alert host at an opportune moment lifted his glass to Humanity" (46) and "They drank Ireland,

---

[13] Kershner, p. 73.

England, France, Hungary, the United States of
America" (*D* 47)--ensure that by the time the game begins
Jimmy will have been thoroughly incapacitated with
emotional overstimulation and the narcotic effects of
excessive drinking.

As the young men stroll through Dublin after their
glamorous dinner, their meeting with the American, Farley,
appears--or is staged to appear--accidental. The narrator
even narrates the exact exchange of surprised greeting, as if
to underline that the meeting is unexpected: "André." "It's
Farley!" (*D* 47). Farley's role in the swindle plot is crucial to
configuring the impending assault on Jimmy's money in
paraerotic terms at the same time that he provides the
historical context to give Jimmy's robbery a gendered social
meaning. On the level of narrative plot, Farley's yacht
provides the remote and secluded venue for the swindle's
consummation that will make Jimmy's escape impossible.
However, the yacht's name--*The Belle of Newport*--sets
Jimmy's misadventure in a specific historical moment, the
dizzyingly rapid industrial expansions of turn-of-the-
century America with their ethically dubious acquisitors of
wealth memorialized in the epithet "robber baron." Further,
the yacht's feminized name conjures the double gender
track that furrows the arriviste universe of new money with
parallel perils for the male world of business and
investment and the female world of the marriage market
and the management of the domestic symbolic order. Joyce
could not have read Edith Wharton's *The House of Mirth*,
which was published in 1905, the year after the publication
of "After the Race" in *The Irish Homestead*. But Wharton had
begun publishing her stories in *Scribner's Magazine* in the
1890s, and Joyce, who is known to have read and liked
some of the short fiction of Henry James, may have been
exposed to this American brand of social criticism to
complicate the genre of the "gentleman's magazine" story

Kershner believes, along with Bernard Huppé, undergirded "After the Race."[14] Wharton's *House of Mirth* retrospectively glosses Farley's world of American Newport society by depicting not only the predations of the marriage market for the "belle of Newport" but also the ravages of the ruinous gambling debts Lily Bart incurs by playing bridge beyond her financial resources. *The Belle of Newport*, I would suggest, overlays the ideological intertextuality of Dumas's Three Musketeers, which Kershner sees as the plot enacted by Jimmy Doyle the night after the race, with a heterosexual configuration of the story's homosociality.

Aboard *The Belle of Newport* the boys' night out mimics a scene of heterosexual play fueled by mirth, liquor, and abandon ("They drank, however: it was Bohemian" [*D* 47]) that devolves into orgy. "Villona played a waltz for Farley and Rivière, Farley acting as cavalier and Rivière as lady. There was an impromptu square dance, the men devising original figures. What merriment! Jimmy took his part with a will; this was seeing life, at least"(*D* 47). As the group plunges into the card game, Villona plays "voluntaries" (*D* 48)--an ironic musical accompaniment to the hidden coercions that force Jimmy to remain in frenzied rounds of games whose pleasure gives way increasingly to unpleasure as Jimmy's losses begin to mount and he loses control of the calculations. The "voluntaries" of improvised music underline the hidden misery of date-rape, the sickening feeling that one has brought it on oneself, that one has no one else to blame: "it was his own fault for he frequently mistook his cards and the other men had to calculate his I.O.U.'s for him" (*D* 48). By the time the narrator utters Jimmy's wish, "They were devils of fellows

---

14 Kershner, p.72.

but he wished they would stop" (*D* 48), his protest
sounds as anguished and futile as that of a rape victim. The
card game, whose ludic surface conceals the rigid code of
"honor" that will ensure brutal enforcement of its financial
consequences, affects Jimmy like an amorous adventure
gone awry and become abusive. By the last game, nothing
is left to chance; Jimmy is scarcely in the running ("[H]e
would lose, of course. How much had he written away?"[*D*
48]), and after a last throb of excitement, the game is over.
Jimmy is left abjectly slumped over the table in a stupor of
incipient pain. Routh, not Ségouin, has won the climactic
game, an outcome that makes it necessary to assume a
collusion between the traditional national enemies, the
Englishman and the Frenchmen, as well as their American
and Hungarian accomplices, to achieve the coup of legally
robbing Jimmy of the planned investment.

But the depth of the conspiracy, as well as the extent
of Jimmy's loss, affects chiefly the degree rather than the
nature of his ruin. Both Jimmy's losses and the scope of his
anagnorisis--the altered self-perception produced by
recognition of "his folly"--remain indeterminate. Are his
losses, though clearly beyond "the limits of reasonable
recklessness" (*D* 44) still recuperable with the aid of a
forgiving father, or has he squandered his birthright, the
"great sum under his control" that represents his entire
capital, the familial portion the twenty-six-year-old
assumed upon attaining his majority? What illuminations
will his anticipated regret bring him with the sobering
daybreak? Will his epiphany embrace his layers of
degradation -- the pain of his father's disgust; self-loathing
for his fatuousness as "a creature driven and derided by
vanity," like that of the boy in "Araby"; anger at the betrayal
by bogus friendship and abused trust? Will it extend to the
more intimate recesses of self-recognition -- to seeing that
his friends' exploitation of him was a form of

counterexploitation, that they exploited his wealth and immaturity as he had exploited their prestige and worldliness? Will he finally recognize that the worth he has lost was always already lost, that he had commanded a spurious regard only on the basis of his detachable appurtenances or phallic signifiers -- his money, Cambridge, smart clothes, and familial indulgence?

The depth of Jimmy Doyle's mourning in the morning is largely incalculable--although we are led to imagine it will exceed the mere detumescence (that promises repeatability) that is the aftermath and denouement of pleasure, the hollowness associated with the morning after, after the ball, when the party's over. We are supplied with at least one measure of Jimmy's ability to calculate his loss: the "solid instinct" that lets him "translate into days' work that lordly car in which he sat"(D 45) and demystify glamour and wealth to recognize its material base in the substance of the body's labor. We are virtually assured that he will be able to quantify his lordly losses in squandered years'--rather than days'--work. But his ability to admit the psychic brutalization to which he has been subjected remains unknowable, and there is every possibility that he could remain in the oblivion into which he sinks himself on the morning after the race, when he blocks out the morning light with his hands and suspends himself in a "dark stupor" that admits no images of loss, betrayal, or self-reproach, by counting only the raw life that remains, "the beats of his temples" (D 48). Such an outcome would insert the dark specters of trauma and repression into the fatuousness and blindness that had once been his innocence.

But the reader who has performed a critical analysis of the fate of Jimmy Doyle must confront the lesson of gender that is inscribed in the specific politics of Jimmy's overdetermined violation in this story. Eve Kosofsky

Sedgwick's parable of social power requires only minor skewing to map effectively her gender dynamism onto the scene in "After the Race." Pointing out that male entitlement "required certain intense male bonds that were not readily distinguishable from the most reprobate bonds," the condition of male entitlement incorporates the threat of social and psychological foreclosure that inspires "homosexual panic."[15] The plot of "After the Race" is precisely the pursuit of male entitlement through intense male bonding, and although what Jimmy experiences is homosocial betrayal rather than homosexual panic, its outcome produces a similar lesson about the arbitrary and manipulable symbolic ground on which masculinity is constituted as a vulnerability. What Jimmy construes as male bonding in the service of consolidating entitlement turns out to have been a charade that concealed his feminization by the Continentals, who covertly translated their refusal to reciprocate his regard into an effective mutilation of his ability to recover the psychic ground from which he could reclaim privilege. His friends stripped Jimmy not only of money but of the membership in homosociality needed to secure the position in the symbolic order that is designated as masculine.

The Continentals have "queered" or feminized Jimmy Doyle--using his naïveté on the one hand, and his aesthetic sensibilities, his appreciation of style, refinement, glamour, and other symbolic excrescences, on the other--to mark the domain in which his "complicity" was manipulated. That complicity is, of course, spurious, since Jimmy is an aspirant to an acculturated masculinism--and the point of masculinity's vulnerability to annihilation

---

[15] Eve Kosofsky Sedgwick, *Epistemology of the Closet* (Berkeley: University of California Press, 1990), p. 185.

inherent in the illusion of its arbitrary and provisional grounding is thereby drawn all the more painfully. Jimmy's extrusion from male privilege demonstrates Teresa de Lauretis's argument that "[t]he term *gender* is, actually, the representation of a relation, that of belonging to a class, a group, a category."[16] Insofar as this positionality of gender is determined by cultural technologies, masculinity in "After the Race" is constructed through such homosocial texts and subtexts as those discussed by Kershner: Dumas's *Three Musketeers*, drinking songs, the choruses of *Cadet Roussel* ("with linked arms, singing *Cadet Roussel* in chorus, stamping their feet at every: '*Ho! Ho! Hohé, vraiment!*'"[D 47]) that guarantee camaraderie and homosocial inclusion without advertising the concomitant requirement of oppressive or exploitive exclusions against which privilege defines itself. Interestingly, Joyce may have achieved an insight into the calculus of masculinity from a curious rejoinder made by Henri Fournier, the prototype of Ségouin, during his 1903 interview. Asked to size up his racing competitors, including a certain Mr. Edge, Fournier demurred by silence. Joyce pressed him by asking, "He won the prize the last time, did he not?" (*CW* 108), to which Fournier replied, "O yes . . . . But, you see, Mr. Edge won, of course, but . . . a man who was last of all, and had no chance of winning might win if the other machines broke"(*CW* 108). Gender, like being a contender, is a matter of positionality.

But the story does not simply present us with an enlightened insight into the end of gender, because the metaphysical masculinity game that hides beneath the social masculinity games in "After the Race" is, after all,

---

[16] Teresa de Lauretis, *Technologies of Gender: Essays on Theory, Film, and Fiction* (Bloomington: Indiana University Press, 1987), p. 4.

only dimly transparent, if not opaque, to the uncritical, or precritical, reader. We have as much trouble "hearing" or comprehending what is going on, as does Jimmy, whose difficulties with communication[17] might serve as a caution to the reader. Like Villona's humming, the narrator's elegant and wry prose distracts us from the holes and silences in his story. Why doesn't the narrative voice that knows enough to ironize the Irish spectators of the Gordon Bennett Cup Race as producing the "cheer of the gratefully oppressed" (D 42) simply tell us of Ségouin's designs on Jimmy's money and describe to us the swindle of the card game that divests Jimmy of money he would gladly have invested? Perhaps I should be obliged to concede that there may be no plot, that the story's donnée may be simply "Jimmy Doyle's Bad Night After the Race." But my question draws attention to the narrative refusal to tell us very much about the Continentals and their orchestrations of this particular evening ending in the debauch, if not complete ruin, of their Irish friend. The narrative reticence illuminates the strangely liminal--and, I would argue, sinister--position of the narrator as one of "them," as a Continental, or a crypto-Continental, who "knows" what is going on, who "knows" the motives and maneuvers of Jimmy's "friends," and who could tell us whether or not there is a conspiracy, a callousness, a carelessness, or some other attitude that contributes to the evening's outcome. By refusing to betray what he knows, the narrator can legitimately be construed as a discursive accomplice to a plot to defraud and humiliate Jimmy Doyle without betraying the conspirators or incriminating himself (a narrator gendered not only as male but as masculinist). The narrator's part in the game of masculinity is to expose

[17] Leonard, p. 114.

Jimmy's foolishness, his vulnerability and fatuousness and its cost, but without, simultaneously, exposing his friends' villainy. The narrator takes care not to compromise Ségouin and his friends as "gentlemen," even though that last word of the story is as ironic as the title opening the next story, "Two Gallants." The effect of this maneuver is troublesome for us, as readers, because it allies us with Jimmy Doyle and positions us, epistemologically, in the same place--as "helpful animals" assisting in our embarrassment, as Kershner puts it, by confusedly apprehending Jimmy's appalling state at story's end, blaming him for it in some inchoate way, sharing with some empathy in his pain, and yet failing to discern fully or clearly the mechanism by which it was achieved. The narrator has contributed to our own proleptic "queering," by giving us the illusion that he confides in us, that we are sharing in the male bonding necessary for entitlement as "knowing" or comprehending readers, while extruding us from the conspiracy by making us helpless to penetrate it or assert our claim to membership in the circle of the cognoscenti and manipulators of the gender system. By having its narrative "perform" the dynamic of masculinism that it thematizes in "After the Race"--the exercise of privilege and male bonding dependent on the marginalization and extrusion of the arbitrarily feminized-- the story's text teaches us masculinity's paradoxical constructions through the experience of our troubled, inconclusive, and imperfect reading.

University of California, Irvine

STANDING THE EMPIRE: DRINKING, MASCULINITY, AND MODERNITY IN "COUNTERPARTS"

PAUL LIN

Abstract. This essay argues that drinking enables the politically and socially disenfranchised working-class male subject under colonial rule to temporarily elude his own subjection by disrupting the hegemonic discourses of colonialism upon which his subjectification is based. However, this practice is not without its drawbacks; for the nationalist overtones of drinking as a response to modernity invariably reproduce what Declan Kiberd calls "the old, familiar tyranny" of colonialism. Hence, in my title and throughout the essay, I use the term "standing" as an analytical pun that encapsulates, in its various meanings, the rituals of Irish drinking and its often contradictory results.

At the end of Joyce's "Counterparts," the decidedly unheroic Farrington reluctantly makes his way home after a deplorable day at work and an even worse evening out on the town. Battered and broke, he violently redirects his anger and chagrin toward his son Tom; bullied at work and at the public houses, he bullies at home. The story closes with the frightened boy literally and figuratively at the mercy of his tyrannous father, offering repeatedly to "say a *Hail Mary* for you" (*D* 98) in order to escape bodily punishment. This scene, on the one hand, is a poignant depiction of domestic violence as the result of alcohol, a social reality in Ireland all too familiar for working-class men and their families. On the other hand, it can also be read as an allegory for the abusive domestic relationship between the English and the Irish that is colonialism. In both cases, the narrative represents an Irish working-class male subject caught in a cycle and a system of oppression, simultaneously identifying him as both a victim and a victimizer.

This essay looks at the praxis of drinking in the Irish metropolis as a function of the construction of a masculine subject and the way in which that construction interfaces with colonial politics and the condition of modernity. Situating "Counterparts" as the focus of my discussion, this essay will examine the complex ways in which drinking is represented by Joyce in both the private and the public sphere, in the workplace and in the public house.[1] In centering the narrative on the problem of intemperance, I will argue that Joyce's text disrupts the intoxicating binary constructions upon which the hegemonic discourses of colonialism and modernity are legitimated and disseminated. In doing so, I will show how "Counterparts" reveals the multiple and paradoxical ways in which Ireland "stands" England -- which, to use the term as a pun for analytical purposes, is to say: "endures," perhaps even "resists," "treats" as in the Irish custom, and finally, "maintains" in an upright position, stable and affirmed.

In his famous 1906 letter to Grant Richards, Joyce indicated that his motive for *Dubliners* was "to write a chapter of the moral history of my country and I chose Dublin for the scene because that city seemed to me to be the centre of paralysis."[2] What the stories subsequently

[1] My distinction between the public and the private spheres follows that of Jürgen Habermas. See "The Public Sphere," in *Rethinking Popular Culture*, ed. Chandra Mukerji and Michael Schudson, *Rethinking Popular Culture* (Berkeley: University of California Press, 1991), pp. 398-404.

[2] This letter, dated 5 May 1906, is the same letter in which Joyce addresses the (English) printer's objections to "Counterparts." *Letters II*, p.

depict is a series of individuals at the defining moments of their lives (it is sometimes suggested that these individuals are all, in fact, synecdoches of the same person). Each of these individuals experiences the conflicting revelation of his or her own psychic fragmentation. In Declan Kiberd's words: the tales betray "an impulse arrested or else enacted to a point where it becomes self-negating: in either case, the gesture of revolt is fated always to have the old, familiar tyranny inscribed in it."[3]

As Farrington demonstrates at the end of "Counterparts," his efforts to counteract the effects of his own abuse is to reproduce the violence, "the old, familiar tyranny," at home. "Counterparts" is a witness to the fact that one of the deepest problems of the Dublin environment may indeed be the use and abuse of alcohol. Throughout *Dubliners*, in fact, drinking is frequently the center of activity; one only needs to think of the primacy of drinking in "A Little Cloud," "Ivy Day in the Committee Room," and "Grace." Additionally, many of the book's most memorable characters--such as Mr. Mooney in "The Boarding House," Joe in "Clay," Emily Sinico in "A Painful Case," Freddy Malins in "The Dead," and, of course, Joe Kernan in "Grace"--have debilitating drinking disorders that render them socially incompetent in the eyes of Dublin's middle class.

Discriminatory attitudes by the English toward the Irish have long centered upon the practice of drinking or as Seamus Deane articulates it, "drunkenness."[4] Elizabeth Malcom observes, "Throughout most of the nineteenth

134.

[3] Declan Kiberd, *Inventing Ireland: The Literature of the Modern Nation* (Cambridge: Harvard University Press, 1995), p. 330.

[4] Seamus Deane, "Civilians and Barbarians," in *Ireland's Field Day* (London: Hutchinson, 1985), p. 37.

century Irish nationalism and the temperance movement were at odds."[5] Throughout Ireland, but most notably in the cities, drinking among the working classes was discouraged as a disruptive force in the "peaceful" operation and maintenance of industry and empire; Malcom continues: "Temperance began as, and for long remained, the exclusive preserve of middle-class, pro-British protestants, who used it to bolster their own position while at the same time denigrating the customs and habits of their catholic social inferiors."[6] Thus in "The Dead," Gabriel Conroy's responsible attempt to sober up Freddy Malins can be seen as characteristic of his West-Briton sensibilities. Gabriel's foil in this respect might be the Citizen in *Ulysses,* whose blind (or rather cyclopean nationalism finds refuge in Barney Kiernan's pub where the anti-treating league, not drink, is denounced as "the curse of Ireland" (*U* 12.684). Neither is portrayed in a particularly sympathetic light, however, and both Gabriel's snobbery and the Citizen's xenophobia, while at odds with one another, are similarly drunk with binaristic imperial, racial, cultural, and sexual attitudes toward Ireland's "historical heritage" and "external culture."[7] This antagonism, manifested in *Dubliners* in the form of intemperance, is motivated by what Georg Simmel interprets as "the resistance of the individual to be levelled, swallowed up in

[5] Elizabeth Malcom, "Temperance and Irish Nationalism," in *Ireland under the Union: Varieties of Tension: Essays in Honour of T. W. Moody,* ed. F. S. L. Lyons and R. A. J. Hawkins, New York: Oxford University Press, 1980), p. 112.

[6] Malcom, p. 112.

[7] Georg Simmel, "The Metropolis and mental Life," trans. Edward A. Shils, in Donald N. Levine, ed. *On Individuality and social Forms: Selected Writings* (Chicago: University of Chicago Press, p. 324.

the socio-technological mechanism."[8] Simmel's figural use of "swallowed" is apropos to Joyce's text, for it signifies the ways in which (bodily) consumption and modernity are inextricably linked.

On a more general scale, some of the transformations in Irish society under the rationale of modernity can be understood via the theorization of the body. In *Discipline and Punish*, Michel Foucault describes the process by which disciplinary power, through the manipulation of space and time, penetrates both the physical and the social body, producing what he has famously termed "docile bodies"-- bodies that are tame, educable, and therefore efficient. Citing Jeremy Bentham's panopticon as the model par excellence, he explains the ways in which extrinsic schemata operating "in a diffused, multiple, polyvalent way" can induce discipline intrinsically in a subject :

> He who is subjected to a field of visibility, and who knows it, assumes responsibility for the constraints of power; he makes them play spontaneously upon himself; he inscribes in himself the power relation in which he simultaneously plays both roles; he becomes the principle of his own subjection.[9]

As the quintessential space of disciplinary power, Joyce's Dublin can be seen in these terms, as the locus of panoptic technologies disseminated throughout the various institutions maintaining and maintained by colonialism and modernity. Thus the temperance retreats in the background of "Grace" and "The Dead" and in the "Nausicaa" episode of *Ulysses*--a chapter that is preoccupied with issues of observation and self-evaluation--can be seen

[8] Simmel, p. 324.

[9] Michel Foucault, *Discipline and Punish: The Birth of the Prison*, trans. Alan Sheridan (New York: Vintage, 1979), pp. 202-3.

as instances of the collaboration between the multiple apparatuses of religion (the backbone of many temperance movements) and modernity. One can also see how disciplinary power is evinced by Father Mathew's crusade during the 1840s, in which temperance readers, pamphlets that promulgated the ideologies of the empire under the guise of literacy, were disseminated throughout the national schools as part of the curriculum in Ireland. In all of these endeavors directed at the level of culture and national politics, the body with its practices becomes the primary site of contestation and struggle.

Within the sphere of the workplace, nowhere do we see the physical embodiment of modernity more evident in "Counterparts" than in the oppressive figure of Farrington's supervisor, Mr. Alleyne. His "piercing North of Ireland accent" (D 86) marks him as a foreigner to Dublin, but one who is clearly aligned with the ruling class, and, hence, with the English. Mr. Alleyne's name, which is perhaps derived from the German *allein* (meaning "alone"),[10] further distinguishes him from the native employees. Isolated in his office upstairs, an outsider on the inside, he is emblematic of the piercing alien presence of modernity in the workplace. But Mr. Alleyne's affinities with the English go beyond his geo-political sensibilities, for it is through his physical disembodiment that Joyce depicts him as the representational embodiment of the apparatus of modernity. He penetrates the narrative as a disembodied sound, "a furious voice" (D 86)--later described as a "shrill voice" (D 86)--that is juxtaposed in the same sentence with an intercom bell which also rings "furiously" (D 86). Reduced to nothing more than the aggressive transmission

---

[10] John Wyse Jackson and Bernard McGinley, eds., *James Joyce's "Dubliners": An Illustrated Edition with Annotations* (New York: St. Martin's Press, 1993), p. 76.

of vibrations, Mr. Alleyne is represented in the story as the depersonalized mimicking of a telecommunicational device. When we finally do see him, he is described as "a little man wearing gold-rimmed glasses on a cleanshaven face. The head itself was so pink and hairless that it seemed like a large egg reposing on the papers" (*D* 87). Streamlined and optically enhanced, Mr. Alleyne's head itself takes on the appearance of the result of a labor. When he later scolds Farrington for his insubordinate yet felicitous remark, "[h]e shook his fist in the man's face till it seemed to vibrate like the knob of some electric machine" (*D* 91).

For Joyce, the product of disciplinary power in the workplace is not simply the division and abstraction of labor; it is also the principles of modernity made manifest in the physical body of Mr. Alleyne; or as Foucault puts it: "Discipline is no longer simply an art of distributing bodies, of extracting time from them and accumulating it, but of composing forces in order to obtain an efficient machine. The body is constituted as part of a multi-segmented machine."[11]

In his zealous absorption of this discipline, Mr. Alleyne does not become solely associated with mechanization, but rather he becomes an interchangeable unit in the machine itself. The automaton-like behavior he evinces is evident in his constant repetition of phrases: "*Mr Shelley said, sir*"; *Mr Shelley says, sir*" (*D* 87); "Do you hear me now?; Do you hear me now?" (*D* 87); "*You--know--nothing. Of course you know nothing*" (*D* 91); "You impertinent ruffian! You impertinent ruffian!" (*D* 91); "You'll apologise to me; you'll apologise to me!" (D 91-2); "you'll quit the office instanter! You'll quit this"(*D* 92). Alleyne throws out commands like a well-oiled piston in a factory assembly

---

[11] Foucault, p. 164.

line.[12]

In stark contrast to Mr. Alleyne is the idle, corpulent Farrington. Whereas Mr. Alleyne's body is the logical outcome of modernity--"polished" (*D* 87) and regulated-- Farrington's body is described as "tall and of great bulk," "hanging," "dark wine-coloured," "bulged forward," and "dirty" (*D* 86); in other words, a body that exceeds the capacity of control. Whereas Mr. Alleyne's movements are abrupt and efficient (Simmel might characterize this as nervousness)--"he shot up his head" (*D* 88), "swivelled his chair" (*D* 90), "tapped a finger then flicked it" (*D* 90), "his mouth twitched" (*D* 91)--Farrington's are plodding and inefficient: he "muttered under his breath" (*D* 86), "pushed back his chair to stand up" (*D* 86), "went heavily upstairs puffing with labour" (*D* 86), "crammed his cap back again into his pocket" (*D* 89), "struggled on with his copy" (*D* 90), and of course, "wrote *Bernard Bernard* instead of *Bernard Bodley*" (*D* 90). Thus within the space of the workplace, as it is discursively constituted by the logic of progress and modernity, the corporeal differences between Mr. Alleyne and Farrington legitimate the former's positional superiority over the latter.

The seemingly antithetical characteristics of Mr. Alleyne and Farrington, as seen within the larger framework of modernity, can be understood as symbolic representations of a colonial distinction; that is, the discursive formation of oppositional categories in discourses of colonialism in order to perpetuate a logic of difference that always puts the colonized in subsidiary relation to the colonizer. This structure is apparent in the

---

[12] Garry Leonard, in *Reading "Dubliners" Again: A Lacanian Perspective* (Syracuse: Syracuse University Press, 1993), also discusses "Counterparts" in terms of repetition and mechanization, but from a psychoanalytic perspective.

long-standing tradition of the "feminization" of Ireland, especially during the nineteenth century when writers such as Ernest Renan and Matthew Arnold were making purportedly "scientific" observations about the Celts, and by implication the Irish. In his essay "Poésie des Races Celtiques," Renan categorizes the Irish in terms of sexual and political congruence: "[I]f it be permitted us to assign sex to nations as to individuals we should have to say without hesitance that the Celtic race . . . is an essentially feminine race."[13] Arnold, in "On the Study of Celtic Literature," draws upon Renan's writings--as well as contemporary philology, ethnology, and anthropology-- and comes to an "objective" conclusion which confirms his Teutonic masculinity: "[N]o doubt the sensibility of the Celtic nature, its nervous exaltation, have something feminine in them, and the Celt is thus particularly disposed to feel the spell of the feminine idiosyncrasy; he has an affinity to it; he is not far from its secret." The somewhat romantic quality he attributes to the Celt, however, is not without the trace of a menace, for in the same paragraph Arnold disparagingly considers the Celt "undisciplined, anarchical, and turbulent,"[14] The somewhat romantic quality he attributes to the Celt, however, is not without the trace of a menace, for in the same paragraph Arnold disparagingly considers the Celt "undisciplined, anarchical, and turbulent," characteristics that Farrington, according to Mr. Alleyne's perceptions, certainly possesses. Thus in order to secure the cultural hegemony of the English in Ireland, Arnold's discussion of the Celtic race, disguised as

[13] Ernest Renan, *The Poetry of the Celtic Races*, trans. W. G. Hutchison (London: Walter Scott, 1897), p. 8.

[14] Matthew Arnold, *On the Study of Celtic Literature and Other Essays* (1910; reprint, New York: Dutton, 1976), p. 86.

scientific   discourse, "produced a procedure for the cultural and political incorporation of the Celts which flattered them into accepting a subsidiary position for themselves vis-à-vis the English."[15]

Inscribed by the paralyzing structures of colonialism and modernity, the hapless Farrington, in his oppositional relationship with Mr. Alleyne, is unavoidably constructed in terms of the category of the "feminine." Joyce recognized this: within this discursive regime, the Irish are always-already constituted according to these terms. At the same time, these same structures legitimate the English as the colonial patriarch of the Celtic races: Mr. Alleyne as Farrington's "masculine" counterpart. As Renan and Arnold have made clear, Farrington's subordinate relationship to his boss has already been predetermined by his Irish sensibilities, which perhaps accounts for his passivity: "He stood still" (*D* 87), "bowed respectfully" (*D* 90)--in Mr. Alleyne's office as he endures, indeed "stands," his often vociferous abuse.

This colonial distinction, however, cannot be seen as simply a categorical imposition; as Jacques Derrida has reminded us, any delimitation is always-already a contamination. These purported observations, therefore, go beyond distinguishing the Irish as "feminine" and by association "passive." Moreover, they go beyond differentiating the English by a simple binary negation--as "masculine" and "aggressive." For, as in the figure of Mr. Alleyne, these observations suggest that the Celt is always-already part of the English. As Peter Stallybrass and Allon White have powerfully argued, this double articulation of consciousness, that of having an underground self with the

---

[15] David Cairns and Shaun Richards, *Writing Ireland: Colonialism, Nationalism and Culture* (Manchester: Manchester University Press, 1988), p. 49.

upper hand, "captures a nexus of power and desire which regularly reappears in the ideological construction of the low-Other." Amending the Hegelian master-slave dynamic by symbolically including the slave within the political unconscious (to use Jameson's terms) of the master, they contend that "[t]he result is a mobile, conflictual fusion of power, fear and desire in the construction of subjectivity: a psychological dependence upon precisely those Others which are being rigorously opposed and excluded at the social level."[16]. As I will explore later, the complex interaction between these two, opposing subjectivities is ultimately the desire for that Other which is demonized in the self.

Joyce disrupts this colonial distinction by representing Farrington as just the "undisciplined, anarchical, and turbulent" Irishman that Arnold pejoratively ascribes to him. For if we revisit the differences between Mr. Alleyne and Farrington, we quickly notice that whereas the former never seems to leave his office, the delimited sphere of modernity, the latter can never seem to stay in one place with his periodic, clandestine visits to the local public house. Within the structured domain of the workplace -- with its rules, divisions, and spatiotemporal discipline -- Farrington is somewhat of an anomaly. By virtue of his bodily excesses, his inability to be contained within the strictures of his occupation, Farrington disrupts the Foucauldian constraints of power. He is recalcitrant to intrinsic discipline, for his itinerant thoughts are repeatedly preoccupied with drinking: "But his head was not clear and his mind wandered away to the glare and rattle of the public-house. It was a night for hot punches" (D 90). Even

---

[16] Peter Stallybrass and Allon White, *The Politics and Poetics of Transgression* (Ithaca: Cornell University Press, 1986), p. 5.

his physical body, when he gazes at Mr. Alleyne's "polished skull" (D 87), resists passivity: "A spasm of rage gripped his throat for a few moments and then passed, leaving after it a sharp sensation of thirst. The man recognised the sensation and felt that he must have a good night's drinking" (D 87). He also resists efficiency: "He couldn't finish it on time. He longed to execrate aloud, to bring his fist down on something violently. His body ached to do something, to rush out and revel in violence" (D 90). While he is forced by the requirements of his job to finish his copy, all he can think about is his inferior (and confined) station at work and his desire for yet another drink in order to escape, however temporarily, his colonial subjectification. For Farrington, subjected as he is to his own "feminization," chemical dependence enables a psychological form of independence, or at the very least it creates in his mind the condition of possibility for his own remasculinization.

Roy Rosenzweig, in his rich essay "The Rise of the Saloon," traces the formation of this working-class, leisure institution within the parameters of repressive nineteenth-century industrial societies. With the increasing prohibition of drinking in the workplace (for it was deemed to compromise the efficiency of modernity), a primarily male working-class labor force increasingly sought spaces where they could congregate outside the workplace and where drinking would be permitted. In his discussion of the culture of the saloon, Rosenzweig emphasizes "the character of the saloon as 'essentially a male refuge' pervaded by an 'aura of free-wheeling masculinity.'"[17] As an emerging social space between labor and domesticity,

[17] Roy Rosenzweig, "The Rise of the Saloon," in Chandra Mukerji and Michael Schudson, eds. *Rethinking Popular culture* (Berkeley: University of Calfornia Press, 1991), p.147.

the saloon allowed the working-class male to construct his subjectivity outside of what Louis Althusser has defined as "ideological state apparatuses,"[18] which tend to reinforce the ruling class. Although the gendered environment of the saloon appeared to uphold and affirm certain values within the dominant culture, its construction as an alternative social space to the workplace allowed its patrons to stand in opposition to modernity, even if in a masculinist way. Thus for Farrington, the public house is not merely a site for male recreation; it is for him also a site for the re-creation and emotional renewal of his masculinity. It is perhaps no surprise then that after his humiliating encounter in Mr. Alleyne's office, where he has been discursively "feminized," and after a particularly difficult time at his desk, Farrington feels compelled to sneak off to O'Neill's for a quick drink.

In his analysis of "Counterparts," Vincent Cheng has argued that the practice of drinking in the story is symptomatic of Farrington's colonial victimization: "[T]here is the resort to drink, the opiate of the oppressed, as a mode of transference of personal and cultural rage."[19] His argument suggests that Farrington's lack of agency at work finds expression in the extremeness of his drinking. One could argue, however, that the practice of drinking enables a politically and socially disenfranchised male subject temporarily to elude his own subjection by disrupting the binary logic of hegemonic discourses upon which his subjectification is based. Farrington's decision to drink,

---

[18] See Louis Althusser, "Ideology and Ideological State Apparatuses (Notes Towards an Investigation)," in *Lenin and Philosophy and Other Essays*, trans. Ben Brewster (New York: Monthly Review Press, 1971), pp. 127-86.

[19] Vincent J. Cheng, *Joyce, Race, and Empire* (Cambridge, Cambridge University Press, 1995), p. 121.

therefore, creates a kind of hallucinogenic state that enables him to recuperate his masculinity by engaging in an activity that clashed with the dominant culture and is recalcitrant to the discourse of colonialism. Indeed, drinking in the public house frequently allows the Irish working-class male to subvert his own "feminized" representation within the colonial regime, deploying what Michel de Certeau has called a "tactic" in order temporarily to disrupt the efficient flows of modernity and to evade in a partial and limited way panoptic discipline. Rather than pathologize drink as symptomatic of violence, I would argue that Joyce distinguishes drinking as an alternative practice to the totalizing force of modernity.

Fortified with drink, Farrington returns to the workplace. There he encounters the "moist pungent odour of perfumes." The presence of Miss Delacour reconfigures the one-to-one relationship between Farrington and Mr. Alleyne. As the "feminine," racial Other, the eroticized figure of a Semitic Miss Delacour "smoothing the handle of her umbrella and nodding the great black feather in her hat" (D 90) (all elements of sexual iconography), becomes the demonized and desired mediator between Farrington and Mr. Alleyne, against which the two must define themselves. Garry Leonard argues, in a parallel analysis, that both men seek Miss Delacour's gaze for validation and a unified sense of a masculine self. When Mr. Alleyne interrogates Farrington about the missing correspondence, he directs his question to both Farrington and Miss Delacour: "Tell me, he added, glancing first for approval to the lady beside him, do you take me for a fool? Do you think me an utter fool?" (D 91). Farrington's slaked response is also made in terms of Miss Delacour:

> The man glanced from the lady's face to the little egg-shaped head
> and back again; and, almost before he was aware of it, his tongue

had   found   a   felicitous   moment:
-- I don't think, sir, he said, that that's a fair question to put to me.
(*D* 91)

The result, of course, is Miss Delacour's smiling approval and Mr. Alleyne's humiliation, one that Joyce represents in terms a colonial stereotype: "Mr Alleyne flushed to the hue of a wild rose [evoking the color of Farrington's own 'wine-coloured' face and his mouth twitched with a dwarf's passion" (*D* 91). Farrington's visit to the public house produces the conditions for his own re-creation and discursively enables his tongue to "stand" against his "feminization." In doing so, he reconstitutes his own "masculinity" by receiving the female acknowledgment of his projected heterosexual desire, an acknowledgment that Leonard similarly reads as the "approving gaze [of] the feminine prize."[20] This triangular scenario is played out again later in the story when Farrington departs from the confines of the workplace and joins his friends in "the comfort of the public-house" (*D* 92), where the Irish subject is at ease.

Departing from the private sphere of the workplace, Farrington next enters the (unofficial) public sphere of the public house, a public sphere that is also private; as Rosenzweig notes, the public house "stood outside the dominant cultural values of the late nineteenth century" by fostering an "ethic of reciprocity and mutuality" among its working-class patrons.[21] With Nosey Flynn, O'Halloran, Paddy Leonard, and Higgins by his side, Farrington celebrates his now famous retort as everyone takes turns "standing" each other "exhilarating" drinks. As Rosenzweig

[20] Leonard, p. 175.

[21] Rosenzweig, p. 147, p. 143.

explains, the social custom of "standing"--that is, treating--"provided the nineteenth-century Irishman with a crucial means of declaring his solidarity and equality with his kin and neighbors"; to refuse a drink was tantamount to an insult. Here then, Farrington's perpetual desire to be in the public house is not just to re-create his own masculinity, but also to put himself on the same level as other Irishmen (as opposed to being downstairs from Mr. Alleyne), to participate in the construction of a unified national identity that can be seen as a kind of recalcitrance to the "feminizing" discourse of colonialism and modernity. It is no surprise then, as Malcolm had indicated, that "Irish nationalism and the temperance movement were at odds."[22] For, as Emer Nolan writes, if "Nationalism seeks to recreate a sense of traditional community within contemporary mass culture,"[23] the ethic of the public house constitutes a "pre-modern," perhaps even "anti-modern," response to the conditions of modernity. This ethic is surely regressive, but it nonetheless constitutes a response. The Irish working-class men represented in "Counterparts" need not *resort* to drink, but rather they *seek* to drink in order to counter temporarily the debilitating effects of their own oppression. By salvaging the practice that is frequently evoked to their discredit, the Irish subjects are able to reclaim a modicum of agency from the ruins of empire. In similar fashion, Nolan finds Joycean modernism and Irish nationalism "significantly analogous discourses,"[24] an assertion which may have merit, but only if we understand both as being more complex than is traditionally perceived: internally

[22] Malcom, p. 112

[23] Emer Nolan, *James Joyce and Nationalism* (London and New York: Routledge, 1995), p. xii.

[24] Nolan, p. xii.

fragmented and sometimes fraught with ambivalences and paradoxes.

For as much as drinking appears to authorize Irish nationalism, Joyce's text quickly disrupts and undermines this celebration of solidarity when Farrington is introduced to the Englishman Weathers. Once again, like the confrontation between Farrington and Mr. Alleyne, the confrontation at the Scotch House reproduces the one-to-one oppositional relationship between Farrington and Weathers. But unlike Mr. Alleyne, Weathers is "an acrobat and knockabout *artiste*" (D 94), which places him outside the conventional circles of English society. However, like Mr. Alleyne, Weathers is a foreigner, and, here, an outsider on the inside. Moreover, his association with the ruling class puts him in a different relationship with other men at the bar; Weathers's presence, in effect, challenges the "ethic of reciprocity and mutuality" of the public house. But as is the custom, "Farrington stood a drink all round" (D 94). As the evening progresses "O'Halloran stood a round and then Farrington stood another round, Weathers protesting that the hospitality was too Irish" (D 94). Weathers exploits the custom of "standing" no longer a means by which to declare one's solidarity and equality with his kin and neighbors, by allowing himself to be provided for at the expense of the Irish. Although Weathers does end up buying the others a round of drinks, he does not participate in the custom of "standing" as it is practiced by the Irishmen; the term is in fact never used in connection with him. Instead, "Weathers made them all have just one little tincture at his expense" (D 94). Thus within the space of the public house, a putative space outside of modernity, the figure of Weathers enslaves the two Irishmen by their own national custom and allegorically reproduces the condition of colonialism.

Next, when at Mulligan's, Farrington is drawn into another triangular scenario when Weathers acknowledges the presence of some his friends:

> Weathers saluted them and told the company that they were out of
> the Tivoli. Farrington's eyes wandered at every moment in the
> direction of one of the young women. There was something
> striking in her appearance. An immense scarf of peacock-blue
> muslin was wound round her hat and knotted in a great bow
> under her chin; and she wore bright yellow gloves, reaching to the
> elbow. Farrington gazed admiringly at the plump arm which she
> moved often and with much grace; and when, after a little time,
> she answered his gaze [...] he admired still more her large dark
> brown eyes.(*D* 95)

In a passage that Joyce was later forced to delete, Weathers
offers to introduce Farrington to a young woman who is
explicitly depicted as a prostitute. Once again, as with Miss
Delacour, the young woman becomes a "demonized" and
desired mediator between Farrington and Weathers,
against whom the two must define themselves. In
constructing his own masculine subjectivity, Farrington
once again directs his heterosexist gaze toward the
"eroticized," female Other. He is struck, bound in his
fascination with her "peacock-blue" scarf and her graceful
movements. And when "she answer[s] his gaze," Farrington
is even more delighted in this frozen moment of
recognition, the recognition of his own masculinity and
heterosexual desire.

But the eyes he sees are "dark brown," like his own
"dirty" eyes, and before he realizes it the young woman gets
up to leave: "She glanced at him once or twice and, when
the party was leaving the room, she brushed against his
chair and said *O, pardon!* in a London accent. He watched
her leave the room in the hope that she would look back at
him, but he was disappointed"(*D* 95). Whereas Miss
Delacour affirmed Farrington's masculinity with her smile,
the young woman in this situation, who turns out to be

English, disrupts--one can even say reverses--her own sexual objectification as the low-Other by revealing herself to be the high-Other. The result is Farrington's anger: "He cursed his want of money and cursed all the rounds he had stood, particularly all the whiskies and Apollinaris which he had stood to Weathers. If there was one thing he hated it was a sponge. He was so angry that he lost count of the conversation with his friends" (D 95); and later, when on the train home,"[h]is heart swelled with fury and, when he thought of the woman in the big hat who had brushed against him and said *Pardon!* his fury nearly choked him" (D 97).

This disabling moment of "smouldering anger and revengefulness" (D 96) can be understood through Jacques Lacan's famous analysis of "the mirror stage," which explains the formative moment at which an infant develops his subjectivity, his ego, his I/eye. Immediately admiring the woman as an Other, a non-self, Farrington initially imagines that he has mastery over her image, which is a surprise, especially considering the fact that he sees his own corpulent body as fragmentary and the woman's as unitary and graceful. He immediately desires her and identifies with her, but he also feels anger toward her because the body of the Other is whole and his is not. This leads to what Lacan believes is the nexus between narcissism and aggressivity. Farrington's construction of his self in opposition to an Other is thus based upon a wrong conception of the self, or what Lacan refers to as "*méconnaissance.*"[25] Therefore, the Other is in actuality not "other" but a projection of the (unconscious) self-image. Thus Farrington realizes that his masculine desire for the

[25] Lacan, *Écrits: A Selection*, trans. Alan Sheridan (New York: Norton, 1972), p. 6.

"feminine Other"--enabled by his drinking--is in actuality the projection of femininity upon himself. Drawn to the color of the woman's scarf--"peacock-blue," the peacock being a symbol of vanity--and the color of her eyes, his narcissism is interrupted by the woman's London accent and by his inability to master her when she disappoints his gaze, no longer the low-Other, but a high-*English*-Other. He realizes that she had been gazing at him, that she had mastery over his gaze, his eye/I, his self. Farrington realizes that he is in fact that low-Other that he saw in her, and what masters him is indeed England. His defeat is only emphasized by his loss to Weathers in their arm-wrestling match, in which he is unable to "uphold the national honour" (*D* 95). Simultaneously enabled and disabled by his drinking, Farrington's double defeat causes him to curse "all the rounds he had stood" (*D* 95). Joyce depicts him in a fury that "nearly choked him" (*D* 97).

Farrington's desire to seek an emotional escape from the panoptic discipline of the workplace results in his being further imprisoned by an English gaze. No longer the space in which his masculinity is re-created and renewed, the public house becomes the place where Farrington's "masculine" identity becomes further dismantled. Like his experience at work, the "feminizing" effect of colonialism becomes here reproduced in his interaction with the English woman, and Farrington, in his dependence upon alcohol, puts himself in the self-reflexive position of coming to the realization of his own self-negation. Ironically, Farrington's psychological independence becomes the means by which he is further made *dependent*--"he had not even got drunk. He began to feel thirsty again and he longed to be back again in the hot reeking public-house" (*D* 97)--so much so that it nearly chokes him. The tragedy is that Farrington's dependence upon masculine, heterosexual validation forces him to reproduce the repressive behavior of which he is so painfully aware.

In his 1843 article in *Nation*, Thomas Davis, one of the principle members of the nationalist organization Young Ireland, attempts to reconcile the problem of intemperance with his own political beliefs:

> [The Irishman] drank nothing for some 350 days in the year; but once or maybe oftener in the month, he got roaring drunk. This occasional debauch was the Lethe-moment of all his sorrows. He then forgot all his wrongs. His cabin was warm, his belly full, his back covered--for an afternoon; but he woke in the morning penniless, broken-headed, guilty, conscious-sore. *During his intoxication he had flung off his chains, and his duties too. He lost sight of his own miseries and the comfort of his wife and children also*; and for this transient flush of intemperance he not only inflicted severer privations on himself, but the hearth of his bosom's wife was colder and the board of his young ones more scanty for months to come. Narrowed means, injured character, and sourest temper, with starvation and quarrels and degradation, were a fearful penalty for a short pleasure. *Still the very greatness of his suffering was his excuse--his natural excuse for making it greater, in order to achieve liberty and luxury for an hour by the magic of intoxication.*[26]

In what may be seen as a virtual sociological reading of Joyce's fictional narrative, this account underscores the paradoxical properties of drinking. In arguing against the temperance movements of his day, Davis contends that drinking may offer possibilities for the nationalist cause, even if at the expense of disrupting the domestic harmony of one's family life. Indeed, he acknowledges that, whatever emancipatory effects drinking may provide, it unfortunately comes at the price of human (usually female or juvenile) suffering. As this document and "Counterparts" show, it is frequently the bodies of wives and children of these drinkers who must bear that cost.

[26] Quoted in Malcom, 81-82; emphasis added.

As Davis makes clear, the Irish practice of drinking, as it struggles with modernity, is deeply implicated in the question of nationalism. For as Nolan explains: "Nationalism ... always seeks to enable people to enter into fully-fledged modernity, but tries to do so by reinventing modernity on its own terms, by retaining something from an archaic, pre-modern form of community."[27] The environment of the public house can be seen as an example of this. But as Joyce reveals, although drinking appears to advance some of the goals of nationalism, it is only possible through an outright transgression of those very principles. Foucault comes to the conclusion that modernity is "an attitude,"[28] rather than a period of history, an attitude that both produces and struggles against its own countermodernity, a condition of recalcitrance within which the original tyranny is unconsciously inscribed. This is perhaps what Kiberd means when he declares that Joyce "began from the premise that to be Irish was to be modern anyway"[29]; or as Marshall Berman writes,"[T]to be fully modern is to be anti-modern. [I]t [is] impossible to grasp and embrace the modern world's potential without loathing and fighting against some of its most palpable realities."[30] For if to be modern means to have an alternative perception of independence-- an independence that is predicted upon fragmentation, self-

[27] Nolan, p. 110.

[28] See Michel Foucault, "What Is Enlightenment?" trans. Catherine Porter, in *The Foucault Reader*, ed. Paul Rabinow, (New York: Pantheon Books, 1984), p. 39.

[29] Kiberd, 266-67.

[30] Marshall Berman, *All That Is Solid Melts into Air: The Experience of Modernity* (London: Verso, 1983), p. 14.

negation, and compromise-- then to be Irish is also to reproduce the multiple subjectivities that we see in Farrington.

The story thus ends where we began--at home. Again: battered and broke, Farrington violently redirects his anger and defeat toward his son Tom; bullied at work and at the public houses, he bullies at home. What had been for Farrington a condition for the possibility of recalcitrance, becomes in this instance also a factor in his own disenfranchisement. Joyce writes, "The man sat down heavily on one of the chairs while the little boy lit the lamp. He began to mimic his son's flat accent, saying half to himself: *At the chapel. At the chapel, if you please!*" (*D* 97-98). He begins to mimic Tom, as Mr. Alleyne had mimicked him and the bell. When he jumps up "furiously" (*D* 98) to exact violence upon his son, we are reminded of the parallel to Mr. Alleyne's and the intercom's furious behavior. Moreover, Farrington's angry declaration, "By God, I'll teach you to do that again" (*D* 98), carries overtones of the tyranny of Father Dolan in *A Portrait* and other disciplinary/ideological apparatuses, which, of course, elicits Tom's panicked attempt at atonement with a "*Hail Mary*" (*D* 98). By the end of the story, Farrington's failed attempt at his own masculine renewal and national identification prompts his son to offer him a renewal of a different, more spiritual, kind. Unfortunately, because of his drinking, Farrington's final attempt at forging his identity takes on the familiar form of violence. As David Lloyd points out, this is the dilemma of most nationalist modes of resistance:

> Even in its oppositional stance, nationalism repeats the master narrative of imperialism, the narrative of development which is always applied with extreme rigour and priority to colonized peoples. . . . [T]he nationalist desire to develop the race into

authenticity, borrowed already from a universalist ideology, produces the hegemonic conditions for the ultimate perpetuation of imperial domination even after independence is achieved.[31]

In his attempt to achieve a unified subjectivity as an Irish man against and within the presence of modernity (and its expression in colonialism), Farrington turns to drinking as a decidedly "pre-" or "anti-modern" form of resistance. However, as with many of the characters in *Dubliners*, this transgressive impulse is enacted "to the point where it becomes self-negating,"[32] a self-reflexive gesture that is crucial to the development of the attitude of modernity. Any form of resistance, therefore, is "fated always to have the old, familiar tyranny inscribed in it."[33] It is here that we can then understand in colonial terms the Gramscian notion of "hegemony," as the internalization of the principles and processes of modernity.

Farrington's predicament seems to offer him no alternative other than that in which he has been unconsciously inscribed. Thus, in sitting down to colonialism, Farrington "stands" England, which, in this final sense, is to maintain in upright position, stable and affirmed. Farrington, by the end of the story, submits to his colonization and the principles of modernity, which for Joyce is a condition of his paralysis. His aggression toward Tom is indicative of that paralysis, for the only way he can hold on to his masculinity is to become a product and a purveyor of discipline and modernity, in other words, the

---

[31] David Lloyd, *Anomalous States: Irish Writing and the Post-Colonial Moment* (Durham, N. C.: Duke University Press, 1993), p. 54.

[32] Kiberd, p. 330.

[33] Kiberd, p. 330.

counterpart of the empire.

University of California, Irvine

DUFFY'S SUBJECTIVATION: THE PSYCHIC LIFE OF "A PAINFUL CASE"

COLLEEN LAMOS

Abstract. This essay examines and critiques the implications of Judith Butler's theory of the construction of the subject in *The Psychic Life of Power*, by means of an application to Joyce's figure of James Duffy, the central character of the story "A Painful Case" in *Dubliners*, whose subjectivation does not allow of any sexual relations.

James Duffy, the central character of "A Painful Case" James Joyce's *Dubliners*, provides what appears to be a textbook illustration of Judith Butler's theory of subjectivation, as elaborated in her recent book, *The Psychic Life of Power: Theories in Subjection*.[1] Precisely because Duffy exemplifies several key elements of the process of becoming a subject, as Butler describes it, Duffy's deviations from her account pose significant problems that point to weaknesses in her theory itself, especially concerning the nature of melancholia, the roles of narcissism and of homosexual foreclosure in melancholia, and, finally, the possibility of the agency of the subject in resisting social power.

In *The Psychic Life of Power*, the trope of turning upon oneself links Butler's discussions of the concepts of the "unhappy consciousness" in Hegel, the "bad conscience" in Nietzsche, interpellation in Louis Althusser, and melancholia in Freud. The common thread that runs throughout the works of these four theorists, according to Butler, is self-reflexivity, and her primary aim is to show

---

[1] Judith Butler, *The Psychic Life of Power: Theories in Subjection* (Stanford: Stanford University Press, 1997).

that this self-reflexive turn gives birth to the subject as such, that is, both as a subject *to* power and as a subject *of* power. This ambivalence of the subject's relation to social power -- on the one hand, as being subordinate to power and, on the other hand, as wielding power -- is the central issue that occupies Butler's book, which she presents as an attempt to bring together Foucault and Freud. Without claiming to have produced a "grand synthesis" of these two thinkers, Butler negotiates a somewhat erratic course between them as she tries to answer the objections of critics to her earlier books, *Gender Trouble* and *Bodies That Matter*, objections that typically focus upon the alleged voluntarism of her theory of gender and sexual performativity. However, there remain in *The Psychic Life of Power* questions concerning agency, questions to which I will return below.

Butler initially claims that the "interiorization of the psyche" or the carving out of an inner, psychic realm, as distinct from an outer, social realm, depends upon and is caused by the internalization of regulatory norms. These norms operate principally not by direct repression but by defining the domain of livable social categories. Western culture offers a limited set of gender and social classifications, such as male and female or gay and straight, within which the subject can recognize him- or herself *as* a viable subject. These classifications also determine the subject's recognition of sanctioned and viable objects of desire. The effectiveness of social regulation stems not only from the internalization of prohibitions and proscriptions in the conscience but from the very production of the conscience itself, as an interior zone of self-reflexivity. Because the capacity for reflection is crucial to Butler's hope for a "resistant" subject, she searches for the presubjective ground of self-consciousness, which would also account for the social origin of the individual conscience.

In Butler's view, the self as we know it emerges from

an inchoate, primitive folding back that retroactively constitutes both the subject and the object. Following Nietzsche's claim that the doer is an effect of the deed, she argues that the subject is the belated product of the act of doubling back upon itself by a not yet constituted presubject. The ego thus arises as an object of itself, resulting in the putatively "inner space" of the conscience. What initiates this inaugural, reflexive turn? A primordial foreclosure, under the pressure of social mandates, compels the emergent ego to turn from the barred object of desire and, incorporating the latter, to take itself as an object, a movement that Butler calls "the melancholic turn."

Expanding upon Freud's essay "Mourning and Melancholia," Butler seizes upon the concept of melancholia, first, because foreclosure, as she sees it, is an originary, "preemptive loss" that precedes and forms the self-reflexive subject and, second, because particular, socially regulated foreclosures are constitutive of "normal" subjectivity in our culture. Specifically, the barring of homosexual desire is "foundational" to what she terms "a certain heterosexual version of the subject."[2] In a word, melancholia is the condition of typical, heterosexual subjectivation in Western, heteronormative culture. Although Butler significantly never mentions the unconscious, she implies that homosexual desire is the unconscious, disavowed abject of heterosexual psychic constitution.

Turning to Joyce's story, "A Painful Case," it is apparent that the main character, James Duffy, has profoundly internalized middle-class norms, including a disdain for the Dublin that he so mundanely embodies. Duffy conforms rigidly to social regulations, although he

[2] Butler, p. 23.

doesn't think so, preferring to believe himself above vulgar "phrasemongers" and the sort of morality that is enforced by the police (D 111). A man with *Thus Spake Zarathustra* and *The Gay Science* on his bookshelf, Duffy is nonetheless hardly an *Übermensch* but a fellow with what Nietzsche terms a "bad conscience." At the beginning of "A Painful Case," Joyce characterizes him by obsessive orderliness, asceticism, and, importantly, self-reflection:

> He lived at a little distance from his body, regarding his own acts with doubtful side-glances. He had an odd autobiographical habit which led him to compose in his mind from time to time a short sentence about himself containing a subject in the third person and a predicate in the past tense. (D 108)

The apple that this otherwise tidy man leaves to rot in his writing desk testifies to Duffy's constrained appetite in general. He derives pleasure from the imperatives of his conscience, so that renunciation simply strengthens his enjoyment of prohibitions. Indeed, Duffy has cultivated a narcissistic attachment to the self-punishment of asceticism, which Freud terms a "negative narcissism." In short, Duffy fits the profile of Butler's "subjectivated" subject. But is he melancholic? What light does his case shed upon Butler's theory of the subject?

On the face of it, Duffy's problem lies in his refusal to love, specifically, in his rejection of Mrs. Sinico's offer of love. One might too easily conclude that Duffy is repressed and that, at the end of the story, he comes to mourn his loss of Mrs. Sinico. Such an interpretation is, I believe, quite wrong. Far from grieving over his loss of Mrs. Sinico's affection or even over her death, Duffy is "disillusioned" that she mistook friendship for sexual passion (D 111), and he is even "revolted" by what he considers her "degraded" venality (D 115). In short, Duffy has, from the start, preemptively denied the possibility of heterosexual love and, hence, the possibility of its loss. Instead of repression, Duffy's is a case of foreclosure that, as Butler explains, entails a "double disavowal, a never having loved, and a never having lost."[3] Having refused both love and the deprivation of it, Duffy does not mourn; precisely his inability to grieve -- his pain*less*ness, as it were -- marks him as a melancholic, in Butler's sense of the term. Duffy displays few, if any, of the symptoms of melancholia, such as dejection and a fall of self-esteem, as described by Freud. However, his consistent albeit negative narcissism and his preemptive foreclosure of Mrs. Sinico's love make it clear that, even before he meets her, he stands in a melancholic (non)relation to the world.

Duffy's constitution as a melancholic subject suggests that melancholia, rather than being an extreme and more or less pathological version of mourning, as Freud would have it, may be characteristic of the way in which subjects in general are formed, as Butler claims. Instead of a psychological process that, under the duress of bereavement, some people unfortunately undergo and that, in Freud's view, they usually pass through successfully, melancholia, in Butler's formulation, is a decisive and apparently universal event in the prehistory of the ego, an originary moment that happens once and for all, and of which the subject is necessarily unaware. It is certainly not an affective state. Without signaling her divergence from Freud, Butler nevertheless makes a clear break with him when she claims that "[m]elancholia does not name a psychic process that might be recounted through an explanatory scheme".[4]

[3] Butler, p. 139-40.

[4] Butler, p.171.

For Butler, melancholia lies at the source of the psyche itself, denoting the primordial turn that generates "the divide between the ego and object." "The [melancholic] turn from the [lost] object to the ego produces the ego" as a "*psychic object*," so that "there can be no ego without melancholia."[5]   In short, the ontological distinction between subject and object is the aftereffect of an "opaque," primal scene in which what will become the subject defends itself against the deprivation of the beloved object by withdrawing the latter into itself. Paradoxically, the ego "is the retroactive product" of this melancholic infolding.[6] In Butler's scenario of the genesis of the reflexive subject, the object appears to preexist the subject, which emerges only upon the withdrawal or incorporation of the lost object into itself, thus becoming, in part, that object. Yet, if the ego is a "belated" consequence of this reflexive turn, so, too, must be the object.

Butler gives a Nietzschean spin to Freud's well-known account of how the melancholic subject refuses to abandon his erotic cathexis on a person whom he has loved and lost. On the one hand, according to Freud, the melancholic internalizes the beloved within the ego, thus identifying with the person, and, on the other hand, he splits off a part of the ego (a part that Freud will later call the "super-ego") which, bearing his denied anger, torments the other part of the ego that identifies with and preserves the beloved, generating a psychic battle that leads to an impasse. Butler, however, ignores Freud's obvious assumption that melancholia is an aberrant response to erotic deprivation -- an experience that befalls an already constituted subject who refuses to come to grips with

[5] Butler, p. 168, p. 170, p. 171.

[6] Butler, p. 177.

reality -- and poses melancholia as the founding moment of subjectivation.

Her reason for so positing melancholia is, apparently, to support her now famous claim that "melancholic identification is central to the process whereby the ego assumes a gendered character" (132-33), a claim initially broached in *Gender Trouble*.[7] That argument, which she repeats in *The Psychic Life of Power*, runs largely as follows: In a heteronormative society, subjects can achieve proper masculinity and femininity only by abandoning early homosexual attachments. Specifically, the subject's renunciation of the parent of the same sex as an object of love requires that both the homosexual aim and object be foreclosed, not transferred onto a substitute. Instead of simply giving up the love of the same-sex parent, the very possibility of such a love must be forsworn and forgotten, resulting in what Butler calls the "never-never" of homosexual disavowal: for the heterosexualized subject, same-sex love never happened and was never lost. That negated love is preserved through "melancholic incorporation" in the form of an identification with the love object that has been disavowed.

Butler's political aim in advancing this in many ways persuasive thesis is, in her words, "to work on the weakness in heterosexual subjectivation and to refute the logic of mutual exclusion by which heterosexism proceeds."[8] However, her work has often had quite different effects, albeit wildly successful, than those that she apparently intends. Her theory of gender performativity is frequently misinterpreted as an endorsement of cross-dressing and

[7] *Gender Trouble: Feminism and the Subversion of Identity* (New York: Routledge, 1990), pp. 57-72.

[8] *Gender Trouble*, p. 148.

other drag styles, leading to facile underestimations of the strength of those regulatory social norms that she describes in *The Psychic Life of Power*. By contrast, Butler's attempt, in this book, to expose the "weakness" in the construction of heterosexuality makes it very difficult to understand how anyone could *not* become heterosexual. By situating homosexual foreclosure at the inaugural moment of the ego, Butler implies that the disavowal of same-sex love is structural to the very formation of the ego. In short, the ego is heterosexualized at birth. A homosexual subject is, as a result, an oxymoron. Moreover, her explanation of heterosexual subjectivation renders homosexuality and heterosexuality poles apart, even mutually exclusive, in psychological terms, a consequence to which Butler is overtly opposed politically.

These and other problems with Butler's theory become evident when we return to "A Painful Case." For Duffy, the foreclosure of same-sex love coincides with the foreclosure of other-sex love; he disavows *both* homosexuality and heterosexuality. Furthermore, his refusal of both directions of desire is explicitly conscious. Two months after breaking off his relations with Mrs. Sinico, Duffy writes in his notes, "Love between man and man is impossible because there must not be sexual intercourse and friendship between man and woman is impossible because there must be sexual intercourse" (*D* 112). The *pro*scription of homosexuality, side by side with the *pre*scription of heterosexuality, suggests that they are equally "impossible" or closed off to him, rather than mutually exclusive modes of subjectivation. Neither does the disavowal of heterosexuality, as it is thematized in "A Painful Case," produce a homosexual subject, nor does the disavowal of homosexuality produce a heterosexual subject. In short, Duffy's position is off the hetero/homo binary grid that Butler's theory maps for subjectivation. He is, as it were, unrecognizable   as a sexual subject in terms of the division between these opposed categories of desire.

Duffy's case poses further complications for Butler's concept of melancholia. His sexual preference, if he can be said to have one, is for himself: he is thoroughly narcissistic. His intimacy with Mrs. Sinico serves primarily, even exclusively, to magnify his ego.

> This union exalted him. . . . Sometimes he caught himself listening to the sound of his own voice. He thought that in her eyes he would ascend to an angelical stature; and, as he attached the fervent nature of his companion more and more closely to him, he heard the strange impersonal voice which he recognised as his own, insisting on the soul's incurable loneliness.(D 111)

Duffy incorporates Mrs. Sinico into his own ego and, even when speaking to her, listens to himself. She is a mere soundingboard for his own reflections on the impossibility of any intersubjective relation. It is no wonder that he is disappointed when he discovers that Mrs. Sinico has mistaken his self-love as love for her!

The misunderstandings between Duffy and Mrs. Sinico issue in a chain of misdirected performances that point toward the problem of agency in Butler's work. Duffy's case is "painful" to him primarily because, his narcissism notwithstanding, he fails to have the complete control that he wishes over the significance of his words and actions. Mrs. Sinico is, as it were, an errant reader of his gestures, temporarily disrupting the autoerotic circuit of his desires. When she takes his hand and presses it to her cheek, she tacitly insists that she be the object of his love; hence, his disgust and, later, his anger when he feels that her passion has degraded him.

Duffy's foreclosure of both heterosexual and homosexual love is in the service of his narcissism. As such, his case confirms Freud's observation that melancholia "represents . . . a *regression* . . . to original narcissism" insofar as the ego surrenders an actual relation to the loved person in order to preserve the erotic cathexis or "love relation" itself, which it substitutes for object-love.[9] By contrast, Butler argues that melancholia operates in a direction directly counter to narcissism, aligning it instead with the death drive. Although the linchpin of melancholia, in Freud's formulation, is narcissism, as both its motive and aim, Butler must reject the constitutive role of narcissism in order to sustain what she claims is the priority of the melancholic turn in the initial construction of the ego.

Despite the deterministic cast of Butler's account of melancholia, she, like Duffy, wants to assert the possibility of subjective agency. As previously noted, much of *The Psychic Life of Power* is implicitly devoted to rebutting the charge of voluntarism that has been leveled at Butler's earlier work. At various moments in her book, she adopts one or more of the following strategies to counter this charge, strategies that are not, however, altogether consistent.

Butler's usual argument for the possibility of resistance to regulatory norms is borrowed from Michel Foucault and is, strictly speaking, a claim not for subjective agency but for the beneficent consequences of accidents. Foucault argues that the conflicts and convergences among powerful discourses produce multivalent effects that may exceed, undermine, or reverse the aims of normalization; in short, power may inadvertently overthrow itself. Butler's particular spin on this argument is her assertion that, because the subject is constituted through reiterated, non-identical performances of itself, iterability offers the

---

[9] Sigmund Freud, "Mourning and Melancholia," in *The Standard Edition of the Complete Psychological Works*, ed. and tr. James Strachey (London: Hogarth Press, 1957) Vol 14, p. 249.

possibility of subversion. Adopting Althusser's idiom, she contends that "subversions are unanticipated effects of symbolic interpellations."[10] The weakness of this claim and Butler's evident skepticism of its efficacy are clear when, immediately after asserting that "the [symbolic] law turns against itself and spawns versions of itself which oppose . . . its animating purposes," she shifts to the first-person plural and asks, "[H]ow can *we* work the power relations by which *we* are worked?"[11] Here and elsewhere, Butler resorts to an unquestioned and untheorized "we" at the moment when, for her, crucial political interests are at stake and she is not content to wait for a fortunate accident.

Butler devotes considerable energy in *The Psychic Life of Power* to examining what she calls the "bind of agency," by which she means that the power exercised by a subject is at once continuous with and at odds with the power that shapes it. This "ambivalence" of power, as both the cause and the effect of the subject, fails to extricate Butler from her own double bind concerning agency, and she is thrown back on the Foucauldian notion that agency is an unintended effect or errant residue of power, the possibility of which lies in the unforeseeable future.

Still dissatisfied with vague aleatory hopes, Butler at other points resorts to the unseen past of the subject, to the psyche or the unconscious. Within psychoanalytic theory, the unconscious is traditionally understood to exceed or resist the demands of the ego and the normalizing discourses of social power. Swerving back and forth from Freud to Foucault on the issue of the relation of the psyche to the symbolic order, Butler finally comes down on the side of Freud, arguing that presubjective, imaginary, erotic

[10] Butler, p. 99.

[11] Butler, p.100 (emphasis added).

investments offer the possibility of resistance to the requirements for a coherent ego identity and obedience to the symbolic law. But Butler's resort to the psyche is ultimately opportunistic, for, when push comes to shove in political matters, the ground for resistance, for her, is pure will. For instance, when discussing insulting or injurious interpellations, such as being called "queer," Butler asserts that "the condition under which resignifying that interpellation becomes possible" is our sense of "alienation" at being hailed by that name.[12] In short, "our" resistance to the social category of homosexuality and our rejection or reworking of interpellations such as "queer" or "dyke" depend upon how comfortable we feel with those designations. Once again, Butler relies upon a presumptive and question-begging "we" at the critical moment in her claim for subjective agency.

In the final pages of *The Psychic Life of Power*, Butler takes a last, brief stab at the problem of agency and, surprisingly, calls for "forfeiting the notion of autonomy" by "accepting the ego's dependence upon the other." Acts of resistance to social power can come about only through "submission to a sociality . . . that makes such acts possible." This submission must be voluntarily performed, though, so it is only to be expected that Butler promptly returns to her faith in the failures of subjectivation as providing what she calls the "possibility for constituting oneself."[13] To conclude, Butler's belief in the self-creating power of the reflexive subject is disabled by her own account of the process of subjectivation. Rather than resistance, much less subversion, the best hope her theory offers is that of errancy and mistakes, such as Mrs. Sinico's misrecognition of

[12] Butler, p. 104.

[13] Butler, pp. 196-97.

Duffy's desires. As it stands, Butler's theory leaves the subject in Duffy's melancholic position, with his narcissistic illusion that he is the master of his fate. Although Butler struggles mightily in *The Psychic Life of Power* to situate the subject within the nexus of social relations, one feels at the end, like Duffy, that one is alone.

Rice University, Houston

"AS IF A MAN WERE AUTHOR OF HIMSELF" LITERATURE , MOURNING, AND MASCULINITY IN "THE DEAD" AND *ULYSSES*

RICHARD BROWN

Abstract. This essay provides cultural-historical and literary contexts to the choice of a literary career around the beginning of the twentieth century. It argues that such a choice, as in the case of Gabriel in "The Dead," might have been considered slightly effeminate. Relating Gabriel's choice to the ambivalent state of mourning and melancholy after the death of the mother, and extrapolating the situation of the hero of "The Dead" to Joyce's other protagonists, this essay argues that Stephen Dedalus finds in Shakespeare's Coriolanus an ideal image which helps him to become "author of himself."

> My mother bows,
> As if Olympus to a molehill should
> In supplication nod; and my young boy
> Hath an aspect of intercession, which
> Great Nature cries. "Deny Not." --Let the Volsces
> Plough Rome and harrow Italy!, I'll never
> Be such a gosling to obey instinct, but stand
> As if a man were author of himself,
> And knew no other kin.
> (Shakespeare, *Coriolanus* V.iii.29-37)

This speech from Shakespeare's *Coriolanus* was, of course,

known to Joyce.[1] Indeed the scene is referred to by Stephen in the "Scylla and Charybdis" episode of *Ulysses* when he claims, of the mother of Shakespeare (who died in 1608 when the play was written), that "Her death brought from him the scene with Volumnia in *Coriolanus*"(*U* 9.881-82). It is, perhaps, because Stephen's mother is traumatically deceased in *Ulysses*, whilst Volumnia is so fully alive in Shakespeare's play, that the two have not been as often connected in critical readings of Joyce as they might have been. Yet Stephen's comment invites a link, especially since, in this speech, it is in terms of a crisis of "authorship" that Coriolanus defines his confrontation with his mother and since both the assertions both of self and of literary authorship seem significantly connected to the maternal in Joyce, both for the Stephen of *Ulysses* who is in mourning for his mother and haunted by her ghost and for Gabriel in "The Dead", whose dead mother, Ellen, the third sister and "brains carrier" of the Morkan family, has defined the future course of his life and career and consequently the predicament in which he finds himself in that story, which I shall attempt to discuss here in terms of his masculinity. Issues of literature, masculinity, and the maternal may also inform our approach to a difficult section of and (the pun seems unavoidable) to the very conception of the "Oxen of the Sun" episode of *Ulysses*, where, as I shall suggest, an association with Coriolanus suggestively recurs.

Strength and weakness, heroism and unheroism, and their paradoxical relations with one another are significant aspects of each of these texts that can be highlighted by linking them in this way. Drawing on some recent work on the play by women critics, it might be said

[1] William Shakespeare *The Complete Works*, ed. Stanley Wells and Gary Taylor (Oxford: Oxford University Press,1988), p. 1096.

of Coriolanus that the strength of his commitments to conventional masculine-heroic codes of military prowess and at the same time to conventional masculine-filial codes of respectful obedience to the maternal proves to be his undoing.[2] The fact that he exhibits a kind of courage and self-denial in recognising the incommensurability of these codes at the climax of the play may give him a kind of tragic strength, we might think, even at the moment of his greatest apparent weakness. There may, at any rate, be something powerfully reminiscent, for Joyceans, in the kind of humbling tragic climax that the play offers, since the conclusions to many of the stories of *Dubliners* are often represented as being themselves humbling recognitions of weakness on the part of the protagonists.

The most direct link between the scene from *Coriolanus* and Joyce would seem to be the scene in "Circe" where Stephen has an equally climactic confrontation with his mother's ghost (*U* 15.4157-4245). For Stephen, as for Coriolanus, "authoring" is something that apparently needs to be performed in a kind of opposition to, or at least at some distance from, the maternal influence, and in both cases, we might observe, the mother appears to voice a demand for the suppression of self to the authority of Rome: in one case, to the city and, in the other, to the Roman Catholic Church. Where Coriolanus succumbs to the maternal plea, Stephen is apparently more successful in dismissing the image of his mother's ghost, perhaps allowing his development away from a debilitating melancholic posture and towards performative authorship

[2] Coppélia Kahn, *Roman Shakespeare* (London: Routledge, 1997), pp.144-59, pursues a relevant line of argument, in the course of which she acknowledges Page du Bois, "A Disturbance of Syntax at the Gates of Rome," *Stanford Literature Review* 2 (1985):185-205.

to proceed. If we take Stephen's exorcistic encounter with his mother's ghost in "Circe" as a step on his way towards becoming the author he wishes to be, then there is even, perhaps, something suggestive of the heroic conflict with the maternal monster that characterises the Anglo-Saxon epic *Beowulf* in this scene. Yet it is perhaps Stephen's comparative weakness (in *Ulysses* he is still an adolescent or young man who has not yet found his place in the world) that allows him to transgress the other side of the traditional heroic code by treating his mother's ghost in this apparently churlish and disrespectful way with some degree of impunity in the reader's eyes. Presumably, we recognise some legitimacy in his intellectual need to assert a priority of secular over religious learning and of cosmopolitan ambitions over local political constraints.

It seems appropriate, in the light of psychoanalytic studies of bereavement that are becoming more regularly invoked in literary critical discourses, that he should need to construct a negative image of (or as Freud puts it, to "bring into the open" an "ambivalence" in relation to) the loved object of his mother, in order to justify its loss to his traumatised ego, thereby allowing the process of healthy mourning, rather than that of debilitating melancholy, to take place.[3] For whatever complex of reasons, this

---

[3] Sigmund Freud, "Mourning and Melancholia (1917), in *On Metapsychology*, Pelican Freud Library, Vol.11 (Harmondsworth: Penguin, 1984), pp.247-68. In "Mourning and Its Relation to Manic Depressive States" (1940), Melanie Klein stresses the importance of reintegrating the "good" image. See Juliet Mitchell, ed., *The Selected Melanie Klein* (Harmondsworth: Peregrine Books, 1986), pp. 146-74. Julia Kristeva's work on melancholy can be found in *Black Sun: Depression and Melancholia*, trans. Leon Roudiez (New York: Columbia University Press, 1989); and a recent contribution to this discourse in Joyce criticism can be found in Hilary Clark, "Legibly Depressed: Shame, Mourning and Melancholia in *Finnegans Wake*," *JJQ* 34.4

apparently Wagnerian/Blakean or Nietzschean moment of heroic self-assertion of the "intellectual imagination" in "Circe" is fraught with contradictions and with an ambivalence that is strongly articulated in Stephen's definitively ambiguous cry of "*Nothung!*"

It is interesting to recall, then, that for Gabriel Conroy, another male character whose literary ambitions can be approached in terms of the maternal, authorship is apparently constructed not so much in opposition to as much as in obedience to the influence of his mother. Reference to Gabriel's mother is subtly but pointedly introduced into "The Dead." It is "thanks to her," we learn, that Gabriel has "taken his degree in the Royal University" (*D* 186-87) and, since she was the eldest of the three Morkan sisters who host the Christmas party, it is in the context of the maternal side of his family that Gabriel enjoys his regular if awkward role as "favourite nephew," literary speech-maker, and substitute patriarch at the annual Christmas gathering (*D* 179).

Gabriel's mother's social ambitions for him have, we are told, led her to disapprove of his choice of the "country-cute" Gretta for a wife (*D* 187), perhaps thereby causing, certainly anticipating, the possible divisions between the couple that the story proceeds to narrate. This negative thought reveals just the kind of ambivalence in his attitude to his mother's memory that, we may infer, has allowed him to mourn her passing in a way that is appropriate, according to the Freudian model.

To some extent, however, the literary role bequeathed to Gabriel by his mother seems to be a problematic one for him to occupy, in the sense that it seems to inhibit aspects of his ability to conform to more

(Summer 1997): 461-72.

conventional masculine/heroic roles. We never learn whether Gabriel's father, "T. J. Conroy of the Port and Docks" (*D* 179), had in mind for him some more conventional masculine career, such as in the administration or operation of the maritime aspect of Anglo-Irish relations. He is to be seen "piloting" the dysfunctional Freddy Malins across the landing at one point (*D* 184), and he chats to his (somewhat domineering) mother about her sea-crossing from Glasgow, but these hints aren't much further developed. Gabriel has become a man of letters by the time the story takes place, and it is in representing the demands and difficulties of maintaining this role, especially, I would like to argue, in terms of its implications for conventional ideas of masculinity and heroism, that much of the intensive focus on his consciousness in the story might be understood.

In contrast to Stephen's hubristic bid for intellectual freedom and "self-authoring," Gabriel's position as an intellectual figure appears to depend upon the awkward realisation that he is not "the author of himself," and he shows an ability to show respect for and to negotiate with the maternal influence and the feminine authority of his hostesses, though this is apparently at some cost to his self-esteem and even to the esteem in which he is held by the others in the story. Lilly and Miss Ivors, for instance, both seem to wish for something else from him than what he is able to give them.

In nineteenth-century Britain, literary work was not always recognised as an appropriately heroic masculine activity and was engaged in a constant struggle for legitimation against the more conventional, especially military, modes of masculine activity. Thomas Carlyle's enormously popular and influential work on *Heroes and*

Heroism is an obvious text to invoke here.[4] Carlyle attempted to reconfigure the concept of the masculine hero for his rapidly secularising Victorian audience by conceptualising the mythological and religious figure as a hero in a paradigm that was drawn from the Norse sagas. Significantly, he felt the need to treat the role of the poet (Dante and Shakespeare) and that of the man of letters (Johnson, Rousseau, Burns), as well as the figure of the religious leader (Mahomet and Christ) in these terms.

However, Victorian critics were not always so keen to register the heroism of their own literary contemporaries. Tennyson, Browning, and increasingly the later Victorian poets often seemed to their contemporaries not to conform adequately to the heroic or masculine role that the persistently military character of the Imperial age demanded. Joseph Bristow's useful collection of Victorian poetic criticism conveniently highlights this aspect of the critical discourse of the time, as, for instance, in the works of critics like the first poet laureate of the new century, Alfred Austin, who characteristically complained of the effeminacy of Tennyson's *Idylls of the King*.[5] A rise in the popularity of nonfictional prose during the period, especially by male writers, might be connected to these concerns.

Some aspects of the drive for linguistic energy and firmness in poetic discourse that is characteristic of some strains of literary modernism and the emerging genre of

[4] *On Heroes and Hero Worship* (London: Chapman and Hall, 1840). The work does not appear among those by Carlyle that were present in Joyce's Trieste library, though an extract from the section, "The Poet as Hero," is included in the Peacock anthology cited below.

[5] Joseph Bristow, *The Victorian Poet: Persona and Poetics* (London: Croom Helm, 1987), pp. 117-26.

First World War writing may also be connected to this and to the increasing needs of the First World War period to legitimate kinds of masculine activity other than the mass sacrificial industrialised carnage of the trenches. Feminist revisionary reconstructions of modernism that have emerged from critics like Scott and Gilbert and Gubar may have usefully foregrounded the importance of women's agency but have done little to prevent the obscuring of this masculine drive.[6]

Joyce's often quoted remark that T. S. Eliot's *The Waste Land* "ends poetry for ladies"[7] seems to be both modernistic and also to draw upon the modernising gender discourse of George Eliot's 1856 essay on "Silly Novels by Lady Novelists" which criticised a certain kind of Victorian writing for women in order to allow her own voice to be heard.[8] Ernest Hemingway's attempt to construct a terse modern prose style for his 1927 publication of *Men without Women* may also be relevant here. So also may be the ideas of Rémy de Gourmont on gender and intelligence that obviously interested Ezra Pound enough for Pound both to write about and to translate his work during the 1920s.[9] The

---

[6] Bonnie Kime Scott, ed., *The Gender of Modernism* (Bloomington: Indiana University Press, 1990); Sandra Gilbert and Susan Gubar, *No Man's Land*, 3 Vols. (New Haven: Yale University Press, 1988, 1989, and 1994).

[7] Richard Ellmann, *James Joyce* (Oxford: Oxford University Press, 1982), p. 495.

[8] George Eliot, "Silly Novels by Lady Novelists," *Westminster Review* (October 1856): 442-61.

[9] Rémy de Gourmont, *Physique de l'amour* (Paris: Mercure de France, 1903), translated by Ezra Pound as *The Natural Philosophy of Love* (London: Casanova Society, 1926). See also Ezra Pound, "Rémy de Gourmont: A Distinction," in *Selected Essays* (London: Faber, 1960).

likelihood that de Gourmont also interested D. H. Lawrence in some respects may also be highly relevant to this debate in ways that it is not possible to explore fully here.

That the problem was exacerbated in the Irish context of the turn of the century might be obvious for all students of literature in the paradigmatic preference shown by Maud Gonne for the man of action, John MacBride, over the man of letters, Yeats, which was repeatedly lamented in his lyric poetry. In Joycean circles, issues of masculinity have been variously opened by Declan Kiberd, Joseph Valente and others, though not, perhaps, precisely in these terms.[10]

Echoes of these Victorian and early modernist concerns can be seen throughout Joyce, as, for instance, in his attempt in entitling the fragmentary *Stephen Hero* as he does to translate the kind of heroism that is conceived in the traditional ballad about the highwayman "Turpin Hero" into the more subtly heroic mode of self-abnegation that may be implied in a narrative shift from first- to third-person narrative discourse. Joyce's letters at one memorable point in 1905 reveal a literary taste that could apparently prefer the popular masculine Victorian adventure fictions of Captain Marryat even to the preeminent literary achievements of Henry James, and indeed the echo of Marryat recurs through Joyce's work,

---

[10] Declan Kiberd, *Men and Feminism in Modern Literature* (London: Macmillan, 1985); Joseph Valente, ed. *Quare Joyce* (Ann Arbor: University of Michigan Press,1998). For some current discussions of masculinity, see Mairtin Mac An Ghaill, *Understanding Masculinities* (Milton Keanes: Open University Press, 1996); J. Hearn and D. Morgan, eds., *Men: Masculinities and Social Theory* (London: Hyman and Unwin, 1990); and H. Brod and M. Kaufman, *Theorising Masculinities* (London: Sage, 1994). See also Andrew Parker, Mary Russo, et al., eds., *Nationalisms and Sexualities* (London: Routledge, 1992).

though not, of course, to the exclusion of the Jamesian dimension.[11]

It is no surprise, therefore, to see that stereotypical modes of masculine heroism -- the Wild West adventure tale, racing fast cars, sexual gallantry, authority in the workplace, political heroism, supposedly heroic feats of alcoholic consumption, and so on -- are repeatedly presented in the *Dubliners* stories and contrasted with the weaker or more sordid realities of Joyce's protagonists when seen in a colder light.[12] Displaced or complicated notions of heroism were the stock-in-trade of prose fiction during the previous century and had been perhaps since the time of Cervantes. William Thackeray's *Vanity Fair* was subtitled "A Novel without a Hero," and Dickens's *David Copperfield* begins, "Whether I shall turn out to be the hero of my own life . . . these pages must show"; yet the more traditional, predominantly masculine adventure tale retained its popularity and even had something of a revival at the end of the century. Indeed in the more serious guises of Joseph Conrad and Rudyard Kipling as well as of R. L. Stevenson (whom Henry James, of course, himself admired) and even Conan Doyle, whose presence in *Finnegans Wake* has recently been demonstrated,[13] it was one of the most

[11] "I have been reading 'Confidence', 'Monsieur Bergeret a Paris' by Anatole France and 'Peter Simple' by Capt. Marryat: and I prefer the last of the three" (*Letters I*, p. 185). Mulligan is half-quoting the title of a Marryat novel when he calls Stephen "Japhet in search of a father" (*U* 1.561).

[12] One recent foray into the popular boy's adventure tale as it figures in "An Encounter" is Chester G. Anderson, "Should Boys Have Sweethearts?" in R. B. Kershner, ed., *Joyce and Popular Culture* (Gainesville: University Press of Florida, 1996), pp. 49-63.

[13] W. D. Jenkins, *The Adventure of the Detected Detective: Sherlock Holmes in James Joyce's "Finnegans Wake"* (Westport: Greenwood Press, 1998). See

interesting as well as most popular and distinctive genres of the period, and Joyce's stories touch on its language and strategies from time to time.

The small boy of the first three stories of *Dubliners* seems especially interesting in relation to the masculine adventure paradigm. This is, perhaps, not insignificant in broader literary historical terms, since Henry James's essay on Stevenson's *Treasure Island* had recognised and celebrated the access to a small boy's psychology that the novel gave, by implication inspiring the subtler and more ironised child perspectives and quests that figure in his own work.[14] Wittingly or unwittingly, Joyce's small boy is Jamesian in this sense. He often appears as a displaced or unsuccessful quester whose loss of satisfactory masculine role models gives him a confused sense of identity and of aspiration that may run to the root of fascination with language and signs. As the stories progress through their series of related experiences, the Carlylean goal of literary heroism -- at least as it appears in the cases of Little Chandler and James Duffy -- becomes a central paradigm of this difficulty of attaining the heroic, and its characteristic paradoxes and difficulties in these terms may be seen as significantly present in "The Dead."

Here, Gabriel's attempts to carry out his primarily literary role during the party are repeatedly subject to a series of jibes, and the text is pointedly full of hints and gestures towards other kinds of more or less heroic masculine roles: the "man o' war suit" worn by Gabriel's

---

also Maria Di Battista and Lucy McDiarmid, eds., *High and Low Modernisms: Literature and Culture, 1889-1939* (New York: Oxford University Press, 1996).

[14] Henry James, "Robert Louis Stevenson, 1887," in *The House of Fiction* (London: Rupert Hart-Davies, 1957), pp. 114-38.

brother in the old photograph of him with his mother; the references to Wellington; the military style of dancing "the lancers"; the much-discussed military overtones of carving the goose, in which task Gabriel is at least momentarily at ease (a detail that we might perhaps fortuitously connect to Coriolanus's reluctance to be a gosling in the speech I have quoted); Lilly's complaint that "the men that is now" are "all palaver" (that is, translating from the Portuguese that is apparently spoken by her unconscious, that they are men of words, or *palabras*, rather than of action); Molly Ivors's nationalist and gender jibes; Malins's drunken sottishness; Browne's geniality; the feats of the great tenors of the past who may not fall like the soldiers in the songs they sing but still achieve the heroic feats of the high C's; the gallery boys who get to be the horses pulling the carriage of some great *prima donna*; the tragi-comic story of Gabriel's maternal grandfather's horse Johnny; the sexual potency of D'Arcy's tenor voice, even or perhaps especially when hoarse with a cold; the romance of Michael Furey who, Gretta feels, has died for love of her; and so on. Whilst not all of these are obviously more heroic or more masculine roles than Gabriel's, they all seem to inform his disabling sense of the awkwardness of his situation.

Gender problems associated with the discourse of English Victorian poetry are also important in the story. A complex of self-conscious repressions and frustrations accompanies Gabriel's selection of a quotation from Browning, a task whose challenge to him is such that, by comparison to it, even the military heroic sacrifice of the Duke of Wellington seems momentarily "more pleasant" (*D*192). His "ten trembling fingers" on the tablecloth (*D* 202) clearly recall the "trembling fingers" of the first line of the nervous first Christmas lyric (lyric 30) of Tennyson's *In Memoriam* and show how deeply Gabriel's self-expression is locked within the idiom of the Tennysonian mode of poetic discourse at its most elegiac.

Frustrated, even in his anticipation of some steamy marital sex at the end of the story, Gabriel's only remaining recourse is to the literary weapon of irony, and, since that is apparently doomed to failure (with Gretta at least), the only outlet for his masculine aspiration is in the confrontation with humiliation and failure that the everyday round of modern life holds out for him in the future -- a decidedly Bloomian kind of "heroism" that consists in compromise, self-effacement, and self-denial.

Gabriel's confrontation with himself in the mirror is a kind of climax in the story in these terms. His "glimmering gilt-rimmed eyeglasses" are not the heroic spectacles in terms of which others would like to see him or he might like to see himself (D 218). The polite rhetoric of his after-dinner speech is all about performed weakness and inadequacy: "my poor powers as a speaker" (D 202), the "princely failing" of hospitality (D 203), the deference towards the more "spacious age"(D 203) of the past, the choosing "beyond my poor powers" (D 204), of not knowing to whom to give the prize (D 205). That, we might say, is its strength, even if it does seem to leave Gabriel inscribed into an extreme version of the very position of rhetorical impotence that his conventionally polite discourse has created for him as a "ludicrous figure, . . . pennyboy, . . . nervous well-meaning sentimentalist, . . . pitiable fatuous fellow," and so on (D 220).
Clearly in some sense Gretta's disloyalty to Gabriel at the end of the story (shown in her failure to render up her conjugal obligation at his moment of triumph and in her nostalgic fantasy for another man) provokes his extraordinary melancholic reverie. It would be neat, from the psychoanalytic point of view, to suggest that it does so

not as a result of sexual jealousy, which he conspicuously does not feel or tries not to feel. Rather, the moment confirms his mother's original criticism of Gretta, which had not prevented him from marrying her but had provided him with grounds for an important and enabling ambivalence about his mother's image. The recognition that his mother might have been right all along (at least in diagnosing Gretta's romanticism for the rural) may prevent Gabriel's ego from maintaining that ambivalence about her that has been necessary for him to convert melancholia into healthy mourning, and this may be thought to cause the melancholia associated with her loss to resurface in his mind at the close.

However, it might equally make sense to point to Gabriel's anxieties as related to the frustration that his civilised literary talents and interests cannot easily be understood by his wife in terms of conventional ideas of heroic masculinity. His retreat into poetic reverie at the end notably involves him in the voicing of a conventional sentiment of the man of action. Indeed there is something almost suicidally masculine and militarist in his declaration that he might "[b]etter pass boldly into that other world in the full glory of some passion than fade and wither dismally with age" (*D* 223). Joyce's intellectual vocation, of course, required that he maintain a distance from such sentiments even in a time of pan-European war.

Amongst recent attempts to redefine cultural representations of masculinity, the work by Peter Middleton in *The Inward Gaze* might seem especially appropriate to the attempted negotiation of the literary and the heroic that is suggested by Joyce's hero.[15] Middleton

[15] Peter Middleton, *The Inward Gaze: Masculinity, Subjectivity, and Modern Culture* (London: Routledge, 1992).

argues that it is in their self-consciousness that many modern literary heroes of the bourgeois world achieve a valid expression of their masculinity. Gabriel is certainly self-conscious, but Joyce's distinctive strategy of narrative objectivity and withdrawal leaves it open to the reader's interpretation or to doubt whether he thinks this position of melancholic self-doubt is really preferable to traditional masculine modes or not. Certainly both Gretta and Gabriel himself have their doubts.

If this conundrum of literature, melancholy, and masculinity is indeed characteristic of Gabriel's situation in "The Dead,",it is just as intensely felt in the developing predicament that Joyce imagines for his embattled and self-legitimating modern man of words, Stephen Dedalus, in *Stephen Hero*,in *A Portrait*, and, most of all, in *Ulysses*, where the expanding range of narrative perspectives and the increasing intensity of Stephen's dilemmas of literary productivity, as well as the ubiquitously collapsing codes of masculine chivalry, all leave the heroic status of his literary activity open to doubt, a doubt that remains one of the major faultlines of Joycean criticism.

It is well beyond the scope of this essay to offer a full review of Stephen's situation in these terms. However it is, I think, especially instructive to return to the remarkable phenomenon of the "Oxen of the Sun" episode of *Ulysses*, not least since it is an episode that may itself sometimes strike the reader as a literary tour de force, a heroic spectacle or feat.

Some of the characteristic puzzles that the episode sets for the reader can be considered in terms of the paradigm I have proposed. Whilst the Stephen of "Circe" struggles for self-definition against a negative image of the mother, the other and more positive side of his image of the maternal may, perhaps, be identified in the metaphors that underpin this episode, for which the womb is the dominating symbol and structural motif. If the "bad mother" is suggested in the demand for deathly sacrifice of the Cathleen ni Houlihan figure, the "good mother" figure may offer itself up in the fertile and nurturing womb of secular English literature.

It may seem clear enough that the content and structure of the episode are connected in terms of the metaphor of "literary gestation" that Joyce gave to Stephen in *A Portrait,* but the deeper relationship between the obstetric and the literary interests of "Oxen" as they unfold is not always so immediately apparent Why, for instance, is an episode dedicated to the womb so masculine in flavour, in terms of the characters who are present, in terms of the foregrounding of the surrogate paternal relationship between Stephen and Bloom and in terms of the writers who are selected by Joyce as models for the pastiches? Why is this canonical womb so full of dead white males?

One answer may well suggest itself in terms of what I have presented as an ambivalence about the maternal image which may be necessary to the process of mourning, to the avoidance of melancholia in Stephen, and to the need on Joyce's part to avoid Gabriel's quasi-suicidal dilemma by demonstrating that the feminised cultural space of literature can also be enabling for masculine agency.

How do we read the famously problematic question of the attitude that may be implied by Joyce's act of parody and/or pastiche of the long historical canon of English authors? Perhaps the "ambivalence" recently defined in it by Andrew Gibson in terms of an opposition emerging from cultural nationality, for example, should be understood as a somewhat more complex ambivalence that occurs within another ambivalence of this post-Freudian gendered kind. Gibson, by contrast with Ezra Pound's *Cantos,* calls the episode the "adulterate antithesis of its sources"; yet it is surprising, as one reads it more and more closely, how much of the episode is built of these very sources, how deeply and subtly those sources have been mined and explored, and how significantly they are re-voiced by Joyce here, almost as if the impulse to reconstruct a lost urban Dublin has a parallel in this episode's memorial reconstruction of a lost history of English literary prose discourse.[16]

It is at any rate interesting to observe that the trace of *Coriolanus* that I began by describing re-emerges in one of the most puzzling passages of the episode, which, since it is a passage drawing on a number of fifteen-century writers who are now best known as having been among Shakespeare's sources, provides a convenient linkage between the two episodes of "Scylla and Charybdis" and "Oxen" that (we might recall) are consecutive incidents in Homer but widely separated in Joyce's resequencing of the narrative. The passage is the one in which Stephen and the assembly debate the respective claims of a mother and her unborn child to live when a choice might be required because of a difficult birth. After Stephen distributes another round of drinks, the paradoxes of the virgin birth and the relation between natural and verbal creativity are explored, and Stephen offers a theory of creativity that might be seen, however provisionally, defensively and mystically to reclaim creative agency for men:

In woman's womb word is made flesh but in the spirit of the maker all flesh that passes becomes the word that shall not pass away. (*U* 14.292-94)

The section is written in part in the memory of a

---

[16] Andrew Gibson, "*Ulysses*, 'Cantos,' and the Shapes of Cultures," in *Pound in Multiple Perspective*, ed. Andrew Gibson (London: Macmillan, 1993), pp. 158-87.

passage of Sir Thomas North's translation of Plutarch's "Life of Coriolanus," which comes from William Peacock's anthology that Joyce used in composing the episode, and which was also Shakespeare's primary source for his play, though the North passage covers the period of Coriolanus's exile rather than that of his return.[17] In this particular passage of "Oxen" the multiple layering of the source passages (Raleigh, Holinshed, Hakluyt, Florio, and Sidney) makes the suppressed narrative paradigms hard to establish. However, North's picture of the banishment of Coriolanus must have sat powerfully in Joyce's imagination, definitive of the state of exile as it is. Indeed, the North passage draws an explicit parallel between Coriolanus's exile among the Volsces and the position of Odysseus in Troy in *Iliad,* book 10, that might have further appealed to Joyce.

The tendency of Joyce's phrase borrowing during the composition episode is to disperse the narrative integrity and contextual significance of the original passages, and the few phrases directly harvested from the passage by Joyce do little to reinforce the larger structural parallel between North's scene and his own.[18] The borrowings do, however,

[17] William Peacock, ed., *English Prose from Mandeville to Ruskin* (Oxford: Oxford University Press, 1903), was first identified as Joyce's principal source by J. S. Atherton and subsequently studied in detail by Phillip Herring and by Robert Janusko.

[18] In *The Sources and Structures of James Joyce's "Oxen"* (Ann Arbor: UMI Research Press, 1983), pp.108-10, Robert Janusko lists the detailed verbal borrowings from North that he finds on the notesheets and in the text, especially in the following: "insomuch as they feasted him for that time in the honourablest manner" (at lines 200-201); "Pricked forward with their jibes wherewith they did malice him" (line 235); and "Which hearing young Stephen was a marvellous glad man" (line 260). It is not untypical of the pattern of borrowing, when studied in detail, to find that these phrases

suggest that aspects of Stephen's defiant intellectual posture in this section of the episode are in part built from the language of North's *Coriolanus*.

The connection suggests that, in broad terms, Joyce imagined an association between Coriolanus's exile and Stephen's intellectualism as he here constructs a typically dense case against the powerful maternal images of the Catholic Church and instead for the kind of masculine birth or creation that can occur in the form of literature.

The section and the episode as a whole would tend to confirm Joyce's recognition both that a literary man may not be "the author of himself," at least not in conventional terms, and yet that the recognition of his indebtedness to others may be at the mysterious basis of literary fertility and agency itself, especially when, as here, the creative female womb gives forth such a masculine product.

Stephen's struggle with the uterine conundrum of creativity in "Oxen" may then anticipate his gesture of exorcism in "Circe" and contrast with the regressive lapse into melancholic reverie that Gabriel experiences in "The Dead." However, the echo of Coriolanus in the passage may also serve to undermine, rather than to support, Stephen's confidence in the longer term, just as the quotation with which I began this essay may seem to do.

The echo of the play serves to establish a link between creativity and heroic codes of masculinity in Stephen's thinking, that he is still, perhaps, in the process of resolving but which he, in possible contrast both to Gabriel and to Bloom, may yet be able to resolve.

---

occur before the start of the third month and "Elizabethan prose chronicle" section, which, it is usually agreed, begins at line 277. Even so, they suggest that Stephen's defiant intellectual posture in the episode is partly built from an association with Coriolanus.

The performance of these moments provides Joyce with an opportunity to present these central author-characters with a dilemma in which they need to validate the legitimacy of their gendered position in order to progress towards true creativity. However temporarily, they may require to maintain for themselves an enabling ambivalence towards the maternal, in order for them to avoid debilitating melancholia and progress through appropriate forms of mourning to become more fully the "authors" of themselves.

University of Leeds

NARRATIVE AUTHORITY AND PROSTITUTION IN JOYCE'S *PORTRAIT* AND FLAUBERT'S *NOVEMBRE*

ELIZABETH BRUNAZZI

Abstract. This essay concerns the intersection of Flaubert's "idea of prostitution" as represented in his correspondence and early writings with Joyce's *Portrait of the Artist as a Young Man.* In both Flaubert and Joyce, I would argue, the exposure of the margin between the repressed feminine teller and the masculine narrator underscores the ambivalent position of masculine authority in modernism. In this reading, Flaubertian texts possibly catalyzed Joyce's construction of an ambivalent narrative authority through the elaboration of a prostitutional discourse extending from *Stephen Hero* and *Portrait* to his massive inscription of Flaubert's *La Tentation de saint Antoine* as the narrative model for "Circe," the brothel episode and visionary "unconscious" of *Ulysses.*

The dictum defining the relationship of author to text as that of an "absent god" working on his manicure has often been isolated and assumed as the "core of the affinity" between Gustave Flaubert and James Joyce.[1] Critics neglect, however, the context in which it appears in *A Portrait of the Artist as a Young Man*:

> [T]he artist, like the God of the creation, remains within or behind or beyond or above his handiwork, invisible, refined out of existence, indifferent, paring his fingernails.
> ____Trying to refine them also out of existence, said Lynch.
> A fine rain began to fall from the high veiled sky and they turned into the duke's lawn, to reach the national library before the shower came.

---

[1] See Richard Cross, *Flaubert and Joyce: The Rite of Fiction* (Princeton: Princeton University Press, 1971), pp. vii-viii; p. 36.

> ____What do you mean, Lynch asked surlily, by prating
> about beauty and the imagination in this miserable God-forsaken
> island? No wonder the artist retired within or behind his
> handiwork after having perpetrated this country.(*P* 215)

Stephen's high-sounding rhetoric is thus immediately deflated by Lynch's reference to the material history of Ireland, much as "history," as Robert Spoo points out, revisits Stephen at the close of "Circe" in the form of an English soldier's fist.[2]

I shall argue that an alternative discourse on the "idea of prostitution," represented in both Flaubert's correspondence and early writings, intersects with Joyce's *Portrait* at crucial points. This discourse, indivisible from Flaubert's "modernism," not only destabilizes the narrative position of the masculine "author-god" but also inaugurates, as Alice Jardine states in *Gynesis*, "the putting into discourse of 'woman' as that process . . . intrinsic to the condition of modernity, . . . to new and necessary modes of thinking, writing, speaking."[3]

In this reading, early Flaubertian texts possibly catalyzed Joyce's construction of an ambivalent narrative authority through the elaboration of a prostitutional discourse extending from *Stephen Hero* and *Portrait* to his massive inscription of Flaubert's *La Tentation de saint Antoine* as the narrative model for "Circe," the brothel episode and visionary "unconscious" of *Ulysses*.[4]

[2] *James Joyce and the Language of History: Dedalus's Nightmare* (Oxford: Oxford University Press, 1994), p. 7.

[3] *Gynesis Configurations of Woman and Modernity* (Ithaca: Cornell University Press), p.25.

[4] It is often ignored that the triumvirate of Pound, Budgen, and Gilbert all accepted and asserted the preeminence of *La Tentation de saint Antoine* as a textual source and narrative model for "Circe." The sheer length and

If, as Ellmann and others hold, a reading of Flaubert's letters indeed informs the figure of the author as an "impersonal god" in Portrait,[5] it is likely that Joyce also read equally significant material in letters to Louise Colet from the same period.[6] Joyce would have read, for example, Flaubert's now-famous letter written in 1853 to Louise Colet describing his "idea of prostitution":

> It is perhaps a perverse taste, but I love prostitution, and for itself, independently of what is beneath. I have never been able to see

---

complexity of *La Tentation de saint Antoine* have rendered it a largely inaccessible text for the contemporary reader, although at the time of its reception in all three versions in the 1910 Conard edition it was an essential vehicle in the rediscovery of a subjective, visionary, "romantic" Flaubert. Pound, Budgen, Gilbert, and Joyce appear to have been both more knowledgeable and more canny in regard to Flaubertian modernism than many subsequent readers. See Ezra Pound, "Ulysses," in *Literary Essays*, ed. T. S. Eliot (New York: New Directions, 1968), p. 403, pp. 406-07; Stuart Gilbert, *James Joyce's "Ulysses"* (New York: Vintage, 1952), pp. 320-22; and Frank Budgen, *James Joyce and the Making of Ulysses* (London: Grayson and Grayson, 1934),p. 245.

[5] Following Richard Ellmann, Robert Scholes and Richard Kain suggest that Joyce may have read Flaubert's letters from 1852-57 in the period preceding the publication of *Portrait*. See *James Joyce* (Oxford: Oxford University Press, 1959), p. 269; and Robert E. Scholes and Richard M. Kain, eds., *The Workshop of Daedalus: James Joyce and the Raw Materials for "A Portrait of the Artist as a Young Man"* (Evanston, Ill.: Northwestern University Press, 1965), pp. 247-48. Ellmann also remarked in the same context: "This creator is not only male but female; Joyce goes on to borrow an image of Flaubert by calling him a 'god,' but he is also a goddess."

[6] Flaubert's letters to Colet on many literary subjects are charged with their personal battles and should therefore be approached with cautious reserve. Flaubert's preoccupation with the "idea of prostitution" is also contained, however, in letters to other intimate correspondents and in fictional writing and thus quite exceeds the context of his correspondence with Colet.

one of those women in   décolleté pass by in the gaslight, in
the rain without a pounding of my heart, just as monk's robes with
their knotted girdles make me shiver in some ascetic and deep
recess of my soul. There is, in this idea of prostitution, a point of
intersection so complex, lust, bitterness, the nothingness of human
relations, the frenzy of muscles, and the ringing of gold, that
looking into it finally makes you dizzy, and you learn so many
things there! And you are so sad! And you dream so well of love!
Ah, writers of elegies, it is not on ruins that you should go lean
your elbow, but on the breasts of these gay woman! . . . During my
first years in Paris, on hot summer evenings, I would go and sit in
front of Tortoni's and, as the sun set, I would watch the prostitutes
pass by. I was consumed with biblical poetry, and I thought of
Isaiah, of "fornication in high places," and I would go back up La
Harpe street, repeating to myself the end of this verse: "And her
throat was softer than oil." I'll be damned if I was ever more
chaste.[7]

These texts represent an immanence of Flaubert in his work
from its inception and an intersection of autobiographical
elements, literary and historical apprehension much closer
to the character and evolution of Joyce's work than might
be suggested by reliance on the monological dictum of the
"impersonal" author. The spatial figuration of history as a
"ruin" inscribed in Flaubert's letter as a structure in the
process of effacement yet paradoxically generative of
knowledge, vision, and writing; and the linking of such a
discourse with the thematics of prostitution belong,

[7] *Gustave Flaubert: Extraits de la Correspondance; ou Préface à la vie
d'écrivain*, ed. Geneviève Bollème (Paris: Éd. du Seuil, 1963), pp. 122-23. I
have followed Charles Bernheimer's translation of this letter in *Figures of Ill
Repute: Representing Prostitution in Nineteenth-Century France* (Cambridge:
Harvard University Press, 1989), p. 134, as I do not believe it can be
improved upon. I have also employed Harry Zohn's translation from the
German of Walter Benjamin's *Charles Baudelaire* and William Hutchison's
translation from the French of Ernest Renan's *Life of Jesus*. Otherwise, all
translations from French texts are my own.

however, to the late phase of Romanticism in mid-nineteenth-century France and are not uniquely Flaubertian.

In his writing on Charles Baudelaire's modernism, Walter Benjamin returns repeatedly to the generative ambiguity of the prostitute in Baudelaire's work as a metonym for the poet's experience of the "stigmata which life in a metropolis inflicts on love."[8] Citing Baudelaire's evocation of "that holy prostitution of the soul which gives itself wholly, poetry and charity, to the unexpected that appears, to the unknown that passes,"[9] Benjamin demonstrates a "profound duplicity" in Baudelaire's stance that renders his poetry complicit in the "threadbare" heroism of the street.[10] Thus, in Benjamin's formulation, the relationship of the masculine writer as invisible, voyeuristic author-god to his material subject is undermined by the ambivalence of the "seer" which exposes him as the accomplice, the "familiar" of the teeming street whose heroine is the prostitute. The "familiar look" of the prostitute metonymizes the eye of the city-dwelling poet who, like the figure of the prostitute, is both commodity and seller in one.[11]

The first publication of all three versions of Flaubert's *La Tentation de saint Antoine* and of his *Oeuvres de jeunesse inédites*, in the Conard edition of 1910, and the appearance of Benjamin's study of Baudelaire, dating from 1919, are exemplary of the European literary and social

[8] *Charles Baudelaire: A Lyric Poet in the Era of High Capitalism*, trans. Harry Zohn (London: Verso, 1997), p. 125.

[9] p. 56.

[10] Benjamin, p. 26, p. 73.

[11] Benjamin, p. 150, p. 171.

climate in the first two decades of the twentieth century. Joyce was already working with a complex of materials in *Stephen Hero* linking the *aporia* of the prostituted woman with the vocation of the artist: the transmission of historical renewal from "below," through its relation to the marginal, the outcast, the repressed, the secret, and the irrational.

In chapter 24 of *Stephen Hero*, just after Stephen has taken leave of the young woman Emma, presumably forever because she does not "give," a woman in "a black straw hat," that is, a streetwalking prostitute, surges from the darkness and greets Stephen with the phrase, "Good night, love." Stephen silently refuses her offer and, "still humming the chant of the passion, transferred his coins to her hand, and continued on his way"(*SH* 189). This encounter gives rise to a musing narration on the nature of love announcing the style of one of Stephen's interior monologues in *Ulysses*; on texts from the French historian Ernest Renan's well-known *Vie de Jésus*; and on the status of the "woman in the black straw hat" within the scheme of value posed by the life of the historical Jesus (*SH* 190). Recalling her words, Stephen repeats to himself, "The greatest lover of all time could not say more than that. Think of that. 'Good night, love.' Mustn't the devil be annoyed to hear her described as an evil creature?" (*SH* 190).

Following this narrated monologue, Stephen and Lynch engage in a conversation in which they agree that it is "impossible not to commit adultery" and conclude the dialogue with the following exchange:

> ____You remember in *The Adoration of the Magi* "When the immortals wish to overthrow the things that are today and wish to bring the things that were yesterday they have no one to help them except one whom the things that are today have cast out."
> ____Yes.

____Who have I to help me   except the woman in the black straw hat? And yet I wish to bring to the world the spiritual renewal which the poet brings to it. . . . No, I have decided. I will not see her anymore.

____The woman in the black straw hat?

____No, the virgin. (*SH* 205)

The text of W. B. Yeats's *The Adoration of the Magi* is of particular interest in the present study, as the parable recounts the visit of three old men, the "magi" seeking wisdom from the "immortals," to a beautiful Irish prostitute dying in a Parisian brothel. The prostitute, consumed by an "unquenchable desire," is the vessel of knowledge, the threshold of the "names" that will usher in a new era in which the Irish, Gaelic past will be reborn and renewed, as "Christianity is going away, and the Immortals are beginning to awake."[12]

The "woman in the black straw hat" and allusions to Renan and to texts by Yeats are suppressed in favor of a different, both more formal and aestheticized textual strategy in *Portrait*, but, I maintain, they continue to function as subtexts to the discourse of prostitution as it concerns Joyce's early apprehension of the "language of history" in the vocation of the artist. The earlier passages are transformed in *Portrait* to become the narration of Stephen's nocturnal wandering through the streets of Dublin in late autumn, uttering words and phrases to himself and expressing repeatedly an intolerable desire for an ideal woman that is nurtured throughout boyhood by the imagination of Romantic literature. Stephen's represented and textual errancy leads to his eventual confession to sexual initiation with a nameless prostitute.

[12] *The Secret Rose, Stories by W. B. Yeats: A Variorium Edition* (Ithaca: Cornell University Press, 1981), pp. 164-72.

There is an important parallel, and a palimpsest of texts, between Joyce's portrayal of Stephen in the period preceding his sexual initiation as seeking in the streets of Dublin another Mercedes, the heroine of *The Count of Monte Cristo*, in another Marseilles (*P* 62-63), and Flaubert's actual voyage south to Marseilles as a young man and his sexual initiation with a prostitute, inscribed as the most enduring of fragments of memory in his early fictional autobiography *Novembre*.

Arguably his most " Baudelairian" work, Flaubert's *Novembre* would necessarily have impressed the young Joyce. A *Künstlerroman* written during 1840-42 when Flaubert was 20-22 years old, *Novembre* was the Flaubertian project most allied with the aspirations of the young Joyce when he began writing *Stephen Hero*.[13] *Novembre* features the account of the narrator's sexual initiation with a prostitute named Marie, based on the experience of the young Flaubert with a woman from Marseilles named Eulalie Foucaud de Langlade. A final, abrupt shift to a

---

[13] Victor Brombert has remarked that "the young man of *Novembre* is more of a potential artist than a fully formed one; he is one of the only two artist-heroes in Flaubert's fictional writing" ("Flaubert and the Status of the Subject," in *Flaubert and Postmodernism* [Lincoln, Neb.: University of Nebraska Press, 1984], p. 113). *Novembre* was not published in the lifetime of either Baudelaire or Flaubert. An excerpt taken from the prostitute's story framed in *Novembre* as an autobiography within an autobiography appears with high praise in Maxime Du Camp's widely read *Souvenirs littéraires* (Paris: Hachette, 1882), Vol.1, p.312. The work first appeared in its entirety in an edition of the previously unpublished *Oeuvres de jeunesse inédites* in the first collection of Flaubert's *Oeuvres complètes* published by Conard in 1910. It is therefore possible that Joyce was acquainted with *Novembre* before it turned up as a book order for his Trieste library in a 1914 two-volume Charpentier edition of Flaubert's *Premières oeuvres*. *La Tentation de saint Antoine*, *Madame Bovary*, and *Salammbô* are also listed by Richard Ellmann in *The Consciousness of Joyce* (London: Faber & Faber, 1977), pp. 108-09.

third-person   narrator   announces the birth of the writer as teller. The patterning of this first successful work of fiction by Flaubert bears attention as a possible source for Joyce's decision to incorporate a specific account of his sexual initiation with a prostitute in his *Portrait of the Artist as a Young Man* and the construction of a narrative authority following the style of Flaubert.

Novembre opens with a Romantic conflation of autumn as the dying season and the surging of memories. Such a movement sets off the precocity of the young man narrating the story, as he states that he senses his own consciousness as containing "the debris of thousands of past lives."[14] From the very beginning, the *pente* of the narration signals a trajectory into the past, the unconscious of memory, and toward a societal and geographic margin, a symbolic underground, which will ultimately be associated with the young man's wandering among city streets. The stages and settings of the boy's memories, the portrayal of his evolving consciousness, and the awakening of desire conflated with both reading and the generation of poetic language announce the movement and construction of the young Joyce's autobiographical texts.

The memories of young Flaubert's narrator initially include brief flashes illuminating childhood: "I saw so recently the cows coming back, lowing as they turned toward the setting sun, the little boy who drove them in front of him with a bramble, shivering under his canvas clothing. They slipped as they went down the muddy embankment, and crushed several apples lying in the grass" (*N* 248). The childhood memory that opens Joyce's *Portrait* is that of the celebrated visual and auditory image of "a

---

[14] Gustave Flaubert, *Novembre*, in *Oeuvres complètes*, 2 vols. (Paris: Éditions du Seuil, 1964), vol. 1, p. 248. Hereafter cited in text as *N*.

moocow coming down along the road" meeting "a nicens little boy named baby tuckoo" (*P* 7). At a later point, Joyce refers to them again: "But when autumn came the cows were driven home from the grass" (*P* 63).[15]

At boarding school, Flaubert's young man experiences the advent of a vague desire in which language, imagination, and writing all converge: "The woman whom I was already trying to discover . . . I began by forcing myself to dream about it, like a poet who wants to create something and provoke inspiration; . . . it was a frenzied racing of the imagination, a prodigious leap out of reality. I made up adventures, I constructed palaces for myself, I was ensconced there as an emperor" (*N* 249). At boarding school, Stephen is also visited by "vague desire" in which the image of the body of woman, the body of words, and the lure of the "real" commingle: "Eileen had long thin cool white hands too because she was a girl. They were like ivory; only soft. That was the meaning of *Tower of Ivory* (*P* 42). Later, at Blackrock, Stephen thinks:

> Words which he did not understand he said over and over to himself till he had learned them by heart: and through them he had glimpses of the real world about him.
>
> . . . .
>
> His evenings were his own; and he pored over a ragged translation of *The Count of Monte Cristo.*

[15] Christine van Boheemen (*The Novel as Family Romance: Language, Gender, and Authority from Fielding to Joyce* [Ithaca and London: Cornell University Press, 1987]) has said of the initiatory passage in *Portrait,* "Stephen's identity as an artist (no less than his potential for becoming a speaking subject) depends on the identification with a father figure, even if that figure is only known as narrative and, through narrative, as an abstract idea (16). To the extent that these passages echo the young Flaubert, Joyce specifically instances the "father figure" of modernist narrative at the threshold of his vocation.

....
[H]e built up on the parlour table an image of the wonderful island cave out of transfers and paper flowers and coloured tissue paper and strips of the silver and golden paper in which chocolate is wrapped. When he had broken up this scenery, weary of its tinsel, there would come to his mind the bright picture of Marseilles, . . . of Mercedes." (*P* 62)

The vague but splendid object of the young Flaubertian narrator's desire is also associated with the sound of certain words: *femme* (woman), *maîtresse* (mistress), *adultère* (adultery). His love of reading and, in particular, of history, converges with his desire: a "mistress" becomes a historic figure reigning over momentous events, and kingdoms rise and fall, as she is the motive force of historical evolution (*N* 249).

Just as Flaubert describes in his letters recalling his student days in Paris, in *Novembre* the urban street becomes the theater of the young man's wanderings and of his desire. In one of the most vivid descriptions in Flaubert's early writing, the young narrator of *Novembre* evokes his simultaneous discovery of prostitution and the multitudinous life of the city:

> In the period when I was a virgin, I took pleasure in looking at prostitutes. I passed through the streets where they lived, I haunted the places where they walk; sometimes I spoke to them in order to tempt myself, I followed them I touched them. . . .
>
> I loved to lose myself in the whirlwind of the streets; I would often engage in inane distractions, such as looking fixedly at each passerby, in order to discover on his face a salient vice or passion. All of the heads passed rapidly in front of me: some smiled, whistling as they went on, the wind in their hair; others were pale, others red, others white; they disappeared quickly as they passed at my side, they slipped away one after the other like street signs seen from a carriage. . . . [A]t the corner of the street, an organ grinder was playing, children in rags were singing, a fruit merchant was pushing his cart, lit up by a red lantern.(*N* 252)

In this passage, the narrator's experience of urban prostitutes is an *ouverture* to immersion in the random, multiple life of the street and to the rhythm of existences inhabiting it. Such experience entails engagement with desire and an encounter with the "Real," that is, in Lacanian terms, the ephemeral trace of the material world as its signs surge in and out of perception. Flaubert's Marseilles street where faces "[slip] away . . . like street signs seen from a carriage" announces Joyce's "Hades." With "an organ grinder" playing, "children in rags" singing, and "a fruit merchant . . . pushing his cart, lit up by a red lantern," we are transferred to the threshold of Circean Nighttown. In *Portrait* Stephen's nocturnal wandering brings him to a similar street and, like the narrator of *Novembre*, to the threshold of sexual initiation with a prostitute: "He returned to his wanderings. The veiled autumnal evenings led him from street to street as they had led him years before along the quiet avenues of Blackrock" (*P* 99).

Flaubert's narrator states that he "loved to lose himself in the whirlwind of the street." Such a loss of "self" within multiplicity, a *descente aux enfers*, "to be matter," as he puts it in *La Tentation de saint Antoine*, is a persistent theme in the work of Flaubert that figures the cyclical recuperation, the resurrection of the creative self, which is at odds with the rhetorical precept of the famously distant, "impersonal" author.[16] Stephen must "lose" the self in order to find his identity as an artist: "He felt some dark presence moving irresistibly upon him from the darkness, a presence subtle and murmurous as a flood filling him wholly with

---

[16] The "doctrine" of the "impersonal author" has been thoroughly questioned within Flaubertian scholarship. See, for example, Jean Bruneau, "La Présence de Flaubert dans *L'Education sentimentale*," in *Langages de Flaubert* (Paris: Minard, 1976), p. 33.

itself. Its murmur besieged   his ears like the murmur of some multitude in sleep; its subtle streams penetrated his being. It broke from him like a wail of despair from a hell of sufferers and died in a wail of furious entreaty, a cry for an iniquitous abandonment" (*P* 100).

The Flaubertian narrator's description of his initiation with "Marie" is considerably more detailed and elaborate than that of Joyce's Stephen, but the descriptions of the women's bodies and their "language" contain common points.   Flaubert's Marie "passed her hand through [my] hair, as if she were playing with a child" (*N* 260). She has "pink, wet lips, open nostrils, fiery eyes, and seems to vibrate beneath the strokes of her thought as, after the artist has departed, the sonorous instrument continues to emit a secret perfume of silent notes" (*N* 262). Joyce's description echoes both the preceding passages and Flaubert's biblical mantra, "and her throat was softer than oil," in his correspondence: "She passed her tinkling hand through his hair, calling him a little rascal. . . . He closed his eyes, surrendering himself to her, body and mind, conscious of nothing in the world but the dark pressure of her softly parting lips. They pressed upon his brain as upon his lips as though they were the vehicle of a vague speech; and between them he felt an unknown and timid pressure, darker than the swoon of sin, softer than sound or odour" (*P* 101).

Both Flaubertian and Joycean accounts of sexual initiation with a prostitute figure the threshold of narrative representation as the advent of a new speech.   The Flaubertian narrator invites "Marie" to tell him her life story and describes what attracts him in the potential accounting: "I glimpsed a thousand terrible passions which must have been driven into her like thunder bolts, judging from the traces that remained" (*N* 264). Marie's story embodies a texture of fragments of consciousness and memory that the young narrator senses as the inscription of his own subjectivity. Within the framework of the Romantic, autobiographical narrator elaborated by the young Flaubert, the inscription of such subjectivity is the matrix of narrative representation. Marie is thus the sister of the Baudelairian prostitute who is so riveting to the poet because, as Benjamin later discusses in quite similar language, she bears the traces of a "thousand natural shocks that the modern city produces."[17]

The story of Marie's life is framed within *Novembre* as an autobiography within an autobiography; she is provisionally a "teller" speaking in her own voice. While the pattern of her story resembles true accounts of prostitutes' lives in the period, her beginnings are abstracted and effaced in the sum of the inscriptions of all the men who have "written upon" her.[18] The parade of nameless, phantom lovers, which like a poet, Marie sells through her confession to a customer, represents an overdetermination of the incipience of writing, of writing as beginning, as the moment of artistic initiation itself. Benjamin remarks of the urban crowd in the work of Baudelaire that it figures "the phantom crowd of words, the fragments, the beginnings of lives."[19]

Both the figure and story of Marie are ultimately repressed, submerged in the wake of a third-person masculine teller who assumes the narrative of *Novembre*. The assertion of narrativity is thus ambivalently predicated on both the recounting of the prostitute's story and her eventual repression from first-person subjectivity. Such an

[17] Benjamin, p. 61.

[18]Flaubert incorporated accounts of real prostitutes' lives in his fiction, for example, Rosanette's account of her life in *Education sentimentale*.

[19] Benjamin, p. 120.

ambivalent, double movement in regard to the fictionalizing of prostitution as the historical reality of the prostituted woman endowed with subjectivity, on the one hand, and her reification in the masculine imagination as a springboard for writing, a machine for making stories, on the other, is reiterated throughout Flaubert's oeuvre.

The Joycean prostitute in *Portrait* is nameless, and the narrative of Stephen's initiation with her includes only the briefest fragments of dialogue: "Good night, Willie dear!" and "Give me a kiss, she said" (*P* 100-101). She is, however, "the vehicle of a vague speech" (*P* 101) and is thus also represented by Joyce as a threshold, the incipience of a new language, the anonymous space of the yet-to-be-named. Throughout Joyce's work feminine discourse is consistently represented as that which is *about to be spoken;* as the movement of an initial, submerged, half-articulate speech which can only be represented by a masculine narrator who overhears it; as speech at the margin between consciousness and unconsciousness; and as speech at a cultural frontier between the repressed feminine and the patriarchal symbolic order.

In both Flaubert and Joyce, I would argue, the exposure of the margin between the repressed feminine teller and the masculine narrator underscores the ambivalent position of masculine authority in modernism. As the origin of creative discourse, such authority is poised between repression of feminine speech and representation through the masculine symbolic order. Such a relationship to language is hardly "detached, indifferent, refined out of existence." The assertion of artistic language is, on the other hand, "interdependent," to borrow a term from Christine van Boheemen, with repressed feminine discourse in its initiation.[20]

---

[20] Van Boheemen, p. 15.

Ultimately, both Flaubert and Joyce ambivalently assert the initiation of writing through contact with the discourse of repressed feminine sexuality, specifically, the marginalized female body as it is projected in the symbolic figure of the prostitute. The initiation of writing, or textual "beginning," in modernism is thus not the assertion of an onto-theological origin, but rather the site of an oscillation between discourses or, as Edward Said puts it, between "authority" and "molestation."[21] If historic repression of female sexuality is a cornerstone of the patriarchal order and the symbolic discourses that represent it, and if, similarly, assertion of female sexuality is fundamental to the project of a "new," antipatriarchal language, as Luce Irigary and others have argued, the discursive margin occasioned by the ambivalence of the masculine narrator in regard to the sexualized body of the prostitute, a metonymy for the repression of the female sexual body in general, is the threshold itself of a "new language."[22]

[21] Edward Said, *Beginnings: Intention and Method* (New York: Basic Books, 1975), pp. 83-84. Joyce, following Flaubert in the order of texts if not of "influence," exposes the ambivalence of masculine authority to the "mirror" of feminine subjectivity as the decentered "origin" of writing itself. I prefer both Mikhail Bakhtin's concept of a dialogical "threshold" and Said's "beginnings" to "origin." The quarrel of both Flaubert and Joyce with the onto-theological, hierarchical tradition asserted in Catholicism, and their mutual assumption of an heretical role through their art, is too complex to bear discussion within the scope of this study. It has occasionally been noted that it was a fundamental common point between them, by, for example, Fritz Senn (in "Trivia Ulysseana IV: Brood of Tempters," *James Joyce Quarterly* 19.2 [1982]: 151-54), but has not been elaborated through the representation of the prostitute and the brothel.

[22] See, for example, Ann Rosalind Jones's essay, "Writing the Body: Toward an Understanding of *l'Écriture Féminine*," in *The New Feminist Criticism: Essays on Women, Literature, and Theory*, ed. Elaine Showalter (New

Fredric Jameson asserts that history, defined as the Althusserian "absent cause" or Lacan's "Real," is not accessible to consciousness other than indirectly through textual, narrative form, and that cultural texts -- specifically, narrative texts -- exhibit dynamics of contradiction and repression that represent the traces of history itself.[23] History, in Jameson's perspective, thus becomes the texture of that which has, as well as that which has not, been made available to consciousness through narrative, with the result that the traditional dichotomy between the "real" and the "written" ceases to apply.[24] Similarly, the dichotomy assumed between sexuality, active or fantasized, and the "historical," conceived as economic or political history, collapses. For Jameson it is possible to "short-circuit the false problem of the priority of the economic over the sexual, or sexual oppression over that of social class. . . . It becomes clear that sexism and the patriarchal are to be grasped as the sedimentation and virulent survival of forms of alienation specific to the oldest mode of production of human history, with its division of labor between men and women, and its division of power between youth and elder."[25]

Charles Bernheimer makes a similar point on ideology and sexuality when he speaks of "the force of ideology in the unconscious, and the force of sexual

---

York: Pantheon Books, 1985), pp. 361-77, for a critical discussion of the positions of Julia Kristeva, Luce Irigaray, and Hélène Cixous on this point.

[23] *The Political Unconscious: Narrative as a Socially Symbolic Act* (Ithaca: Cornell University Press, 1981), pp. 34-35. My remarks summarize principal points in Jameson's first chapter, "On Interpretation: Literature as a Socially Symbolic Act," pp. 17-102.

[24] Jameson, pp. 42-49.

[25] Jameson, p. 100.

fantasies in ideological formations."[26] The narratives of "history" and the cultural texts that contain them may be interpreted as networks of such ideological formations forged over time, indivisibly, out of both event and fantasy.

The youthful works of Flaubert and Joyce, *Novembre* and *Portrait*, assert the indivisibility of the phenomenon of prostitution and a vision of history: the prostitute is the figure at the crossroads, the intersection between the past and the contemporary, or between "history" conceived as a linkage of external events and as the current of interiority. As a transgressive, marginalized, outcast figure, she represents a repressed stratum whose traces are perpetually pushing up into historical view, thus becoming the present signs of the future.

Toward the end of *Portrait*, Joyce merges the discourse of prostitution with his ambition to write a new, collective Irish history, "the uncreated conscience of his race." As Stephen views the Irish "patricians" through the window of Maple Hotel, he muses specifically on the fate of Ireland in the form of Irish womanhood, asking himself how he might "cast his shadow over the imaginations of their daughters" (*P* 238). Shortly afterward, he recalls the figure of the Irish peasant woman offering herself to Davin from the doorway of her house, literally standing on the threshold. She is a complex figure of the poverty of life and culture as well as of the nobility, beauty, and innocence Joyce found in the Irish context. It is here that the palimpsest of texts in *Portrait* is most apposite. The effaced layers of *Stephen Hero* beneath the specific account in *Portrait* of Stephen's sexual initiation with a prostitute include, as discussed earlier in this essay, Renan's remarks

[26] Charles Bernheimer, p. 53.

from the *Vie de Jésus* in   which the "fallen" woman is the type of sinner most cherished by Jesus as a springboard for redemption; and Yeats's parable of *The Adoration of the Magi* in which the Irish beauty outcast and dying in a Parisian brothel is the vessel of a new Irish history, the threshold of its "names."[27]

It is plausible that a broader reading of Flaubertian modernism than is generally supposed, supported by the choice of Flaubertian texts in Joyce's Trieste library, informed Joyce's selection of a narrative solution to his rejection of the Catholic, hierarchical grid of culture. In this reading, Flaubertian narrative offered Joyce a mirror of his own ambivalence toward women as "origin," while permitting him to remain within "the blueprint of patriarchy."[28] Joyce thus circumvented the problem posed by his rejection of the onto-theological tradition by incorporating Flaubert as a modernist "father," one whose legacy to the discourses that propel modernist narratives is difficult to overestimate.

Princeton, New Jersey

[27] *Life of Jesus*, trans. and intro. by William G. Hutchison (London: Scott Publishing, 1897),p. 97: "[The] Magdalene was . . . the principal agent by which faith in the resurrection was established." Jacques Aubert has said of the girl Stephen glimpses on the strand, "A figure of the Virgin in her inaccessibility, she is also the reverse, just as Eve, according to good theology, evokes and justifies the Madonna; . . . she figures Woman, which is to say . . . the hieroglyphic function of language, the interdependence of image and letter: she is for Joyce the luminous, literally epiphanic emblem of writing itself" (preface, *Portrait de l'artiste en jeune homme*, trans. Ludmila Savitzky, revised by Jacques Aubert [Paris: Gallimard, 1992], p. 25. It is arguable that Joyce's "Magdalenes," including both the nameless prostitute and the woman who stands in the doorway beckoning Davin, are transformations of the same discursive complex.

[28] Van Boheemen, p. 16.

"DO YOU CALL THAT A MAN?": THE CULTURE OF ANXIOUS MASCULINITY IN JOYCE'S *ULYSSES*

TRACEY TEETS SCHWARZE

Abstract. Throughout the nineteenth century, definitions of manhood and masculinity fluctuated and evolved in response to various social challenges to patriarchal authority; such challenges led to the formation of a masculine discourse subtended by an anxious awareness of its own instability. Defining itself against feminine and racial Others, Charles Kingsley's "Christian manliness" (derogatorily known as "muscular Christianity") had achieved an uneasy hegemony both socially and politically by the latter half of the century; ideas of "manhood" and "nationhood" converged as the construction of national identity became dependent upon the new masculine ethos. Joyce's *Ulysses* illustrates the cultural domination of Kingsleyan discourse in 1904 Dublin, its Other-driven anxiety, its deep-seated fears of emasculation, and its extensive ramifications for the Irish nationalist project.

Gerty MacDowell's self-conscious construction of a "feminine" identity at the confluence of various social discourses--the sentimental novels of Maria Susannah Cummins, the mythology of the Blessed Virgin, the poetry of Louis J. Walsh ("Art thou real, my ideal?"), and the advertisements of the *Lady's Pictorial*--has been well documented by critics such as Suzette Henke, Kimberly Devlin, and Garry Leonard.[1] Gerty becomes the signifier of

---

[1] See Suzette Henke, "Gerty MacDowell: Joyce's Sentimental Heroine," in *Women in Joyce*, ed. Suzette Henke and Elaine Unkeless (Urbana: University of Illinois Press, 1982), pp. 132-49; Kimberly Devlin, "The Romance Heroine Exposed: 'Nausicaa' and *The Lamplighter*," *James Joyce Quarterly* 22.4 (1985): 383-96; and Garry Leonard, "The Virgin Mary and the Urge in Gerty: The Packaging of Desire in the 'Nausicaa' Chapter of

a culturally constructed-- and contested--femininity, a surface that draws attention to itself by continually gesturing toward its constructedness, a facade that is constantly threatened by contentious disruptions ("little monkeys common as ditchwater" [U 13.468]) or contradictions within the sources themselves. Molly Bloom is similarly engaged in a process of contested self-representation, as recent essays by Devlin and Cheryl Herr have argued.[2] Molly, like Gerty, plays out the various gender "roles"--replete with their inherent contradictions--that the culture of 1904 Dublin has assigned to her. What has received considerably less attention than these important recontextualizations of feminine gender identities, however, is Joyce's depiction of masculinity as an equally constructed--and deeply conflicted--ideology. I wish to consider the social construction of middle-class masculinity and its various Others as they are posited within Ulysses; I will suggest that the insistent "difference" of Leopold Bloom, manifest both in his status as the "new womanly man" and in his racial Otherness, reveals his conflicted position in relation to the masculinist discourse that had achieved an uneasy hegemony in England and Ireland by the late nineteenth century: Charles Kingsley's "Christian manliness."[3]

Ulysses," University of Hartford Studies in Literature 23.1 (1991): 3-23.

[2] See Kimberly Devlin, "Pretending in 'Penelope': Masquerade, Mimicry, and Molly Bloom, " in Molly Blooms: A Polylogue on "Penelope" and Cultural Studies, ed. Richard Pearce (Madison: University of Wisconsin Press, 1994), pp. 80-102; and Cheryl Herr, "'Penelope' as Period Piece," in Pearce, pp. 63-79.

[3] A variety of masculine discourses circulated throughout the Victorian era and competed with Kingsley's ideal man: Thomas Carlyle proposed the cerebral "man of letters" as the hero of the age, while aesthetes such as Algernon Charles Swinburne, Walter Pater, and Oscar Wilde offered still

Most recent gender   critics who have turned their attention to the constructed nature of masculinity would argue that the phrase "anxious masculinity" is in fact redundant, as the question of what constitutes "masculinity" or "manliness" is "always bound up with negotiations about power, and is therefore often experienced as tenuous."[4] Definitions of manhood and masculinity in nineteenth-century England were no exceptions to this observation; they fluctuated and evolved in response to various social challenges to patriarchal authority, such as Chartism, feminism, and threats to empire, issues that were themselves often framed in terms of gender, as David Rosen notes: "The debate over who should rule often devolved into a debate over who belonged to that privileged group called 'men'"[5] As

---

another model of manliness, one which challenged Kingsleyan notions of moral asceticism and utilitarianism and attempted to re-imagine masculinity in terms of male-male desire.   Each of these discourses, however, was effectively "othered" by the Kingsleyan ethos by the century's end and contributed to the anxiety/instability subtending the Kingsleyan construct. For more on Carlyle, see *On Heroes, Hero-Worship and the Heroic in History* (London: Chapman and Hall, 1894), as well as Norma Clarke's analysis, "Strenuous Idleness: Thomas Carlyle and the Man of Letters as Hero," in *Manful Assertions: Masculinities in Britain since 1800*, ed. Michael Roper and John Tosh (London and New York: Routledge, 1991), pp. 25-43. For more on the Aesthetes, see Richard Dellamora, *Masculine Desire: The Sexual Politics of Victorian Aestheticism* (Chapel Hill: University of North Carolina Press, 1990); James Eli Adams, "Pater's Muscular Aestheticism," in *Muscular Christianity: Embodying the Victorian Age*, ed. Donald E. Hall (Cambridge: Cambridge University Press, 1994), pp. 215-38; and Thaïs E. Morgan, "Reimagining Masculinity in Victorian Criticism: Swinburne and Pater," *Victorian Studies* 36.3 (1993): 315-33.

[4] Roper and Tosh, p.18.

[5] David Rosen, "The Volcano and the Cathedral: Muscular Christianity and the Origins of Primal Manliness," in Hall, *Muscular Christianity*, p. 21.

definitions of this "privileged group" expanded or contracted in accordance with political expedience, manhood was exposed as not an "essence" but as a socially constructed--and therefore socially vulnerable--phenomenon. The vulnerability was ubiquitous: the shifting of political power from the aristocracy to the middle classes was achieved in what *The Times* would later call a "menacing" atmosphere of social unrest[6] as Chartist agitations for universal suffrage in the 1830s to 40s erupted into riots in London, Liverpool and Glasgow in 1848, violent colonial uprisings rocked India during the Sepoy Rebellion in 1857, and the Irish stepped up their demands for both land reform and home rule.[7] Such events at home and abroad deeply disturbed the Victorian psyche; significantly, the fears of decline that subtended the Condition of England debates at mid-century were expressed not only in terms of diminishing nationhood but also in terms of disintegrating manhood: in 1843 Thomas Carlyle conflated the two as he bemoaned the waste of poverty and workhouses--in them, Carlyle argued, were squandered "noble . . . national virtues [and] . . . valiant manful habits, soul of a nation's worth."[8] In 1848 Charles Kingsley urged Chartist agitators, the "workmen of

---

[6] "Queen Victoria's Jubilee," 20 June 1887, rpt. in *The Portable Victorian Reader*, ed. Gordon Haight (New York: Viking, 1972), p. 44.

[7] The Irish Republican Brotherhood was born in the late 1850s; Michael Davitt's Irish National Land League helped to liberalize tenancy restrictions during the "land war" of 1879-82; the Home Rule movement gained momentum under Parnell's leadership in the 1880s. For more, see R. F. Foster, "Ascendancy and Union," in *The Oxford History of Ireland*, ed. R. F. Foster (Oxford: Oxford University Press, 1992), pp. 134-73; and David Fitzpatrick, "Ireland since 1870," in Foster, pp. 174-229.

[8] Thomas Carlyle, *Past and Present* (New York: New York University Press, 1965), p. 9.

England," toward a manly readiness to rule, imploring them to "be fit to be free" before increasing their political demands;[9] in 1853 John Ruskin lamented British industrialization and efficiency in decidedly gendered terms: "We manufacture everything . . . but men."[10]

As a result of this sense of progressive social and political emasculation, masculinist movements of the mid-century moved self-consciously to reconstruct "manhood" as a less ambiguous and physically harder phenomenon than the reflective and morally earnest notion that characterized the earlier half century, when the term "manliness"--connoting a "blend of compassion and courage, gentleness and strength, self-control and native purity"--was applied androgynously to both women and men.[11] Anglican minister Charles Kingsley not only advocated, but also came to embody the new ideal of a virile and distinctly heterosexual manliness, one that required "'boldness,' 'honesty,' and 'plainness'; a defiance of authority; stoic patience; and violent energy."[12] In an 1857 parody of Kingsley's own rhetoric, the *Saturday Review* dubbed his philosophy "muscular Christianity" and described his paragon as a man who "fears God and can walk a thousand miles in a thousand hours--who . . . breathes God's free air on God's rich earth and at the same time can hit a woodcock, doctor a horse and twist a poker

---

[9] *Charles Kingsley: His Letters and Memories of His Life*, ed. Frances Eliza Grenfell Kingsley (his wife) (London: Kegan Paul, Trench, 1888), pp. 63-64.

[10] John Ruskin, *The Stones of Venice*, in *Unto This Last and Other Writings* (New York: Viking-Penguin, 1985), p. 87.

[11] Claudia Nelson, *Boys Will Be Girls: The Feminine Ethic and British Children's Fiction, 1857-1917* (New Brunswick: Rutgers University Press, 1991), p. 37.

[12] Rosen, "Volcano," pp. 18-19.

around his fingers."[13] Yet this revised masculinity also registered an intense awareness of its own instability as it began to define itself discursively against feminine and racial Others. Kingsley despised what he called "Mariolatry," or worship of the Virgin Mary, and exhorted his followers to go "not to the Mother but to the Son--not to the indulgent Virgin, but to the strong *man,* Christ Jesus."[14] He valued the robust strength of Esau over the intellectual softness of Jacob but "trembled" at England's dependence on the latter.[15] He problematically attempted to brand the colonized subject with sub-human status in order to justify British rule and affirm British manhood, not an unusual move in colonial discourse,[16] but Kingsley's 1860 account of the Gaelic peasantry evinces an extraordinary agitation over racial similarity which gestures toward the precariousness of these constructs.

> I am haunted by the human chimpanzees I saw along that hundred miles of horrible country. I don't believe they are our fault. I believe there are not only many more of them than of old, but that they are happier, better, more comfortably fed and lodged under our rule than they ever were. But to see *white* chimpanzees is dreadful; if they were black, one would not feel it so much but their skins, except where tanned by exposure, are as white as ours.[17]

---

[13] Rpt.in Bruce Haley, *The Healthy Body and Victorian Culture* (Cambridge: Harvard University Press, 1978), p. 108.

[14] Kingsley, p. 104.

[15] Kingsley, pp. 214-15.

[16] See Homi K. Bhabha's seminal essay, "The Other Question," in *The Location of Culture* (London: Routledge, 1994), pp. 66-84.

[17] Kingsley, p. 236. Simianized images of the Gaels were not unique to Kingsley; they saturated the popular press, appearing in publications such as *Punch* and *Harper's Weekly*. For an excellent discussion and reproductions of these images, see Vincent Cheng, "Catching the Conscience

As it (unsuccessfully) attempts to mark racial difference, this letter also exposes the intense anxiety which lies at the heart of Othering. Kingsley's insistence here on referring to the Gaels as "chimpanzees" rather than "men" suggests the portentous dependence of masculinity on its Others: if difference collapses, then dominance is lost, and so is English manhood.

As the century progressed, the Kingsleyan ethos moved to secure its hegemony in the culture at large as it focused intently on marking Otherness. What Maurizia Boscagli has called "the paranoid fear of racial decay"[18] merged with an obsession to avoid "womanishness" and fueled a curious cultural admixture of male purity and muscle flexing. Organizations such as the Young Men's Christian Association (1844) aimed to show "the average Victorian . . . that religion was not really about 'feminine' piety . . . but was instead a robust and manly affair in the Kingsley mould," while the Boys' Brigade (1874) and the later Boy Scouts drilled military discipline, citizenship, and personal hygiene into their memberships.[19] Masculinity

---

of a Race," in *Joyce, Race, and Empire* (Cambridge: Cambridge University Press, 1995), pp. 15-56.

[18] Maurizia Boscagli, *Eye on the Flesh:: Fashions of Masculinity in the Early Twentieth Century* (Boulder: Westview Press-HarperCollins, 1996), p. 3.

[19] For more, see John Springhall, "Building Character in the British Boy: The Attempt to Extend Christian Manliness to Working-Class Adolescents, 1880-1914," in *Manliness and Morality: Middle-Class Masculinity in Britain and America, 1800-1940*, ed. J. A. Mangan and James Walvin (New York: St. Martin's, 1986), pp. 52-74. Allen Warren also notes that the founder of the Boy Scouts, Robert Baden Powell, addressed the issue of physical purity on a variety of levels; he assailed "self-abuse" in the 1908 handbook, *Scouting for Boys*, and extolled the virtues of "clean blood" and "regular bowel movements." See Allen Warren, "Popular Manliness: Baden Powell, Scouting and the Development of Manly Character," in J.A. Mangan, "Social

became a state of muscle as compulsory sport invaded the boys' public school curricula between 1860 and 1880 and further promoted the ideals of physical manliness; J. A. Mangan has convincingly argued that the new masculinity also actualized "an implicit, if not explicit, crude Darwinism" embodied in aphorisms: "life is conflict, strength comes through struggle and success is the prerogative of the strong."[20] According to Boscagli, the cleansed and hardened male body thus came to signify "the body of the nation," the health or demise of the state inscribed upon its musculature.[21]

Kingsley's "Christian manliness" and its Other-driven anxiety infused Ireland as well, establishing itself as the dominant social and political discourse as early as 1860, when the *Dublin Review* complained of the invasion of a Kingsleyan ethos in the schools, remonstrating that manhood had been reduced "to a mere question of tissues and tendons--[its only goal] to bring out muscle, pluck, self-reliance, independence--the animal man."[22] In spite of such protestations, however, late-nineteenth and early-twentieth-century nationalist movements in Ireland adopted this hard, masculinist ideology as they absorbed--and attempted to defy--a colonial discourse that defined them as "effeminate"[23] and racially "inferior." As their

---

Darwinism and Upper-Class Education in Late Victorian and Edwardian England," in *Manliness and Morality*, p. 202.

[20] J. A. Mangan, p. 142.

[21] Boscagli, p. 114, p. 117.

[22] Quoted in Mangan, p. 145.

[23] Joseph Valente has helpfully detailed some of the feminized images of Ireland which permeated British colonial discourse and has observed the gendered nature of colonial rule there, noting that "gender hierarchy and male control were naturalized as the ultimate referents of the colonial

British counterparts did, the   Gaels began to equate a sturdy, rugged maleness with nationhood, and, as Mary Condren reports, the "recovery of 'manhood' . . . became synonymous with the discovery of the Irish national soul."[24] Like Great Britain, Ireland turned to sport to re-define the body of the nation; the Gaelic Athletic Association (1884) promoted this new muscular manhood, advocating distinctly "Irish" games such as hurling, handball, and Gaelic football over English sports such as rugby, field hockey, and polo. Irish nationalists also engaged in their own brand of Other-driven anxiety, defining Irish manhood not only against effeminacy but also against ethnic impurity. The Gaelic League (1893) insisted on a return to the Irish language, while Revivalist literature proclaimed against "too many strangers in the house."[25] Such attempts to purge the Saxon influence and to assert Irish manhood through fitness and purity movements were not only deeply ironic--they in fact validated the British ethos of middle-class manliness[26]--they were also

---

mission." See "The Myth of Sovereignty: Gender in the Literature of Irish Nationalism," *English Literary History* 61 (1994): 189.

[24] Mary Condren, "Sacrifice and Political Legitimation: The Production of a Gendered Social Order," *Journal of Women's History* 6.4 (1995): 167. Among the examples Condren cites, for instance, is the rhetoric of Patrick Pearse, which equated nationalistic violence with manly virility: "Bloodshed is a cleansing and sanctifying thing, and the nation which regards it as the final horror has lost its manhood" (Condren: 160-61).

[25] William Butler Yeats, *Cathleen ni Hoolihan*, in *Eleven Plays of William Butler Yeats*, ed. A. Norman Jeffares (New York: Macmillan, 1964), p. 226.

[26] As Valente has observed: "[This strategy] ultimately accommodates the very transference between racial and sexual dominion that it appears to interdict . . . [and] concedes, *via negativa* that the colonial subjacency of the Irish people would in fact be justified if they did in truth harbor the feminine characteristics attributed to them" (Valente: 193).

complicated by Ireland's persistent self-mythologization as a female figure. *Ulysses* illustrates the hegemonic nature of Kingsleyan discourse in Ireland, its anxious dependence on its racial and feminine Others, as well as its awareness of the threat presented by the imminent collapse or inversion of this difference. The masculine self is defined throughout the text against a feminized, Semitic Other which embodies the paradox of difference as well as reveals the intricate interconnectedness of Irish definitions with their British forms. On the one hand, the feminized Jew[27] appears to make those men who measure themselves against him feel more "manly" (consider the convergence of the racial and feminine Others disported by J. J. O'Molloy in "Cyclops": "every jew is in a tall state of excitement . . . till he knows if he's a father or a mother" [*U* 12.1647-48]); on the other, the figure also menaces the men who encounter it with economic emasculation. The Englishman, Haines, is the first man in the novel to register the fear of "racial decay" of which Boscagli writes; in conversation with Stephen Dedalus, Haines slurs the "German jews," noting that they are "our national problem, I'm afraid, just now" (*U* 1.668). The thread is woven through the various nationalities and political persuasions represented in the novel. Garrett Deasy, the Protestant unionist, tells Stephen that the Englishman's

---

[27] For more on the sociohistorical context of this figure, especially its sources in Richard von Krafft-Ebing's *Psychopathia Sexualis* and Otto Weininger's *Sex and Character*, see Robert Byrnes, "Bloom's Sexual Tropes: Stigmata of the 'Degenerate' Jew," *James Joyce Quarterly* 27.2 (1990): 303-23. For more recent analysis, see Marilyn Reizbaum, "Weininger and the Bloom of Jewish Self-Hatred in Joyce's *Ulysses*," in *Jews and Gender: Responses to Otto Weininger*, ed. Nancy A. Harrowitz and Barbara Hyams (Philadelphia: Temple University Press, 1995), pp. 207-14; and Natania Rosenfeld, "James Joyce's Womanly Wandering Jew," in Harrowitz, pp. 215-26.

most cherished boast is "I   paid my way," and then he
characterizes Britain's "jew merchants" as usurping this
financial manhood and sapping "the nation's vital strength"
(*U* 2.348); from the funeral carriage of "Hades," Parnellite
Simon Dedalus and Dublin Castle clerk Martin
Cunningham localize and personalize the identical
sentiment as they deride an elderly Jew, "a curved hand
open on his spine," ostensibly for usury (*U* 6.253). Even
Bloom, who comes to embody this racial and feminine
Otherness, attempts to measure his own manliness against
it and locate this Other outside himself: he notes that
Reuben J. Dodd, punished by a judge for his moneylending
activities, is--unlike himself--"*really* what they call a dirty
jew" (*U* 8.1159; emphasis added).

Bloom provides perhaps the best example of the
extent to which the tenets of British Victorian masculinity
had permeated Irish social discourse in 1904; he
demonstrates not only the cultural domination of
Kingsleyan dogma but also the extent of the unease that
surrounded it. That Bloom has been steeped in the model
of muscular manhood as well as its acute, Other-driven
discomfiture is made clear throughout *Ulysses*; Bloom
constantly measures himself against a standard of "hard"
masculinity and continually comes up short, a pattern
which produces for him several anxious masculine
moments which recur in his psyche like primal scenes.
Bloom's turns as the "new womanly man"--especially his
dramatic transformation in "Circe"--have been read
profitably from psychoanalytic, feminist, and cultural
vantage points;[28] I would argue that the anxious androgyny

---

[28] See Suzette A. Henke, *James Joyce and the Politics of Desire* (New York:
Routledge, 1990), especially chap. 4; Colleen R. Lamos, "Joyce and Gender
Justice in *Ulysses*," in *Joyce in Context*, ed. Vincent J. Cheng and Timothy
Martin (Cambridge: Cambridge University Press, 1992), pp. 91-99; Cheryl

associated with Bloom is also significantly indebted to broader societal apprehensions over the instability of the masculine signifier, a position supported by the evident compulsion of various Dublin men to gauge their own manhood against the racial and feminine Other that Bloom comes to embody.

Bloom is, of course, the *Ulysses* character who most consciously--and anxiously--engages the question of masculinity, and he is well aware of the Kingsleyan paragon. During Paddy Dignam's funeral service, Bloom notes the rugged appearance of the presiding priest, Father Coffey, and applies to him the very term the *Saturday Review* used to describe Kingsley in 1857: "Bully about the muzzle he looks. Bosses the show. *Muscular christian.* Woe betide anyone that looks crooked at him: priest. Thou art Peter" (*U* 6.596-97; emphasis added). But Bloom himself does not meet this standard of rock-hard virility, either physically or philosophically. Bloom attempts throughout the novel to reimagine manliness outside the Kingsleyan mode, rejecting both Social Darwinism and physical violence, as well as endeavoring to collapse the notion of difference so integral to masculine identity (consider, for instance, his definition of a nation: "the same people living in the same place" [*U* 12.1422]). But in spite of these efforts, Bloom is ultimately unable to escape the hegemony of the Kingsleyan discourse; that he is a much "softer" version of manhood than Victorian education aimed to produce causes him great consternation and prompts him to compensatory explanations--a revisionist history of his own masculinity--whenever possible. Throughout the day he

---

Herr, *Joyce's Anatomy of Culture* (Urbana: University of Illinois Press, 1986), especially chaps. 4 and 5; and Kimberly Devlin, "Castration and Its Discontents: A Lacanian Approach to Ulysses" *James Joyce Quarterly* 29.1 (1991): 117-44.

anxiously interrogates his own physical manliness, coming up soft at every turn. He imagines the blind stripling in "Lestrygonians" to be "sizing me up . . . from my hand," but since Bloom's touch is admittedly gentle (and therefore womanish), he decides the stripling "knows I'm a man" from his voice (*U* 8.1098, 1102); he speculates in "Nausicaa" whether women detect a "mansmell" about the male, and he inserts his nose into his waistcoat to discern his own odor which is distinctly, sweetly, feminine ("Hm . . . Hm . . . Almonds or. No. Lemons it is"), produced as it is by Molly's soap (*U* 13.1043); he frets throughout the novel about not having resumed Sandow's exercises and congratulates himself on not having allowed Gerty MacDowell to view him in profile, perhaps to elide her vision of his soft stomach as his Semitic features. Bloom even attempted in earlier years to solidify his masculine hardness by masquerading as that poet dubbed by Kingsley as the most "manly" of the Romantics--George Gordon, Lord Byron--while he courted Molly. In an essay, "Thoughts on Shelley and Byron," Kingsley touted Byron-- "the sturdy peer, proud of his bull neck and his boxing"--as the embodiment of rugged virility and branded the "womanish" Shelley as his effeminate Other.[29] Bloom, Molly tells us, has wooed as Byron, presenting her with a volume of poems and even going so far as "trying to look like" the poet (*U* 18.185, 209). But Bloom's Byronic self-construction is again undercut by an unmanly softness, a Shelleyan Other: Molly remembers Bloom not only as "very handsome" but also as "too beautiful for a man" (*U* 18.208-10), an androgynous assessment that recalls common physical descriptions of Shelley offered by both women and

---

[29] Qtd. in Walter E. Houghton, *The Victorian Frame of Mind, 1830-1870* (New Haven: Yale University Press, 1985), p. 202.

men alike.[30] Bloom perhaps carries with him a subconscious awareness of this softness which undermined his performance: in "Lotus Eaters" his loose allusions to both Byron's early volume, *Hours of Idleness* (1808), and Shelley's poem, "The Sensitive Plant" (1820)--"Flowers of idleness . . . . Sensitive plants" (*U* 5.34-35)--conflate the two poets into a single image and neutralize the Byronic virility that Kingsley praised.[31]

To combat this softness, Bloom has availed himself of various products which promise--either explicitly or implicitly--to "make a new man" of their purchasers, but these items themselves also inscribe masculine anxiety by collapsing the difference integral to male identity. Gadgets like the Wonderworker and the exercises prescribed in Eugene Sandow's *Physical Strength and How to Obtain It* trade on a profound sense of masculine insufficiency and inadequacy. The Wonderworker promises to make "a new man of you," peddling not only flatulence relief but also a reconstructed, purged, and purified masculine identity in the Kingsleyan mode (*U* 17.1829); Sandow's program is similarly engaged in shoring up hard, physical manliness, offering powerful physiques to men whose "sedentary

---

[30] In his essay on Shelley, Matthew Arnold reports both female and male perspectives; the "feminine enthusiasm" of a "Miss Rose" is confirmed by a "Captain Kennedy," who, though expected by Arnold to "Keep his head," reported Shelley's beauty in terms even more effusive than the ones Rose selected. See Matthew Arnold, "Shelley," in *Poetry and Criticism of Matthew Arnold*, ed. A. Dwight Culler (Boston: Houghton Mifflin, 1961), pp. 379-80.

[31] Other male characters besides Bloom are similarly undercut by a "feminization" of their masculine performances: as Devlin has observed, the "assertively phallic" stances of both Malachi "Buck" Mulligan and Hugh "Blazes" Boylan are also subtended by their "interest in flamboyant clothing and their exhibitionist postures." See "Castration": 133.

occupations" have caused their muscles to soften with disuse (*U* 17.515). But even as they offer an improved male body, these cultural artifacts also manage to textualize Edwardian anxiety over the masculine signifier by compressing not only the spaces between heterosexuality and homosexuality but also those between "hard" and "soft" masculinities. The Wonderworker, advertised as being of service to women as well as to men, has been misdirected to *Mrs. L.* Bloom, rendering its promise to make "a new man" of the addressee ("Dear Madam") more than a little ironic: if women can become "new men" by "insert[ing the] long round end" into the rectum, then, one must ask, what do men in this same position--certainly suggestive of anal intercourse--become? Just as the Wonderworker's "new man" subversively contracts the space between heterosexuality and homosexuality, so also the image of the strongman manages to conflate the notions of "hard" and "soft" masculinity. Boscagli has argued convincingly that Sandow's hypermasculine, specularized body also inscribes an intense masculine anxiety, one that gestures toward the spaces of femininity and loss as it disperses the phallus throughout its musculature.[32] The enhanced male body evolves here from Kingsleyan utility to aesthetic pleasure: Sandow's exercises were to be performed in front of a mirror--a pose which enhances the specular nature of both process and product--in order "to bring into play the various families of muscles and produce successively a *pleasant* rigidity, a *more pleasant* relaxation and the *most pleasant* repristination of juvenile agility" (U 17.512-18; emphasis added). Thus the hypermasculine male body, as it becomes the pleasure-giving object, inscribes within itself a feminized--and fetishized--site of Otherness, produced by

---

[32] Boscagli, p. 4, p. 114.

the very musculature which   was intended to signify its manliness.

Bloom's investment in the Kingsleyan ethos and his anxiety over the collapse of difference in himself are best illustrated by his attempts to reconstruct the history of his own masculinity to make it "harder." Born in 1866, Bloom recalls school experiences which seem to affirm Victorian Ireland's emphasis on physical development, in spite of the *Dublin Review's* protestations:

> Though ringweight lifting had been beyond his strength and the full circle gyration his courage yet as a High school scholar he had excelled in his stable and protracted execution of the half lever movement on the parallel bars in consequence of his abnormally developed abdominal muscles. (*U* 17.520-24)

Significantly, Bloom fails to meet the specified requirement for biceps, though he here substitutes another set of muscles to atone for his deficiency. His description of this demonstration of athleticism reveals its debt to Kingsleyan manliness not only in its emphasis on physical strength but also in its assessment of the "courage" required to complete the maneuver, which Bloom noticeably lacks as well. As he reevaluates his performance, Bloom's need to assert another kind of physical potency, rather than, say, intellectual prowess (which we might reasonably expect, given the quasi-intellectualism that Bloom displays throughout the novel and for which he is disparaged by the "Cyclops" narrator), suggests the depth of his investment in this ethos. Mangan has noted the "ambivalence" with which the masculinity movement treated intellectualism,[33] and Bloom's revision of his inadequacy in physical terms suggests his awareness that cerebral gyrations were no

---

[33] Mangan, p.149.

substitute   for   those   performed   by   sinewy
tendons.

The most telling evidence of Bloom's implication in
the discourse of Kingsleyan manliness, however, may be his
altercation with the Citizen. Here again, in the aftermath of
the event, Bloom repeatedly takes stock of his performance,
which, in spite of his rejection of physical violence, he
perceives as deficient--he has delivered only linguistic
punches, rather than physical blows. In the Kingsleyan
world view, the physical contest was crucial to masculine
prowess, as this excerpt from *Tom Brown's School Days*
illustrates:

> After all, what would life be without fighting . . . ? From the cradle
> to the grave, fighting, rightly understood, is the business, the real,
> highest, honestest [*sic*] business of every son of man. Every one
> who is worth his salt has his enemies, who must be beaten, be they
> evil thoughts and habits in himself, or spiritual wickedness in high
> places, or Russians, or Border-ruffians . . . who will not let him live
> his life in quiet till he has thrashed them.[34]

Bloom seems to have absorbed something of this ethos in
that he refuses to back down from the racial confrontation
in Kiernan's pub, hurling his defiant declaration, "Your God
was a jew. Christ was a jew like me," back into the bar even
as he is hustled out the door and into the jarvey by Martin
Cunningham (*U* 12.1808-09). But Bloom's reflections will
return to the scene's violence several times during the
course of the evening; he will wonder whether by missing
the physical confrontation, he has somehow violated the
conventions of "manliness." His anxiety is on display as he
vacillates between the poles of "manly" defense of one's

---

[34] Thomas Hughes, *Tom Brown's School Days* (New York: Cornwall,
1911), p. 277.

honor in the Kingsleyan mode and a more "effeminate" appeasement:

> Got my own back there. Drunken ranters what I said about his God made him wince. Mistake to hit back. Or? No. Ought to go home and laugh at themselves. Always want to be swilling in company. Afraid to be alone like a child of two. Suppose he hit me. Look at it other way round. Not so bad then. Perhaps not to hurt he meant. Three cheers for Israel. (*U* 13.1215-20)

Bloom's confused "Mistake to hit back. Or? No" weakens the muscular ethos, even as it attempts to affirm it, and gestures toward the fissure contained within the Kingsleyan ideal itself; unlike Kingsley, Christ taught his followers not to "hit back" but to "turn the other cheek." Bloom's willingness to accord the Citizen the benefit of the doubt ("perhaps not to hurt he meant") while at the same time trying to position himself in a more "masculine" light, having retaliated against the Citizen's abuse, in fact serves as an emasculation of his enemy, a linguistic sleight that reduces the Citizen's brute physicality and even his sarcasm to sentimental cheerleading: "Three cheers for Israel." Such a move enables Bloom to cast himself in the more "manly" role, one he will continue to refine throughout the day.

In "Eumaeus," Bloom continues this pattern of vacillation, first congratulating himself on his cool and manly reliance on "plain facts" in the face of the Citizen's emotional, anti-Semitic outburst, then seeking Stephen's approbation for his response, appealing to yet another precept of Christian pacifism that further undermines the Kingsleyan paragon: "A soft answer turns away wrath. He hadn't a word to say for himself as everyone saw. Am I not right?" (*U* 16.1085-87). While Bloom here asks for vindication of his action, Stephen's muttered Latinate response ("*Ex quibus . . . Christus . . . secundum carnem*" [*U* 16.1091-3]) affirms only the fact of his claim--that Christ was indeed a Jew--and not its appropriateness. In this vacuum, Bloom continues to obsess over the encounter, re-imagining it and recasting his response until it resonates with the appropriate level of manfulness. Declaring to Stephen with "dramatic force" that "I'm . . . as good an Irishman as that rude person I told you about at the outset" (*U* 16.1131-33), Bloom reconstructs his physical pacifism until he convinces himself that he not only had not avoided an engagement, but also that he was its victor. Within a few more lines, Bloom has perfected his revisionist history of the encounter: "[H]e, though often considerably misunderstood and the least pugnacious of mortals, . . . departed from his customary habit to give him (metaphorically) one in the gizzard" (*U* 16.1597-99). Bloom's use of the "manly" colloquialism here--"to give him . . . one in the gizzard"--to describe the verbal fisticuffs in which he has engaged reveals his deep-seated need to transform an intellectual victory into proof of physical prowess, according to the conventions of his age.

The "hypermasculine" nationalism on display in the "Cyclops" chapter appears to contrast sharply with Bloom's masculine oscillations, yet it also reveals the hegemony of the Kingsleyan ethos and the anxiety that subtended it. Like the social constructions of masculinity in Edwardian Dublin, political postures owed a great deal to Kingsleyan dogma as the discourses of manhood and nationhood converged; in spite of his overtly phallic, "knockmedown cigar," Bloom is transformed by the men of this episode into the racial and feminine Other on which these discourses--and their own masculine identities--depend.[35] Acting "like a man" preoccupies the "Cyclops" denizens as intensely as it

---

[35] Devlin has argued convincingly for the Lacanian apparatus that underpins this episode, noting that the "Cyclops" bar-stoolers are impelled by their universal "fear of lack." See "Castration": 125.

disturbs Bloom, but the bar- stoolers repeatedly assure themselves of their collective masculinity by comparing themselves to Bloom's lack. For John Wyse Nolan, behaving "like men" involves standing up to injustice "with force" (*U* 12.1475), but Bloom uses words; for the nameless narrator, acting "like a man" requires one to "put . . . up a pint of stuff" (*U* 12.1663), whereas Bloom will neither drink nor buy. To J. J. O'Molloy, Jack Power, Ned Lambert, and the Citizen, being a man evidently has something to do with fathering children and then disregarding them. They disparage Bloom for buying a tin of Neave's food six weeks before Rudy was born: "Do you call that a man?" the Citizen wants to know (*U* 12.1654).

To combat perceptions of themselves as racially inferior, the Gaels required their own racialized Other against which they could measure their manhoods, and in *Ulysses* it appears they have located it in Bloom, the Irish Jew. Bloom's racial difference is overtly displayed in this episode, and anti-Semitic slurs abound: Bloom is called a "perverted jew" by Martin Cunningham (*U* 12.1635) and is suspected by the narrator of smelling like a "jewie" (*U* 12.452); he is even challenged to name his nation, which he does: "Ireland . . . I was born here. Ireland" (*U* 12.1422). Obsessed with Bloom's ethnicity, these men are desperately trying to maintain the difference their own masculine identities require, but Bloom appears bent on erasing such difference. His definition of a nation is predicated on sameness--"a nation is the same people living in the same place" (*U* 12.1422) -- and even the distinction he draws between his nation (Ireland) and his race (the Jews) seems designed to elide the difference between Bloom and his interrogators: the Jews, according to Bloom, comprise a race "that is hated and persecuted" (*U* 12.1467),[36] a description consistent with the Citizen's rendition of Irish

---

[36] Erwin R. Steinberg has verified Bloom's claim of Jewish persecution in Morocco; see "Persecuted . . . sold . . . in Morocco like slaves," *James Joyce Quarterly* 29.3 (1992): 615-22.

mistreatment at British hands. Thus Bloom's final sally, "Your God was a jew. Christ was a jew like me" (*U* 12.1808-9), inspires such rage in the Citizen because it collapses the racial difference upon which his masculine identity depends, and he responds with a physical gesture that attempts to reinforce their remaining locus of difference--between the man who talks and the one who fights.

Certainly Dublin men besides Bloom are Othered by effeminacy in this episode; Denis Breen is branded a "bloody old pantaloon," an old man in bathslippers, feminized by his foolishness (*U* 12.253), and Bob Doran is able to control neither his tears nor his exhibitionist wife (*U* 12.401-01). But it is Bloom who comes in for the brunt of this impulse as the masculinized, nationalist body attempts to locate effeminacy outside the self and within the body of the Other. In just one example, the narrator identifies Bloom as "one of those mixed middlings. . . . Lying up in the hotel . . . once a month with headache like a totty with her courses" (*U* 12. 1658-60). In contrast to these "womanish" men sits the Citizen, whose "broadshouldered deepchested stronglimbed frankeyed" manliness epitomizes the new national body, purged of its racial impurity and its feminization. But the de-feminization of this body does not end with Bloom; it also extends to attempts to re-imagine and re-personify the mythology of Ireland in masculine, rather than feminine, terms. It is no coincidence that the chapter of *Ulysses* most concerned with building Irish manhood/nationhood is also the one most fixated on feminine betrayal. Despite the physical absence of women from the bar, their faithless images appear repeatedly in narrative or dialogic form, from Polly Doran's exposure of herself to her husband's associates, to the faithless wife of the *Police Gazette* and, finally, to the "blushing bride elect" of Robert Emmet, who deserts him at his hanging for an Oxford graduate with a healthy bank account (*U* 12.636). In addition, forms of betrayal not particularly associated with women--the colt Sceptre's loss at Ascot, for instance--are also perceived here in terms which nonetheless suggest feminine responsibility. Lenehan laments his loss in terms which lay the blame distinctly at woman's door: "Frailty, thy name is *Sceptre*" (*U* 12. 1227-28). Similarly, the Citizen blames a woman (incorrectly, it seems) for smoothing the way of Saxon invaders even as he evokes the words of Cathleen ni Houlihan--"we want no more strangers in our house" (*U* 12.1150-51)--and undercuts the conventional heroism of this female image: "Our own fault. We let them come in. We brought them in. The adulteress and her paramour brought the Saxon robbers here" (*U* 12.1156-58).[37] I would contend that this obsession with feminine betrayal is the manifestation of a masculinity attempting to disassociate itself from Ireland's own self-mythologization as a female figure. Condren has noted a misogynistic pattern in nationalist rhetoric, observing that "there was a constant fear of impotence, of 'becoming women,' or even worse: becoming 'old women.'"[38] Such rhetoric would have been difficult to reconcile with an Ireland that consistently allegorized itself in just such gendered terms: Cathleen ni Houlihan and Granuaile represented the innocent woman-nation in need of liberation, while Caillaic Beare (the Hag of Beare) embodied its sovereignty.[39] Nationalist manhood attempted to redress this

---

[37] The event alluded to is Dermot MacMurrough's request of Henry II in 1166 for assistance in securing his throne against Rory O'Connor, the new high king of Ireland. While MacMurrough had carried off the wife of another rival, the Citizen's unfounded charge suggests that the Norman invasion was instigated by this woman. See Katharine Simms, "The Norman Invasion and the Gaelic Recovery," in *The Oxford History of Ireland*, ed. R. F. Foster (Oxford: Oxford University Press, 1992), pp. 47-48.

[38] Condren, p. 167.

[39] For discussions of these images, see Valente; and Declan Kiberd, "Irish Literature and Irish History," in *The Oxford History of Ireland*, pp. 235-40. For revivalist representations of Cathleen ni Houlihan, see *Cathleen ni Houlihan*, in Yeats, pp. 221-31, and *The Countess Cathleen* (London: T. Fisher Unwin, 1912); for representations of Granuaile, also see Lady Augusta Gregory, *The*

dissonance between its masculinist rhetoric and Ireland's feminine identity by characterizing the female as the tainted betrayer of manhood-nationhood; its purity lost, the feminized image could no longer personify the nation. In its place, revisionist mythology turned, as Charles Kingsley did, from the image of the mother to that of the Son: significantly, according to the Citizen, it is the "*sons* of Granuaile, the *champions* of Kathleen [*sic*] ni Houlihan" who will free Ireland and "come again with a vengeance" (*U* 12.1374-75; emphasis added).

Both socially and politically, then, *Ulysses* reveals Edwardian Ireland to be ironically infused with the ethos of Kingsleyan manliness even as it attempts to reject British hegemony. Both Bloom and the Irish nationalists endeavor to re-masculinize their identities according to the Kingsleyan code, revising their personal histories and national mythologies to enable them to fulfill their culture's ideal of "manliness." Bloom himself tries to locate outside himself the racial and feminine Others so critical to masculine identity, but ultimately he is unable to do so and becomes himself the signifier of Otherness for the various men who have similarly absorbed the codes of middle-class manliness. Ultimately, the representation of masculine anxiety in *Ulysses* reveals masculinity to be not a reified concept against which other social constructs can be measured, but yet another oscillating signifier which remains paradoxically dependent on the existence of Others for its survival and lives in fear that this difference--and finally identity itself--will collapse. Like their female counterparts, Gerty MacDowell and Molly Bloom, the men of Dublin chase the uneasy signifiers of a culturally constructed and contested gender identity.

Auburn University, Auburn, Alabama

Rising of the Moon (Dublin: Maunsel, 1907).

ULYSSES AND THE END OF GENDER

VICKI MAHAFFEY

Abstract. In designing *Ulysses*, Joyce first identified what the socially conditioned reader is most likely to want and expect from male and female characters of different ages, and then he provides his readers with characters who frustrate and implicitly challenge that desire. Defying the traditions of epic and romance, Joyce redefines a male hero as neither brave nor vengeful but as cautious, realistic, and slowly willing to contemplate the possibility that his relation to those he loves has inadvertently been hurtful. The result is designed to expose the gender system itself as an arbitrary and inadequate fiction.

It is easiest to begin a discussion of Joyce's gender politics in *Ulysses* by identifying the positions he does not adopt: his is not an activist stance, nor is he an advocate for disenfranchised groups--whether women or the Irish. Joyce disavows that he is a feminist; as he playfully employs the term in the "Circe" episode of *Ulysses*, feminism is concerned primarily with action (as opposed to thought) and with a desire to appropriate (rather than redistribute) male privilege. When Bloom is being hailed as the world's greatest reformer, a group of women whisper his praises in such a way as to highlight not his but their own attributes: a millionairess appreciates him "richly," a noblewoman lauds him "nobly," and a feminist commends his numerous accomplishments "masculinely" (*U* 15.1461-66). Joyce here presents feminism as a paradoxically masculine, action-oriented position, from which he implicitly differentiates his own practices.

To say, however, that Joyce dissociates himself from the feminist movements of his time does not mean that

Joyce was unconcerned with the social construction of gender and its subtle ramifications. On the contrary, he repeatedly traces many apparently different failures of communication--between Irish and English, between men and men, between women and men, between women and women, between parents and children--to the fault line of sexuality as it has been socially and historically defined. His characters discover again and again that there is no sexual, textual, or parental relation;[1] that the call of desire evokes only fantasy and despair. As early as *Dubliners* Joyce links the paralysis of desire to society's insistence on the commodification of the beloved, which he associates with the sin of simony, and on the rigidly heterosexual imperatives that turn characters such as Father Flynn of "The Sisters" and the stranger in "An Encounter" into "gnomons," geometrical figures of spiritual and sexual incompleteness. As Mr. Duffy writes after breaking off his relation with Mrs. Sinico in "A Painful Case," "Love between man and man is impossible because there must not be sexual intercourse and friendship between man and woman is impossible because there must be sexual intercourse" (*D* 112).

If *Dubliners* records the longing of isolated individuals for meaningful connection, counterpointing their poignant but futile yearning against the rules of a social system that effectively (if not intentionally) prohibits relation in favor of idealized admiration, manipulation, and competition, *Ulysses* takes a lighter attitude towards the impossibility of communication. If *Dubliners* aims to expose

---

[1] I am echoing Jacques Lacan's famous assertion that there is no sexual relation. He first makes this argument in Seminar XX, *Encore* (1972-73); see *Feminine Sexuality: Jacques Lacan and the École Freudienne*, ed. Juliet Mitchell and Jacqueline Rose (New York: Norton, 1982), p. 138. He then repeats the claim several times in his seminars.

the vision of human connection as a mirage, precluded by the very social mechanisms that promote it, *Ulysses* begins with the literally utopian conviction that there is no place (*u-topia*) where such connection can happen because there is no discursive or conceptual space free from the implied rules of gendered (non)relation. Writing is an address, a letter from writer to reader and from one time and place to another; one writer alone cannot rewrite the play of social interaction and communication because he or she is always writing against a background of expectation and desire that is socially programmed and often unconscious. Even if the writer's own intentions are revisionary, those intentions can be derailed by the reader's wishes, which may not cooperate to produce the intended meaning. In designing *Ulysses*, Joyce first identified what the socially conditioned reader is most likely to want and expect from male and female characters of different ages, and then he provides his readers with characters who frustrate and implicitly challenge that desire. The bewildering friction that results is designed to expose the gender system itself as an arbitrary and inadequate fiction, to measure its isolating mechanisms against the urgent complexity of personal desire. Joyce turns the threnody of non-relation in *Dubliners* into the stuff of comedy in *Ulysses* by composing characters who violate popular preconceptions of what makes men and women admirable.[2]

---

[2] Compare the project proposed by Lieutenant Puddock and Captain Devereux in Sheridan Le Fanu's *The House by the Churchyard*, Introduction by Thomas Kilroy (Belfast: Appletree, 1992), which Joyce would later use as a point of reference in *Finnegans Wake*. Puddock suggests that he and Devereux devise an Irish variation upon the plays of Shakespeare:" seriously, by sometimes changing an old person to a young, sometimes a comical to a melancholy, or the reverse, sometimes a male for a female, or a female for a male--I assure you, you can so entirely disguise the piece, and yet produce situations so new and surprising." (135) Devereux

Joyce begins his dialogue with the acculturated reader by offering an anti-portrait of the young male "hero." Even a cursory review of the epic tradition confirms that the young male hero is defined by courage and physical strength; Joyce counters that expectation with Stephen Dedalus, who fears dogs, thunderstorms, and drowning and is easily felled by a drunken British soldier. If the frame were mythological instead of epic, the hero would be a fearless, brawny, handsome prince, heir to a just and well-managed kingdom. Joyce evokes the dream of the charming prince through the twin shadows of Telemachus and Hamlet, only to puncture it by presenting his readers with a scrawny intellectual who is poor, physically dirty, periodically infested with vermin, and a coward. Even Stephen's disposition violates generic expectations; instead of being optimistic, confident, and determined, he is morose and riddled with guilt. Unlike Telemachus in the *Odyssey*, who resolves to perform whatever feats are necessary to gain information about his father, confronting Nestor and appealing to Menelaus in his determined effort to gain control of his home, Stephen, depressed by the crass "wisdom" of Mr. Deasy, struggles blindly with the sea

---

responds by proposing a new version of *Othello*, in which "[a] gay young Venetian nobleman, of singular beauty, charmed by her tales of 'anthropophagites and men whose heads do grow beneath their shoulders,' is seduced from his father's house and married by a middle-aged, somewhat hard-featured black woman, Juno, or Dido."(135) Joyce's project in *Ulysses*, although it is a variation upon not one but two literary works (the *Odyssey* and *Hamlet*), resembles that of Puddock and Devereux in its comic design to expose the hero as a gendered construction, defined not only by sex but also by age, race, and class. The different roles in a Shakespeare play (or in a Homeric epic) are not reversible without dramatic alterations in meaning, for the simple reason that the meanings of sex, age, and class inhere in the culture; the text merely plays against them.

changes of language and philosophy, only to drink himself into a stupor and go berserk in a whorehouse. As a troubled protagonist, Stephen is temperamentally most akin to Shakespeare's Hamlet, who *is* a prince, but a prince who disdains the corruption he is heir to. Joyce darkens the portrait of disaffected youth still further in his portrayal of Stephen, whose indulgence in obscure thought is more oblique than Hamlet's affected madness, and who -- as a freethinking Irish Catholic youth in a poor, colonized country -- occupies a dramatically reduced economic and social position.

The portrait of Stephen, offered as a replacement for that of the conventional young male hero, is not a narcissistic celebration of Joyce's own vulgarity, as some early readers charged. Its function, on the contrary, is to provoke a reappraisal of the criteria for heroism in western culture. Why admire young men whose courage is due partly to the accident of age and health and partly to a rash refusal to assess danger realistically? Why privilege the accident of class and social position, which insulates young "heroes" from more lethal dangers that spring from need, hopelessness, and deprivation? Why is the avoidance of humiliation and degradation (through birth, appearance, and youth) valued more highly than the experience and survival of injustice? Joyce's depiction of Stephen against a grain of expectation makes him an ugly duckling from the perspective of what we were prepared to admire, but at the same time it exposes the hidden basis of our admiration. It becomes clear in retrospect that what makes a young male hero in the popular sense is not bravery, but luck. The hero does not *earn* admiration at all; he merely makes use of the blessings of strength and riches. Moreover, valuing luck gives us no way of differentiating between heroes and villains, since a successful -- or lucky -- villain is indistinguishable from a hero.[3] When Joyce presents us with "twin" heroes at the beginning of *Ulysses* in the characters of Stephen and Buck Mulligan, he uses them to make just such a point. Buck is the conventional hero -- not only is he endowed with the sunny disposition, good health, and financial solvency of the hero, but he is also clean and well-groomed, and he has saved a man from drowning. Stephen uncertainly tries to determine whether he would do what Buck did:

> He saved men from drowning and you shake at a cur's yelping. But the courtiers who mocked Guido in Or san Michele were in their own house. House of . . .We don't want any of your medieval abstrusiosities. Would you do what he did? A boat would be near, a lifebuoy. *Natürlich*, put there for you. Would you or would you not? . . . The truth, spit it out. I would want to. I would try. I am not a strong swimmer. . . .If I had land under my feet. I want his life still to be his, mine to be mine. A drowning man. His human eyes scream to me out of horror of his death. I . . . With him together down. . . . I could not save her. Waters: bitter death: lost. (*U* 3.317-30)

Set against Buck's animal health, Stephen's honest interrogation of his strengths ("I am not a strong swimmer") and his memory of failure at saving others, especially his mother ("I could not save her"), emerge as thoughtful and realistic. His values are less competitive than egalitarian ("I

---

[3] In Le Fanu's *The House by the Churchyard*, the villain, whom everyone had taken for a powerful and successful man, declares his "heroic" faith when he is unmasked: "I believe in luck, Sir, and there's the sum of my creed." He argues, with coldly logical social criticism, that his actions were perpetrated in the name of the same principle that his accusers evoke in putting him to death, "justice, which means only the collective selfishness of my fellow-creatures" (412). The book builds to the climactic (and significant) revelation that the much-admired Paul Dangerfield and the villainous Charles Archer are the same man.

want his life still to be his,　mine to be mine"). Instead of idealizing the feat of salvation, Stephen tries to focus on the reality of support "("A boat would be near, a lifebuoy"). Very gradually, as Joyce explained to Frank Budgen, the reader should begin to appreciate the slow discipline of Stephen's ethics, contrasting it to the easier panache of Buck's.

The next model of male heroism that Joyce proceeds to display and partly dismantle is that of the mature man, epitomized by Ulysses. The heroism of an older man is more complex than that of a younger one, but ultimately it still depends upon the exercise of ruthless physical strength. The *Odyssey* suggests that the mature male hero is cunning, patient, and adept at lying and disguise. He has the capacity to sustain hardships for a very long time, but ultimately he too gathers his resources for a violent, merciless confrontation in which he slaughters his opponents and reclaims his possessions (which include his wife). Joyce endows Bloom with Odysseus's more unconventional characteristics--his adaptability, his taste for disguise, and above all his capacity for survival -- but he translates Odysseus's bloody slaughter of the suitors into Bloom's rational dismissal of his scruples in "Ithaca";[4] moreover, he stretches Odysseus's talent for deception to include a tendency toward self-deception.

In a powerful critique of the ethos of manly heroism (in *Finnegans Wake* Joyce renames the beloved hero a "zero," or *"belowes hero,"* FW 343.17), Joyce intimates that it is the

---

[4] In the schema he gave Stuart Gilbert, Joyce suggests that instead of violently slaughtering Molly's suitors, like Odysseus, Bloom used reason to destroy his scruples. Under "Correspondences" for the "Ithaca" episode, Joyce identifies the suitors as "scruples" and the bow with which Ulysses slaughtered them as "reason." See Don Gifford with Robert J. Seidman, *Ulysses Annotated: Notes for James Joyce's "Ulysses,"* rev. and expanded edition (Berkeley: University of California Press, 1988), p. 566.

powerful and subtle temptation to deceive oneself, to which everyone is susceptible, that renders self-righteous confrontation and retribution suspect rather than heroic. By building his complex verbal structure around a protagonist who tries to avoid the knowledge that his wife has a sexual assignation with another man on that very day, Joyce implicitly challenges two of the most common assumptions about heroism: that the hero is fully aware of his motives for acting, and that those motives are simple, unconflicted, and completely endorsed by the society he epitomizes. In contrast to the stock hero, Bloom is as suspicious of himself as he is of others. Bloom's caution, his propensity to delay action, and his distrust of reprisal make him a different kind of hero, one who will never be guilty of violent abuse. Like Stephen, Bloom aims not to "be master of others or their slave" (*U* 3.295-96), a goal that prods him to question -- half unconsciously -- his own complicity in his wife's desire for other men. Bloom's bipartisan refusal of mastery and enslavement prevents him from becoming like Farrington in "Counterparts," driven to deny his socio-political impotence by ignobly beating a child. Moreover, Bloom's half-conscious preoccupation with the painful knowledge he is trying to disown also signals his refusal to detach himself from Molly by employing the easy, self-congratulatory mechanisms of contempt. His rejection of detachment as a solution to the problems of relation is what differentiates him from cold and haunted characters such as Mr. Duffy in "A Painful Case."

Defying the traditions of epic and romance, Joyce redefines a male hero as neither brave nor vengeful but as cautious, realistic, and slowly willing to contemplate the possibility that his relation to those he loves has inadvertently been hurtful. Joyce's most sympathetic male characters see themselves, painfully, as fallible; their heroism grows, not out of boundless confidence in the rightness of physical might, but out of what might be called the moral courage to imagine freshly the perspectives of people they have wronged. Although Stephen is unable to change his relations with his dead mother and unwilling to show gratitude to Bloom for Bloom's tactful solicitude, his appreciation of Jewish merchants as patient and knowing (*U* 2.364-73) and his vision of Muslim and Jewish intellectuals as "dark men in mien and movement, flashing in their mocking mirrors the obscure soul of the world, a darkness shining in brightness which brightness could not comprehend (*U* 2.158-60)," suggest that he feels an empathy with other races and other times that he is not yet capable of experiencing in the present at the level of individual relations. Stephen's view of woman is also sympathetic, if abstract. Stephen sees her as irresistible, lonely, overburdened, and weary; he calls her the handmaid of the moon, journeying ever westward, "followed by the sun's flaming sword" (*U* 3.391-92), pulling the tide in her wake. Stephen also sees tides within woman -- blood, "a winedark sea" -- a red flood that attracts man, in his role of vampire, toward her (*U* 3.394-98). As the moon, she wearily gathers and releases the waves in splendid isolation; in her perpetual toil, she (like the harp in "Two Gallants") cares nothing for her lovers: "Weary too in sight of lovers, lascivious men, a naked woman shining in her courts, she draws a toil of waters" (*U* 3.468-69).

Although Stephen romanticizes and denigrates women by turns,[5] he is also able to picture to himself the loneliness, toil, pain, and even the indifference of women. Bloom, too, is led by "ruth" (*U* 14.73), "Woman's woe with wonder pondering" (*U* 14.186); "Ruth red him, love led on with will to wander, loth to leave" (*U* 14. 201). Bloom is

---

[5] He expresses disgust at "woman's unclean loins, of man's flesh made not in God's likeness, the serpent's prey" (*U* 1.421-22).

sensitive not only to the travail of women in childbirth but also to the deprivation and creeping despair of Josie Breen, who is caring for a crazed husband: Bloom notes with compassion her worn clothes, the lines around her mouth, the cruel eye of a passing woman upon her (*U* 8.265-69). He is also quick to sympathize with Gerty MacDowell when he realizes she is lame, "Poor girl!" (*U* 13.772), and he even imagines how difficult rejection must be for whores-in-training: "Aho! If you don't answer when they solicit must be horrible for them till they harden" (*U* 13.869-70). Most importantly, Bloom is able to sympathize with women's hardships without sentimentalizing them; he stops short of condescending to women as innocent (and therefore childlike) victims of brutal male desire. He knows, for example, that Gerty was soliciting his gaze, that she is driven by powerful yearnings that she cannot identify to herself as sexual. Bloom is quick to adopt the woman's perspective in a variety of situations, but in his awareness of the manifold compromises of relation, he is wary of delivering definitive judgments. He imagines the feelings of a woman who is married to a drunk:

> Husband rolling in drunk, stink of pub off him like a polecat. Have that in your nose in the dark, whiff of stale boose. Then ask in the morning: was I drunk last night? Bad policy however to fault the husband. Chickens come home to roost. They stick by one another like glue. Maybe the women's fault also.(*U* 13.964-68)

Bloom sees women as capable and possibly culpable, but his reluctance to judge never prevents him from imagining himself vividly in their place: "Have that in your nose in the dark, whiff of stale boose."

The image of male heroism embedded in western culture is emphatically physical; as the male hero ages, his courage is supplemented by cunning, but the basis of his appeal is the power of brute   force and a willingness to use that force to protect (and simultaneously to restrict) women in particular and the community in general. In *Ulysses*, Joyce constructs a verbal edifice that promises to house popular epic heroes, but what the reader finds within it instead are thinking, caring men who are -- like most people -- prone to self-deception and error. The only men in the novel who pride themselves on their physical prowess are an adulterer and a bigot: the exaggeratedly hot Blazes Boylan and the hypocritical Citizen. The reader's expectation clashes loudly with the actual experience of reading *Ulysses*, and the cacophony that results brings the currency of our cultural definition of gender categories comically into question.

Given the premium placed on physical strength in men, it is perhaps surprising that cultural prescriptions for women demand an erasure or concealment of the body and of sexual power. If male heroes should be strong and active, female heroes must be aesthetically pleasing and passive; moreover, they should be immature, the innocent cause and reward of man's desire. The ideal role of the female heroine is to serve as an inspirational icon who is also the prize in a patriarchal contest, as Joyce suggests in *Finnegans Wake* by rendering "beauty" as "booty" (*FW* 560.20). In a typically compressed fashion, Joyce suggests that romantic love, in the popular imagination, is epitomized by the story of "booty with the bedst" [Beauty and the Beast], a tale of rapine in which the brawny man--simultaneously identified as "best" and "beast" --aims to land his "booty" in bed.[6]

Joyce's critique of popular culture's objectification of the young "heroine" -- who learns to see herself from the

[6] "Booty" is also a boot, or a glass slipper, a fetish that represents the hero's desire for her to contain his foot (or "*foutre*"), while remaining inert.

outside and to advertise herself even in her thoughts as a desirable commodity on the marriage market -- is perhaps his most trenchant exposée of the ludicrous cultural prescriptions for women. (As Issy notes in *Finnegans Wake*, in partial response to her name, "I sold/Isolde" -- "One must sell it to some one, the sacred name of love" [*FW* 268 n.1].) In "Nausicaa," Joyce introduces us to the thoughts of Gerty MacDowell, who is so thoroughly indoctrinated with the image of the culturally desirable young woman that she cannot own or realize her own desires, revealing them by indirection, cloaking them with narrative fantasies, burying them in the sand on which she sits. From Gerty we learn that a heroine should be an inanimate objet d'art -- "ivorylike," "Greekly perfect," "hands . . . of finely veined alabaster" (*U* 13.88-89), and that she resembles a fairytale heroine. Like Cinderella, she has small feet: "Edy Boardman prided herself that she was very *petite* but she never had a foot like Gerty MacDowell, a five, and never would ash, oak or elm" (*U* 13.165-67).[7] Also like Cinderella, her inborn qualities reveal her as belonging to a more privileged class from which an unkind fate has exiled her:

> There was an innate refinement, a languid queenly *hauteur* about Gerty which was unmistakably evidenced in her delicate hands and higharched instep. Had kind fate but willed her to be born a gentlewoman of high degree in her own right and had she only received the benefit of a good education Gerty MacDowell might easily have held her own beside any lady in the land.(*U* 13.96-102)

Most poignantly, we observe that although Gerty is careful

---

[7] In *Finnegans Wake*, Joyce stresses the relation between Cinderella and her ashes, which signify the mortality her story denies, more emphatically than he does here by issuing a warning to Cinderella in language that echoes that of the Ash Wednesday service: "Remember, maid, thou dust art powder but Cinderella thou must return" (*FW* 440.26-27).

to deck her body for constant display, she herself is discouraged from inhabiting it: she cannot refer to bodily functions or even the place where they occur. She is uncomfortable both with eating ("she didn't like the eating part when there were any people that made her shy and often she wondered why you couldn't eat something poetical like violets or roses," (*U* 13.228-30) and with elimination. When Cissy refers to a part of the body, "the beeoteetom," Gerty "bent down her head and crimsoned at the idea of Cissy saying an unladylike thing like that out loud she'd be ashamed of her life to say" (*U* 13.263-66). And when she goes to "that place where she never forgot every fortnight the chlorate of lime" (*U* 13.332-33), she distracts herself from what she is doing by gazing at a:

> picture of halcyon days where a young gentleman in the costume they used to wear then with a threecornered hat was offering a bunch of flowers to his ladylove with oldtime chivalry. . . . She often looked at them dreamily when she went there for a certain purpose and felt her own arms that were white and soft just like hers.(*U* 13.334-41).

Although Gerty is physically mature, she is unable to realize that maturity and accept the complexity of physical being because she must constantly identify herself in her own mind with beauty. Even in the outhouse she must block out her surroundings by staring at a picture of old-fashioned gallantry. Gerty relentlessly censors her thoughts and perceptions, vigilantly replacing them with sentimental pictures: of herself as a model in a fashion magazine decked out in "[a] neat blouse of electric blue . . . and a navy threequarter skirt cut to the stride" (*U* 13.150-55); of herself as rescued by "a manly man with a strong quiet face who had not found his ideal, perhaps his hair slightly flecked with grey, and who would understand, take her in his sheltering arms, strain her to him in all the strength of his deep passionate nature and comfort her with a long long kiss" (*U* 13.210-14). She paints a highly touched-up picture of marriage, complete with "a beautifully appointed drawingroom with pictures and engravings" and "that silver toastrack in Clery's summer jumble sales" (*U* 13.231-34), where her tall husband with broad shoulders and "glistening white teeth under his carefully trimmed sweeping moustache" (*U* 13.236-37) has "brekky" with her every morning, "simple but perfectly served." "[B]efore he went out to business he would give his dear little wifey a good hearty hug and gaze for a moment deep down into her eyes." (*U* 13.240-42).

In accordance with what Joyce identified as the meaning of this episode, "The Projected Mirage,"[8] Gerty has replaced herself with a series of aesthetically pleasing pictures, or mirages, that serve the function of advertisements (and that are in fact modeled on advertisements). Gerty has read the signs of popular culture accurately, and she has done as directed by turning herself into something to be seen, like a painting (the "art" of the episode is "painting"). Gerty has fashioned herself quite literally into a heroine, "as fair a specimen of winsome Irish girlhood as one could wish to see" (*U* 13.80-81), and she seems to epitomize the most admirable aspects of her age and gender: virginity, innocence, a deep longing to minister to the needs of men, aesthetic appeal enhanced by the judicious and thrifty use of clothes and cosmetics, religious faith, and "sweet girlish shyness" (*U* 13.121). One of her favorite poems is called "*Art thou real, my ideal?*" by "Louis J Walsh, Magherafelt" (*U* 13.645-46), and she has constructed herself as an answer to that question. Gerty represents the Irish feminine ideal that Irish audiences so hotly defended

---

[8] According to the Linati schema, the "Sense (Meaning)" of the episode is "The Projected Mirage," and its symbol is "Onanism: Female: Hypocrisy." See Gifford, p. 384.

in their protests against W. B. Yeats's *The Countess Cathleen*(1899) and J. M. Synge's *The Playboy of the Western World* (1907),[9] but Joyce examines the implications of this ideal more carefully than did the nationalist protesters; he exposes its pathetic limitations, reducing a real, potentially complex woman to a lonely caricature and common cliché, although one that is tremendously exciting to men at a distance.

Moreover, Joyce uses Gerty to show that an icon of purity carries within it the seeds of a necessary defilement; this is what Joyce somewhat imprecisely refers to in his schema as the hypocrisy equivalent to female onanism: "Onanism: Female: Hypocrisy." What is hypocritical is the autoeroticism not of women but of the feminine ideal, which in "Circe" is represented by the immortal nymph (*U* 15.3232). The nymph advertises herself as "stonecold and pure" (*U* 15.3393) as she castigates Bloom for his furtive indecencies, but then she begins to undergo a transformation. She first turns into an eyeless nun,

---

[9] The *Playboy* riots erupted after Christy Mahon, the playboy, tells the Widow Quin, "It's Pegeen I'm seeking only, and what'd I care if you brought me a drift of chosen females, standing in their shifts itself, maybe, from this place to the Eastern World?" (J. M. Synge, *The Playboy of the Western World*, act 3, in *Modern Irish Drama*, ed. John P. Harrington [New York: Norton, 1991], p. 115). Joseph Holloway, in a theater journal entry for Thursday, 31 January 31, 1907, refers to this as filth and libel of the Irish peasant girl on the stage (Harrington, p 459). In a letter to the *Freeman's Journal* on 28 January, 1907, an Irishwoman writes, "[I]n no part of Ireland are the women so wanting in modesty as to make advances to a total stranger, much less to a criminal" (cited in James Kilroy, *The Playboy Riots* [Dublin: Dolmen, 1971], p. 10). Interestingly, *The Playboy of the Western World* takes as its subject the difference between the *image* of heroism and its ugly realities. The townspeople in Synge's play celebrate Christy's heroic pose as a man who killed his father, but they revile him when they see actual evidence of the attempt, much as a reader might expect Gerty to remain a picture but express shock when she is actually looked at with desire.

intoning, "No more desire.. . . Only the ethereal" (*U* 15.3436-37); then she starts showing "a large moist stain"; and finally "her plaster cast" cracks, emitting a "cloud of stench" (*U* 15.3457, 3469-70). The ideal is itselfcorrupt, and it cannot hide that corruption indefinitely.

Like the nymph-nun in "Circe," Gerty, by constructing herself as pure and by censoring any indelicate thoughts, renders herself defenseless against the pressure of natural desires. As the ideal female, Gerty is a "sleeping beauty," which Joyce translates in *Finnegans Wake* as a "slipping beauty"(*FW* 477.23); Gerty's unawareness of her own desires is precisely what makes her vulnerable to the penetration of Bloom's gaze.[10] What Joyce shows -- by having Gerty swing her shoe buckle and then her leg for Bloom and lean far back until "he had a full view high up above her knee where no-one not even on the swing or wading and she wasn't ashamed and he wasn't either to look in that immodest way" (*U* 13.728-30) -- is that her behavior is totally consistent with her cultural definition as something to be looked at.

Although "[f]rom everything in the least indelicate her finebred nature instinctively recoiled" (*U* 13.660-61), Gerty can picture her self-display as a romantic dream-encounter:

[10] Joyce's insistence on the interdependence of "sleeping" and "slipping" is reinforced by different variants of the "Sleeping Beauty" tale that portray sleeping as an end to innocence. In an Irish version, "The Queen of Tubber Tintye," or "The King of Erin and the Queen of the Lonesome Island," the queen is not only impregnated but also gives birth while sleeping (she awakens when her son is six years old). And in *The Pentamerone of Giambattista Basile*, "Sole, Luna, e Talia," Sleeping Beauty is again raped while sleeping, whereupon she gives birth to two children, Sun and Moon. See P. L. Travers, *About the Sleeping Beauty* (London: Collins, 1975), pp. 96-123.

She had to go but they   would meet again, there, and she
would dream of that till then, tomorrow, of her dream of yester
eve.____Their souls met in a last lingering glance and the eyes that |
reached her heart, full of a strange shining, hung enraptured on her
sweet flowerlike face. She half smiled at him wanly, a sweet
forgiving smile, a smile that verged on tears, and then they parted.
(*U* 13.760-65).

Even her image of physical perfection is unveiled as a
mirage, when she is revealed as lame.

   The attitude that *Ulysses* takes toward female beauty
is exuberantly unconventional. Joyce depicts beauty as a
sleight-of-hand, a trick of costume, an accident of lighting, a
by-product of style, designed to make women feel less
ordinary and to provoke sexual desire in men. The
language of beauty is rooted in the language of magic; as
Gerty amply˙ demonstrates, the desired transformation is
risibly, poignantly transitory. However, those who counsel
women in the deception of beauty do so, unethically, in the
name of truth:

> Time was when those brows were not so silkily seductive. It was
> Madame Vera Verity [true truth], directress of the Woman
> Beautiful page of the Princess Novelette, who had first advised her
> to try eyebrowleine which gave that haunting expression to the
> eyes, so becoming in leaders of fashion. (*U* 13.108-12)

Beauty traffics in the illusion that a woman's body may
transcend "those discharges she used to get and that tired
feeling" (*U* 13.86-87), that she may be transformed into a
spiritual, young, and virginal vision of unstained
perfection, a lady whose "innate refinement" refutes the
indignities of her present station (*U* 13.97).

   By humorously dissecting the magic of cosmetic
transformation and by exposing the purposes that the cult
of beauty serves for men and women, Joyce derails the

reader's desire for a beautiful, faithful heroine and spotlights its implied misogyny. If what we want is a heroine with a "waxen pallor. . . almost spiritual in its ivorylike purity" (*U* 13.87-88), then we are simultaneously expressing a distaste for real women, with the physical afflictions and imperfections that make them long for the magical transformations promised by cosmetics.

Joyce's exposure of the ideal that Gerty worships and imitates as both false and blind (her "little strangled cry" aligns her with the blind bat that flies out at dusk "with a tiny lost cry," *U* 13.735, 626-27) helps to contextualize his decision to design his mature female heroine along radically unpopular lines. Joyce rejects "beauty parlous" (beauty parlors, parlous beauty) (*FW* 454.19-20) as the source of Molly Bloom's attractiveness. Molly is not beautiful in the cosmetic sense, although she is powerfully attractive in the gravitational sense. Moreover, part of what makes her attractive is precisely what prevents her from being conventionally beautiful in fairy-tale terms: her large mass. Attractive, not beautiful, Molly exercises considerable sexual power instead of becoming "booty."

Molly was never designed to "represent" Joyce's idea of womanhood, which would indeed make her a problematic character;[11] instead, her character is a

---

[11] See, for example, Karen Lawrence's discussion of Sandra Gilbert and Susan Gubar's attack on Joyce's "misogyny" in "Joyce and Feminism," *The Cambridge Companion to James Joyce*, ed. Derek Attridge (Cambridge: Cambridge University Press, 1990), pp. 237-58. Gilbert and Gubar object that Joyce identifies Woman too completely with "matter"; Lawrence lends some credence to this view by pointing out Joyce's expressions of guilt over his treatment of women in his fiction and his dreams, but then she goes on to argue that "a catalogue of misogynistic images or female stereotypes in Joyce's work fails to account for his undermining of the grounds of representation" (p. 240). She suggests that "woman in writing is beyond [Joyce's] control and might stand for a play of language that always exceeds

supplement, an antiphonal   answer to the popular (and risibly anemic) idea of a heroine. She is, in a sense, an anti-Gerty, if Gerty is understood to typify someone who, under strong cultural pressure, has replaced herself as she is in biological reality with a picture of what a young woman should be. If Gerty's introjected ideal image is feminine, Joyce has Molly project herself as aggressive and even masculine ("the missus is master," [*U* 15.2759]). If Gerty airbrushes her body out of consciousness, clothing her body parts in a conscientious effort to deny and replace them,[12] Molly takes pleasure in her ample flesh and consciously registers her all aspects of her physical existence -- from sexual arousal and climax to urination and menstruation ("wait O Jesus wait yes that thing has come on me yes now wouldnt that afflict you of course all the poking and rooting

---

the writer's intention" (p. 240), and that woman "becomes the figure for illegitimacy, errancy, and forgery rather than patriarchal signature" (p. 241). My own emphasis is somewhat different, in that I see Molly less as a principle of excess than as an embodiment of physical realities that are conspicuously missing from what might be called the compound cultural self-image against which all women are called upon to measure themselves against.

[12] Interestingly, what Gerty "reveals" to Bloom is not her body but her underclothing, the fetishized substitute for her body that corresponds to the picture she has substituted for herself. To allow the reader a glimpse of what Gerty fears about the body, the narrator (speaking in Gerty's idiom) refers to underwear as "undies," thereby highlighting not only Gerty's taste for common diminutives but also underscoring the fact that clothes, unlike the body, don't die: "As for undies they were Gerty's chief care and who that knows the fluttering hopes and fears of sweet seventeen (though Gerty would never see seventeen again) can find it in his heart to blame her?" (*U* 13.171-73). Gerty is exceptionally conscious of the passing of time, since she has passed the most marriageable age: "Then they could talk about her till they went blue in the face, Bertha Supple too, and Edy, little spitfire, because she would be twentytwo in November"(*U* 13.220-22).

and ploughing he had up in   me," (*U* 18.1104-06). If Gerty is defined by the clothes she uses simultaneously to reveal and conceal herself, Molly is either minimally clothed or nude, like the picture over the bed, *The Bath of the Nymph*, that reminds Bloom of her: "Not unlike her with her hair down: slimmer. . . . Naked nymphs" (*U* 4.371-73). Instead of looking at her clothes, Bloom looks through Molly's clothes to appreciate her "ample bedwarmed flesh" (*U* 4.238-39): "He looked calmly down on her bulk and between her large soft bubs, sloping within her nightdress like a shegoat's udder" (*U* 4.304-05). All we see of Molly in "Wandering Rocks" is "[a] plump bare generous arm" shining "from a white petticoatbodice and taut shiftstraps" (*U* 10.251-52). Molly is presented in a shift, that item of clothing that it was controversial for actors even to name in *The Playboy of the Western World*; an Irishwoman in a letter to the *Freeman's Journal* declared that the word used to indicate this "essential item of female attire" was one that a "lady would probably never utter in ordinary circumstances, even to herself."[13]

Unlike Gerty, Molly is triumphantly, painfully presented as "a nature full and volatile in its free state" that is naturally "the agent and reagent of attraction" (*U* 17.2163-64). In sharp contrast to Gerty's self-advertising picture of feminine underwear, the last image we are given of Molly before she begins to speak is an unprecedentedly alluring image of her nude breasts and rump:

> adipose anterior and posterior female hemispheres, redolent of milk and honey and of excretory sanguine and seminal warmth, reminiscent of secular families of curves of amplitude, insusceptible of moods of impression or of contrarieties of expression, expressive of mute immutable mature animality. (*U* 17.2232-36)

[13] Kilroy, *The Playboy Riots*, p. 10.

Joyce refuses to reduce Molly to the fat tissue of her rump,
but where else in literature or culture can we find a
comparable instance of appreciation for female
corporeality? To a culture that protested raucously against
the use of the word "shift" as a libel upon womanhood,
Joyce offers an image of Bloom kissing "the plump mellow
yellow smellow melons of [a woman's] rump, on each
plump melonous hemisphere, in their mellow yellow
furrow" (U 17.2241-42). Which is the more misogynist
stance, the one that celebrates the full experience of female
flesh, or the one that censors even the mention of intimate
articles of female clothing? In a culture in which thousands
of anorectic young women are trying to melt the flesh off
their bodies while amenorrheal from the attempt to eat
nothing but "violets and roses," how can a representation of
ample female flesh as something more beautiful than any
work of art, something as vital as the earth itself, be
considered misogynist? And when Molly starts to speak,
the reader learns that she is far more than the "2 lumps of
lard" to which she fears Bloom has reduced her (U 18.1404):
she is full of memory and desire, sensation and longing,
poetry and dross. Unlike so many women who think of
themselves even in the third person, she speaks for herself--
powerfully, lyrically, sometimes crudely, and without
inhibition. Unlike Gerty, who has so pitifully suppressed
hers, Molly has a voracious appetite for life, and as a result
she sometimes cannot find "this mortal world enough."[14]
But her famous affirmation with which the book ends
expresses her willed acceptance of life *and* loss, her
resistance to attenuation and despair, to being turned to
stone by a realistic sight of the world as it is, not a romantic

---

[14] W. H. Auden, "Lullaby," in *The Norton Anthology of English
Literature*, 4th ed., Vol. 2 (New York: W. W. Norton, 1979), p. 2397.

world of faery.

Even Nora, Joyce's wife, was not immune to the shock of being asked to read against the grain of glossy fashion images by seeing Molly as a female hero. When asked if she was a model for Molly Bloom, Nora denied it, claiming with some vanity that Molly was fatter than she was.[15] Although men have long appreciated the proportional relation of size and power (a relation that made small men like Napoleon famously anxious), women as a rule do not interrogate the possible correlation of a petite figure and powerlessness. Although Joyce certainly could have made Molly more intellectual (more like her namesake Molly Ivors in "The Dead"), the role of resistant intellectual had already been assigned to Stephen as a way of countering the expectation that heroes *must be* physical. The characters of Stephen and Molly were designed to violate cultural prescriptions insisting that men must be physical and women may not be physical, a prescription that seems to preclude any meaningful heterosexual connection. But neither Stephen nor Molly is presented as a counter-ideal; Joyce's attack is upon the unreality and counterproductiveness of ideals in general, as well as upon specific, mutually exclusive ideals for men and women, in particular.

Joyce sees woman as powerful; where he differs radically from the culture at large is that he does not brand female sexual power as evil.[16] *Ulysses* is shot through with

[15] Brenda Maddox, *Nora: A Biography of Nora Joyce* (New York: Fawcett Columbine, 1988), p. 198.

[16] There are very few representations of mature female sexual power that are not demonized as evil. Shakespeare's portrait of Cleopatra in *Antony and Cleopatra* may be one, although Cleopatra is far from triumphant at the end; Queen Elizabeth consolidated her political power by refusing to allow it to be interpreted as sexual, billing herself as "The Virgin Queen." The notion of the femme fatale sums up the prevailing sense that female

references to powerful female figures: Ann Hathaway, Helen of Troy, Kitty O'Shea, "naked Eve." As Stephen thinks of Eve, "She had no navel. Gaze. Belly without blemish, bulging big, a buckler of taut vellum, no, whiteheaped corn, orient and immortal, standing from everlasting to everlasting" (*U* 3.41-44). Although men like Garrett Deasy blame women for our "many errors and many sins" (*U* 2.389-90), Joyce dismisses such bigotry as an insidiously disguised personal complaint (Deasy's wife is an unpredictable alcoholic), focusing instead on women's loneliness, a loneliness enhanced by a legacy of shame. Although *Ulysses* is built around a single decisive event, Molly's adultery, Joyce refuses to categorize Molly as an evil or corrupt woman; like Thomas Hardy, who controversially described Tess of the d'Urbervilles as "A Pure Woman," Joyce levels his criticism not at the individual but at the institutions that ravage her, reminding the reader that "[f]rom outrage (matrimony) to outrage (adultery) there arose nought but outrage (copulation)" (*U* 17.2196-97). Joyce makes it clear that the "debility of the female" has been "fallaciously inferred" (*U* 17.2215-16), and along with Bloom, he asserts "the futility of triumph or protest or vindication," spurning "the inanity of extolled virtue" (*U* 17.2224-25).

Ulysses is unusual in that it expresses neither fear nor denigration nor denial of the power of female sexuality. The burden of Stephen's theory of Shakespeare is that Shakespeare's productivity grew out of his encounter with a sexually powerful woman, a woman whose capacity for desire--like that of Queen Gertrude in *Hamlet*--is read by

---

sexual power is dangerous, at best, and fatal, at worst, and there are no almost examples of good-intentioned, successful women who are physically strong and resistant to oppression (even Joan of Arc was martyred).

others as faithlessness.[17] Stephen tells his listeners that Ann Hathaway was no mere mistake of Shakespeare's youth; she was the portal of discovery through which he passed without ever really learning the significance of what his writing everywhere reveals, the central importance of his early receptivity to an older, assured woman: "he passes on towards eternity in undiminished personality, untaught by the wisdom he has written or by the laws he has revealed" (U 9.476-78). The "events which cast their shadow over the hell of time of *King Lear, Othello, Hamlet, Troilus and Cressida*" (U 9.400-401) are the events that surrounded Shakespeare's seduction by Ann Hathaway, who tumbled "in a cornfield a lover younger than herself" (U 9.260). What his experience of a sexually powerful, physically alive woman produces in Shakespeare is--crucially--ambivalence, an ambivalence that makes him "Ravisher and ravished," pursuing "what he would but would not" (U 9.472-3); "Belief in himself has been untimely killed" (U 9.455-56), and his ego is splintered in painfully productive ways. He has lost the assured ease of judgmental condemnation but gained the capacity to find himself in all his characters, finding "in the world without as actual what was in his world within as possible" (U 9.1041-42). It is not Ann Hathaway's beauty that produces such a harvest (as "beautifulinsadness Best" says to "ugling Eglinton," "The sense of beauty leads us astray" [U 9.735]) but her vivid reality, the physical and erotic strength that society would debar to women.

Cultural stereotypes, ideals, even gender differences themselves (insofar as they prescribe differences in thought and behavior) are attempts to contain and sterilize the

[17] Compare Virginia Woolf's famous imaginary account of Shakespeare's "sister" in *A Room of One's Own* (1929; New York and London: Harcourt Brace Jovanovich, 1957).

contaminating power of a   reality that, like mortality itself, ultimately destroys all categories. Joyce's war with convention in *Ulysses* highlights the vitality of eschewing judgment and embracing the catalytic force of change. Perhaps Joyce is mistaken in his view that women, having been sharply forbidden fleshly indulgence for at least a millennium, have a capacity to experience physical life exceeding that of men. Virginia Woolf certainly thought that Joyce underestimated the effects on women of centuries of repression. But what Joyce systematically attacks throughout *Ulysses* are those compound cultural images that crowd out individual apprehension, experimentation, and thought, the products and prescriptions of what Gerty calls "Society with a big ess" (*U* 13.666). Gender difference is one such delibilating mirage; boundaries, as Joyce describes them, are heuristic borders designed to be surpassed--not lightly, but at the appropriate time, to initiate new stages of cognitive and emotional development. *Ulysses* is designed to inculcate "heterodox resistance" to simplistic cultural constructions (*U* 17.23); it both protests and mourns the increasing "restriction of the . . . domain of interindividual relations" (*U* 17.64-65). Instead of feminine young women and masculine young men, it offers its readers the fuller, surer touch of a "firm full masculine feminine passive active hand" (*U* 17.289-90). Its categories are mixed, controversial, changing, and alive; its stance is a feminist one in the sense that it prefers "sins of excess" to "sins of denial."[18] Like Bloom, Joyce expresses in *Ulysses* a desire "to amend many social conditions, the product of inequality and avarice and international animosity" (*U* 17.990-92), and in *Ulysses*, he commits himself fully to "the convulsions of

[18] Jeanette Winterson, *Sexing the Cherry* (New York: Random House, 1989), p. 70.

metamorphosis, from infancy through maturity to decay" (*U* 17.1005-06). *Ulysses* affirms "the fact of vital growth" (*U* 17.1005), not artificial categories such as "gender," a word with an "end" in it.

University of Pennsylvania, Philadelphia

"TWENTY POCKETS ARENT ENOUGH FOR THEIR LIES": POCKETED OBJECTS AS PROPS OF BLOOM'S MASCULINITY IN *ULYSSES*

KAREN R. LAWRENCE

Abstract. The male characters in *Ulysses*, Leopold Bloom, in particular, play a shell game in the many pockets of their suits. Way stations between the public and the private, Bloom's pockets provide a safe haven for the objects that he cherishes, ritualistically transfers from place to place on his person, and occasionally imports from and exports to others. From the outside the suit helps consolidate the bourgeois masculine image of self-possession and restraint; it provides hidden spaces in which resources are kept close to the body, available for use but hidden from view. Bloom's pocketed objects buttress the performance of his masculinity. The fondled amulets and fetish objects, such as his talismanic potato, arm him in his encounter with the public world and serve as props in the construction of his private sense of manhood. They enable him as well to bend commodity culture to his own idiosyncratic desires. For unlike Marx, who viewed the fetish worshiper as deluded into believing that an inanimate object would "comply with his desires, Joyce presents a fluid view of the flow of desire between an individual and society's commodities as he represents the mysterious process in which masculine subjectivity is constructed amid commodity exchange.

We are all familiar with the famous photograph of Joyce taken by C. P. Curran when Joyce was twenty-two.[1] Joyce adopts a stance of studied casualness: hips slightly forward, hands in pockets, head cocked slightly to one side, he mildly challenges the camera with an expression that gives nothing away. The gesture of the hands in the pockets is an integral part of the stance of self-containment, composing

---

[1] The photograph is reproduced in *JJII*, plate VIII.

the subject in a closed circuit. His hands and his thoughts are hidden from view. The pose teased the photographer into asking what was on Joyce's mind. A viewer might wonder what is in his pockets.

As we all know from Richard Ellmann, Joyce was reported to have replied to the photographer's question, "I was wondering would he lend me five shillings" (caption under plate VIII), suggesting that the mind may be full of schemes but the pockets are almost empty. In the hypothetical afterlife of the photograph, Joyce will attempt to con the photographer. His wits will have to compensate for his empty pockets. In contrast, the mock-priest, Mulligan, does perform a coin trick in the first chapter of *Ulysses*. The old woman delivering tea to the tower needs to be paid, Haines reminds them. The cost of the tea is two shillings twopence.

> Buck Mulligan sighed and, having filled his mouth with a crust
> thickly buttered on both sides, stretched forth his legs and began to
> search his trouser pockets.
> --Pay up and look pleasant, Haines said to him, smiling.
> Stephen filled a third cup, a spoonful of tea colouring faintly the
> thick rich milk. Buck Mulligan brought up a florin, twisted it
> round in his fingers and cried:
> --A miracle! (*U* 1.446-53)

Mulligan is a magician, a miracle maker who can pull a rabbit out of a hat, a florin from a habitually empty Irish trouser pocket. As we know, much is made in *Ulysses* of what is not found in men's trouser pockets. Money, especially, is scarce. Latchkeys, too, are absent or misplaced: Bloom begins his day by remembering that he left his latchkey in the pocket of another pair of trousers; Stephen begins his day by momentarily pocketing the "huge key" to the tower (*U* 1.530), only to relinquish it soon after. Money and keys, of course, signify one's stake in society's property and one's   claim to a proper share of its commodities. Mulligan's sleight of hand allows him to mystify the origins of money in colonial labor in a show of shamanistic powers.[2] In constrast, Stephen eschews Mulligan's pretense of magical powers. After pocketing the coins he has been paid by Mr. Deasy, he thinks: "A lump in my pocket: symbols soiled by greed and misery" (*U* 2.227-28). The telltale bulge in the trouser pocket only *seems* to symbolize the potency of possession; indeed, shortly after this Stephen emphasizes his sense of impotence, with a phrase that resonates beyond its specific reference in the chapter: "The lump I have is useless" (*U* 2.259).

A whole performance of "to have and to have not," of bulging pockets and useless lumps, pervades the multiple references to pockets in *Ulysses*. The novel is full of ritualized performances in which all sorts of everyday objects are hoarded, relinquished, exchanged, and transferred via male pockets. Mulligan's magic act underscores the way pockets function as repositories of props for the performance of character in general and masculinity in particular, props that are invested with magical powers. The "20 pockets" in the male suit, suspiciously viewed by Molly as not enough "for their lies" (*U* 18.1236-37) contain resources for charming the world. Yet Mulligan's hocus pocus disguises the phallic anxiety attached to the performance of the self and the characters' nagging suspicions that the lumps in their trousers are indeed useless.

Fetishism provides the link between everyday objects and the magical investments of desire; it provides as well a clue to the compensatory functions of material

---

[2] This sleight of hand, what Marx called the capitalist "trick" of commodity fetishism, mystifies the connection between labor and capital. I will discuss fetishism in more detail below.

objects for the characters that circulate through
Dublin in *Ulysses*. In an essay in *Fetishism as Cultural
Discourse*, an excellent collection coedited with Emily Apter,
William Pietz explains that the word "fetishism" originally
referred to the primitive religious practice of worshipping
"terrestrial, material objects."[3] Through Marx and Freud, the
older anthropological discourse came to highlight the
investments of desire in objects that circulate and are
exchanged in modern society, with Marx focusing on the
collectively valued commodity and Freud on the more
personal and idiosyncratic projections of desire. In both
Marxist and Freudian discourse, however, "[o]bjects are
revealed as provocations to desire and possession," as
Apter puts it.[4] It is, of course, in classical psychoanalysis
that the fetish object is viewed as a substitute phallus,
revealing and concealing the "fact" of maternal castration.
Yet, as revisionary work on fetishism has shown, "the idea
stipulated by classical psychoanalysis that virtually any
object -- fur, velvet, chair legs, shoelaces, apron strings,
hatbands, feather boas, etc. -- can become a candidate for
fetishization once it is placed on the great metonymic chain
of phallic substitutions ultimately undermines the
presupposition of a phallic *ur*-form, or *objet*-type."[5]

Bloom's thought, "no key, but potato," captures the
way he props up his sagging masculinity with the magic
charms in his pockets. An updated version of Odysseus's
moly, the potato is associated with Bloom's mother. It is his
talisman, the fetish object that he endows with all the

[3] William Pietz, "Fetishism and Materialism: The Limits of Theory in
Marx," in *Fetishism as Cultural Discourse*, ed. Emily Apter and William Pietz
(Ithaca and London: Cornell University Press, 1993), p. 131.

[4] Emily Apter, "Introduction" in *Fetishism as Cultural Discourse*, p. 2.

[5] Apter, p. 4.

powers of possession that   he lacks. "Potato I have," he reassures himself, as he embarks on his circulation through Dublin (*U* 4.73), and in "Circe," after a near miss with the sandstrewer, the stage directions tell us that Bloom "feels his trouser pocket" for comfort in "poor mamma's panacea" (*U* 15.201-02). In the same chapter, Zoe asks Bloom, "How's the nuts?" (*U* 15.1299), and puts her hand in his pocket and feels instead the potato, which she calls a "hard chancre" (*U* 15.1304), bawdily linking the tuber and syphylitic phallus.[6] Although he lacks the patriarchal keys to Dublin society, most of the day Bloom gains authority and confidence from his protective amulet. In his classic study *The Psychology of Clothes*, J. C. Flugel describes the carrying of amulets on the person to ward off evil spirits: "it is extremely convenient," he says, "to carry about some amulet which can be trusted to ward off the evil influences without the necessity of active intervention.   For this purpose various objects, supposed to possess magical properties, were hung or otherwise attached to the body."[7] "Without the necessity of active intervention," Bloom arms himself for passive combat, one could say; in the modern suit, however, the amulet is pocketed conveniently rather than hung on the body. In returning magical properties to things, the fetishist locates a potency that he otherwise lacks.

In a way, all the small objects that Bloom carries in his pockets are amulets, for pockets in *Ulysses* are reservoirs of possessions and self-possession, the daily arsenals with which the male characters leave their houses, armed for

---

[6] After writing this essay and delivering it as a talk at the Joyce Symposium in Rome, I became aware of Peter Sims's fine article entitled "A Pocket Guide to 'Ulysses,'" *JJQ* 26 (Winter 1989): 239-58.

[7] J. C. Flugel, *The Psychology of Clothes* (New York: International Universities Press, Inc., 1930), p. 72.

circulation in society ("A potato, don't leave home without it," one might say). Pockets are temporary havens for the characters' private property as they navigate their way through city streets. We might think of pockets as the material counterparts of the interior monologue, containers that harbor and construct the domain of the private. In being temporary and portable, pockets contain objects that contrast with the more official and societal "secrets" of the drawer inventoried in the "Ithaca" chapter of *Ulysses*. Birth certificate, bank passbook, stock certificate, insurance policy, graveplot purchase document and official records of a name change -- these contents of Bloom's second drawer establish the more permanent record of Bloom as a stakeholder in society. Coins, rather than bankbooks; cards with pseudonyms, rather than official records; daily newspapers and advertisements of paradisal communities; food and soap--these are the more perishable and vulnerable commodities protected in the portable pouches of the pockets. As Flugel puts it, "[C]lothes, like the house, are protective; but, being nearer the body and actually supported on it, they are (unlike the house) portable. With their help, we carry --like snails and tortoises -- a sort of home upon our backs, and enjoy the advantages of shelter without the disadvantage of becoming sessile."[8]

According to Anne Hollander in *Sex and Suits*, the man's suit--Bloom's suit, with waistcoat, trousers and vest--

---

[8] Flugel, p. 83. See Vincent Pecora's description of the persistence of an archaic "*oikos*," or "noble household," in modern literature and philosophy, which includes a discussion of Bloom's household property, specifically, his potato. Pecora concentrates on the way in which a certain tradition of thought from Durkheim to Mauss viewed fetishism, with its nostalgic magic, as potentially liberating "things deadened by rationality, profit [and] utility" (Vincent P. Pecora, *Households of the Soul* (Baltimore and London: Johns Hopkins University Press, 1997), p. 47.

consolidated the "modern masculine image," a consolidation virtually in place by 1820. In contrast to women's fashion, the masculine suit, she says, "suggests probity and restraint, prudence and detachment."[9] This image of prudence and self-possession is an important part of Bloom's self representation of his bourgeois masculine image; pockets allow for the careful arrangement and concealment of one's personal effects (think of Bloom's self-conscious gesture of "prudently pocketing" Molly's photo in the cabman's shelter [U 16.1644]). Pockets provide cover for Bloom's elaborately constructed rituals of docking imports and exports momentarily on his person -- elaborate shell games in which he receives, fondles, transfers, and replaces objects. Things virtually appear and disappear into the separate compartments of Bloom's "inner pocket," "handkerchief pocket," "sidepocket," "heart pocket," and "trouser pocket." These pockets provide ordering and circulating spaces in a private economy under Bloom's control. Martha's flower and Molly's soap are punctiliously rearranged and separated on Bloom's person, allowing for the literal compartmentalizing, one might say, rationalizing, of his desires ("Change that soap now. Mr. Bloom's hand unbuttoned his hip pocket swiftly and transferred the paperstuck soap to his inner handkerchief pocket" [U 6.494-96]). Indeed, Molly herself focuses on the number of secret chambers enabling male deception: "I'll see if he has that French letter still in his pocketbook I suppose he thinks I don't know deceitful men all their 20 pockets arent enough for their lies" (U 18.1235-37). Slipping Martha's letter and his own Henry Flower card into his sidepocket, Bloom carefully arranges an alibi, a screen, for his deflowering of

[9] Anne Hollander, *Sex and Suits* (New York: Alfred A. Knopf, 1994), p. 55.

Martha's letter: "His hand   went into his pocket and a forefinger felt its way under the flap of the envelope, ripping it open in jerks" (*U* 5.77-78). Martha's letter is a kind of prophylactic (or French letter); the penetration of the envelope in the pocket is safe and prudent sex, a honeymoon in the hidden hand.

Yet if they harbor the domain of the private, Bloom's pockets house as well his passports to the public sphere. As a middle man between the economic base and the superstructure, as Jennifer Wicke has put it in describing Bloom's job as an ad canvasser, Bloom is a willing and active participant in the circulation of commodities.[10] Unlike Stephen, he welcomes commercial exchanges. Indeed, his pleasure in the accumulation and manipulation of the objects in his pockets distinguishes him from the more critical and parsimonious Stephen, whose gestures include divestment more than inventory. This commerce with the world is crucial to constructing Bloom's bourgeois masculinity, his participation in the public sphere.

Thus, as way stations between private and societal domains, pockets are portable spaces that facilitate Bloom's illusion of controlling the exchanges in which he participates. He buys a kidney -- "His hand accepted the moist tender gland and slid it into a sidepocket. Then it fetched up three coins from his trousers' pocket and laid them on the rubber prickles. They lay, were read quickly and quickly slid, disc by disc, into the till" (*U* 4.181-83). The sensuous symmetry between the gland sliding into his pocket and his own coins sliding quickly into the till conveys the tactile, even sexual, pleasure that Bloom derives from his role in commodity culture, in the rituals of

---

[10] See Jennifer Wicke, *Advertising Fictions: Literature, Advertisement, and Social Reading* (New York: Columbia University Press, 1988), p. 128.

buying and selling. We might remember Apter's idea that all sorts of objects can function as fetishes if they exist on the metonymic chain of phallic substitutions, as "moist glands" are wont to do. Yet, what the tactile pleasure of the fetish suggests in the above example is the way in which pockets are the spaces where characters struggle to personalize commodity culture, to invest the objects in circulation with their particular desires and magical projections. As Pietz observes, Marx saw the fetish-worshipper as deceived into believing that an inanimate object would "comply with his desires."[11] Joyce seems to have a more fluid view of the flow of desire between an individual and society's commodities and represents a more mysterious process in which subjectivity is constructed amid commodity exchange.[12]

So Bloom's private rituals depend on and attempt to refashion commodities, for example, as when the daily newspaper -- a symbol of the urban everyday -- serves Bloom as a detachable phallus, his own fetish object for masculine display. To gird himself for his trip to the post office to see if Martha Clifford has responded to him, Bloom draws the *Freeman* from his sidepocket, in a bravura show of his masculinity: "As he walked he took the folded *Freeman* from his sidepocket, unfolded it, rolled it lengthwise in a baton and tapped it at each sauntering step against his trouserleg" (*U* 5.48-50). Imitating the wide-

---

[11] Pietz, p. 136.

[12] Pietz attributes this view of the fetish as an expression of subjectivity to Hegel, whose view countered the more "objective" view of the fetish from Kant: "In contrast to Kant, Hegel emphasized the importance of random association and contingency in fetishism, which he viewed as the first spiritual expression of human subjectivity per se, in the form of arbitrary caprice and particular desire, projected and objectified as power in some (any) material object" (p.124, n.14).

hipped sauntering girl who purchased sausages, no less, in Dlugacz's earlier in the morning, Bloom orchestrates his performance of masculinity with the prop of his "baton," wearing the phallus on the outside. As with Martha's unpocketed letter, the unpocketed *Freeman* shows how Bloom commandeers circulating language, fetishizing textual objects, investing them with his own desire.

Yet Bloom's ritual management of masculine props cannot protect him from exposure and humiliation. Such exposure comes when M'Coy interrupts him and asks, "How's the body?" (*U* 5.86), and "Who's getting it up?" (*U* 5.153), questions that remind us of the lack the fetish object is deployed to conceal. Another moment comes when Bloom, unexpectedly spying Boylan, desperately inventories his ammunition, like a turtle who retreats into its shell:

> Look for something I.
> His hasty hand went quickly into a pocket, took out, read unfolded Agendath Netaim. Where did I?
> Busy looking.
> He thrust back quick Agendath.
> Afternoon she said.
> I am looking for that. Yes, that. Try all pockets. Handker. *Freeman*. Where did I? Ah, yes. Trousers. Potato. Purse. Where?
> Hurry. Walk quietly. Moment more. My heart.
> His hand looking for the where did I put found in his hip pocket soap lotion have to call tepid paper stuck. Ah soap there I yes. Gate.
> Safe! (*U* 8.1182-93)

The analogy between pockets and consciousness is never clearer than here; Bloom's anxious thoughts and his things spill willy-nilly about, the syntax unable to compartmentalize effectively the disparate contents of and on his person. "Try all pockets," Bloom vainly instructs himself. In this passage, Bloom anticipates Beckett's Molloy, who performs the most famous pocket ritual in modern literature -- the distribution into four pockets of sixteen sucking stones, individually sucked and deposited.[13] Molloy's stripped down version of appropriation and self-possession seems a far cry from Bloom's bourgeois delight, yet the futility of trying to control the placements, replacements, and displacements of desire is poignant in both cases -- and comic.

It is in "Circe" that this futility is dramatized in theatrical spectacle as Bloom's inner pockets are picked, his privacy anything but inviolate: "Beware of pickpockets" (*U* 15.245), Bloom warns early in the chapter. The objects prudently pocketed or relinquished now speak their own desires rebelliously,like Molly's soap or the watch which Bloom has earlier drawn from his pocket in embarrassment, caught in the act of masturbation by Cissy Caffrey. It is emphasized in "Circe" that Bloom's pocketed objects are mostly fetishes associated with women: Molly's "wandering soap," his mother's "potato preservative," Molly's *Sweets of*

[13] "I distributed them equally among my four pockets, and sucked them turn and turn about. This raised a problem which I first solved in the following way. I had say sixteen stones, four in each of my four pockets these being the two pockets of my trousers and the two pockets of my greatcoat. Taking a stone from the right pocket of my greatcoat, and putting it in my mouth, I replaced it in the right pocket of my greatcoat by a stone from the right pocket of my trousers, which I replaced by a stone from the left pocket of my trousers, which I replaced by a stone from the left pocket of my greatcoat, which I replaced by the stone which was in my mouth, as soon as I had finished sucking it. Thus there were still four stones in each of my four pockets, but not quite the same stones" (Samuel Beckett, *Molloy*, in *Three Novels by Samuel Beckett: "Molloy," "Malone Dies," "The Unnamable"* [New York: Grove Press, 1955], p. 69). In this ritual performance, Molloy appears as a wildly exaggerated incarnation of Bloom's punctiliousness and obsessiveness.

Sin.[14] These commodity fetishes, in Marxist fashion, literally take on a life of their own, refusing to sit still for Bloom's displacements. Indeed, the metonymic "slide" of phallic substitutions reaches its apotheosis as sticks, "stiff" legs, a "stiff walk" (U 15.207), and "stiffpointed" tails (*U* 15.1252) abound in the chapter. The prosthetic baton Bloom has made of the *Freeman* is now replaced by Cissy Caffrey's "the leg of the duck," which she distributes to Molly and to Nelly to strap on wherever they please. The phallic mothers have their revenge. Indeed, the sexual differentiation that pockets signify -- women carry their objects in their purses, men carry them in their pockets -- is itself undermined. After Tommy and Jacky run into Bloom at the beginning of the chapter, Bloom "pats with parcelled hands, watchfob, pocketbookpocket, pursepoke, sweets of sin, potatosoap" (*U* 15.242-43), trying to remain in possession of his possessions, which form unnerving combinations and substitutions within his pouches. The pocket is now a "pocketbookpocket"; "purse" and phallic "poke" are combined in "pursepoke." It is in "Circe" most of all that the "thing itself," the phallus, is revealed as a prop. The pocket, by day associated with the masculine suit, by night reveals its female properties, specifically, its pouchlike, womblike function. The props of masculinity and femininity circulate and combine in the heated compression of the chapter. The fetishes, provocations to desire and possession, reveal the way desire is an errant thing not possessed or pocketed but always misplaced and displaced. Finally, for all Bloom's intimate and fond contact with the possessions he harbors,

---

[14] Sims says that in "Circe" Bloom's pockets "play an important role as sources of comfort and prophylactic protection. . . . The potato, soap, and condom form a trinity of hygienic talismans, each addressing a different requirement of the phallus' protection" (245). My point is that in "Circe" Bloom's pockets are turned inside out in a risky gesture of exposure.

his elaborate pocket rituals can neither conceal his sense of lack nor make commodities conform to his own desires. The comic animism of the fetish in "Circe" signals the slippery slope of substitution, once the metonymic chain of displacement begins.

It stages as well a certain demystification of the artist's conjuring act, a resistance to his magical powers. There is a link between the talismanic potency of the fetish and the seduction of details that contribute to realism's power. It is a connection implicit in the following description in Hugh Kenner's *The Stoic Comedians*: "But Joyce tended to fondle data which comes in finite sets, and to enumerate these sets, and when the data is as protean as the life of a great city, he avails himself of various delimiting devices -- single day, a city directory, a newspaper--to give at least the appearance of a finite set."[15]

In *Ulysses* the narrative fondles, invests, and inventories data in the manner of Bloom. In the narration of *Ulysses* we are made to see the sleight of hand performed in all representation -- the conjuring of the "things" of the world, "the hidden hand . . . again at its old game" (*U* 15.975). Watch carefully as the baton waves -- take your mind off the narration and a scene has been moved, objects magically appear without being properly introduced. Anti-realism and realism merge in this fiat, this performance. But if we are careful, we must see through the deliberate mystifications of pulling rabbits out of hats, that is, the aesthetic of art's autonomous creation out of the "deep pocket" of the author's mind; for if the fetish reminds us of the mysterious workings of fantasy and desire, it also reminds us of the material object and its putative value in

[15] Hugh Kenner, *The Stoic Comedians: Flaubert, Joyce, and Beckett* (Berkeley, Los Angeles, and London: University of California Press, 1962), p. 105.

circulation. The fondling of   data and the investment of everyday objects with desire, provide a corrective to the view that art is cut off from the world.

University of California, Irvine

DEALING IN SHAME: POWER/GENDER IN "CIRCE"

SHELDON BRIVIC

Abstract: Joyce allowed himself to be called "Shame's Voice," and he makes the expression of shame central to his work because he recognizes shame as a central factor not only in personal feelings but in art, in gender, and in social economy. "Circe" develops Joyce's idea that shame is the crucial medium of exchange in modern society. Sylvan Tompkins's argument that shame plays a foundational role in political systems is parallel to Joyce's view of shame as the substance that holds social bonds together. Moreover, Leon Wurmser opposes shame, as the feeling of someone violated, to guilt, as the feeling of the violator, and this suggests that shame constitutes the stereotype of femininity, while guilt constitutes that of masculinity. Therefore Joyce reverses conventional genders and hierarchy by indicating through Leopold Bloom that shame is the grounding principle in the life of the average man.

The women whom Bloom imagines attacking him in "Circe" suggest his own need to attack himself, but also keep him from perceiving it. His shame at being in the brothel defends against a deeper level in which he enjoys shame. This is the level of abjection in which identity disintegrates, and Bloom subjects himself to a power of women that has to be defined as masculine, their power to reshape men. This power is identified with Circe, who, in Kristeva's terms, is a goddess of defilement.

In the ordinary world (the world that gives orders) Bloom defends against the inner desire for shame by using the outward level of shame to connect with the social system. An examination of his performance at his job reveals that his main effort   goes into bearing shame at the hands of his customers. He is shown as a Jew asking favors from Christian clients who treat him with contempt. His ability to make contact with those on higher social levels is an index of his success and depends on his ability to sustain shame. Joyce implies that the hardest work of most jobs consists of being shamed. There are people who advance themselves by shaming others, but Joyce insists that they are morally reprehensible. The choice of shame, shame's choice of self-development through feminization is the only possible action of the Joycean male protagonist.

In *Our Exagmination round His Factification for Incamination of Work in Progress* (1929), there is a letter of protest against *Finnegans Wake* written somewhat in the style of that work in progress.[1] At one point it addresses the author it criticizes as "mysterre Shame's Voice." Many readers of this collection must have assumed that Joyce wrote the letter, for its tone accords with his portrayal of the shameful sham Shem. In fact, as the signature of the letter indicates, a follower of Joyce named Vladimir Dixon is the true author.[2] Joyce, however, approved of the publication of the letter in a book he organized, and he may have seen truth in the suggestion that what spoke in his work was shame.

Late in *Giacomo Joyce*, after giving Amalia Popper a copy of *A Portrait*, Joyce reflects, "Those quiet cold fingers

[1] Samuel Beckett et al., *Our Exagmination round His Factification for Incamination of Work in Progress* (New York: New Directions, 1972), pp. 193-94. This collection does not have an editor and appears to have been assembled by Joyce.

[2] Dixon is identified in Thomas A. Goldwasser, "Who Was Vladimir Dixon? Was He Vladimir Dixon?" *James Joyce Quarterly* 16 (Spring 1979): 219-22. Goldwasser pointed out that up to that time even Richard Ellmann thought that Dixon's letter was written by Joyce.

have touched the pages, foul and fair, on which my shame shall glow forever" (*GJ* 13). If Joyce thought of *Portrait* as radiating with his shame, he must have seen *Ulysses* as burning brightly with it, especially "Circe," which enacts versions of some of his most debased fantasies in the longest and most climactic episode. Joyce makes the expression of shame central to his work because he recognizes shame as a central factor not only in personal feelings but in masculinity, in art, and in social economy. "Circe" develops Joyce's idea that shame is the crucial medium of exchange in modern society.

In his analysis of the emotions Sylvan Tomkins says: "In contrast to all other affects, shame is an experience of the self by the self."[3] Tomkins links shame to shyness and a withdrawal from stressful contacts with people one does not know. Self-regard may be fundamentally intertwined with shame, and both may be linked by Joyce to the origin of his writing. In *Portrait*, when Stephen Dedalus begins to record his epiphanies around the age of fourteen, we are told that "he chronicled with patience what he saw, detaching himself from it and testing its mortifying flavour in secret"(*P* 67). This is parallel to Judith Butler's argument (following Julia Kristeva) that the subject defines itself by separating itself from what it designates as unclean or abject.[4] Yet Stephen, as a semi-colonial artist aligned with the colonized, recognizes his dependence on the impurities he focuses on.

Tomkins argues that shame plays a foundational role in political systems. He says that hierarchical relations are

[3] *Shame and Its Sisters: A Sylvan Tomkins Reader*, ed. Eve Kosofsky Sedgwick and Adam Frank (Durham: Duke University Press , 1995), p. 136.

[4] Judith Butler, *Gender Trouble: Feminism and the Subversion of Identity* (New York: Routledge, 1990), p. 133.

based on the oppressor feeling contempt and the oppressed feeling either contempt for himself or shame.[5] This is parallel to Joyce's recognition that shame is the substance that holds social bonds together. Tomkins asks, "Why are shame and pride such central motives?[6] In most situations in life, people strive to avoid shame and maintain pride; yet Joyce as an artist reverses these strivings.

This may be because the Romantic myth of the artist, which Stephen derives at this stage from Dumas's *The Count of Monte Cristo* and Byron (and which remains fundamental to Joyce's art through the influence of Symbolism), takes the position of the colonized, the shamed. The Church actually promotes such an attitude in its own way, for the Jesuits, followers of the "despised and rejected" (Isa. 53:3) Jew Jesus, see themselves as a band of outsiders bent on self-mortification. Joyce's reversal of conventional vision as an artist who seeks mortification allows him to see how pride and shame are misused in society.

Moreover, the opposition between shame and pride is parallel to, and may in fact be the basis of, the traditional distinction between femininity and masculinity, which generates the shameful pudendum and the proud phallus. The stereotype of males as active and females as passive tends to make shame appear as a feminine feeling; and Toby Olson wrote a fine novel called *The Woman Who Escaped from Shame*, implying that this woman's accomplishment was remarkable.[7]

Further indication of the gender bearing of shame may be found in *The Mask of Shame*, by Leon Wurmser.

[5] Tomkins, p. 139.

[6] Tomkins, p. 136.

[7] (New York: Random House, 1986).

Wurmser opposes shame, the feeling of the loser, to guilt, the feeling of the winner.[8] Shame is the feeling of someone violated, and guilt is the feeling of the violator.[9] Wurmser adds that the unconscious "threat implied in" shame is "abandonment," while the threat in guilt is castration.[10] This seems to confirm the gender division, since women are more inclined to worry about abandonment, and men, about castration.

The traditional double standard produces a situation in which the man feels guilty for cheating and his women feel shamed by his infidelity. Yet to feel guilt does not keep one from feeling contempt. Like Germans and white people, men are great at feeling guilt, but at the same time, that guilt allows them to feel that they have more integrity than their victims. Wurmser quotes Nietzsche from *Beyond Good and Evil: "Wer sich selbst verachtet, achtet sich doch immer noch dabei als Verachter"* [He who has contempt for himself still thereby respects himself as the scorner].[11] Shame, on the contrary, is a feeling of not having integrity, of being unable to control oneself.[12]

Self-contempt may be seen as the more masculine reaction in traditional terms because it cannot be reconciled to the oppressor, whereas shame is the one that corresponds to femininity because women have often *had* to be reconciled to their oppressors. If shame is linked to femininity, then for a man to focus on it is to reverse stereotypes, and Tomkins's editors, Eve Kosofsky Sedgwick

[8] (Baltimore: Johns Hopkins University. Press), p. 28.

[9] p. 62.

[10] p. 73.

[11] p. 68.

[12] p. 35.

and Adam Frank, argue that Tomkins's realistic examination of affects serves to oppose heterosexist views.[13] Likewise, Joyce's insistence on the power of shame--in his own development and in social operations--is part of his attack on and reversal of conventional genders and hierarchical ideology. Through Leopold Bloom, he suggests that shame is a key grounding principle in the life of the average man.

"Circe" is organized along what Donald Nathanson calls the shame/pride axis, the interplay of these inseparable feelings.[14] In the hallucinatory plot of "Circe," Stephen tries to hold himself aloft with pride--"No, I flew. My foes beneath me" (*U* 15.3935)--but ends up getting knocked down into a shameful position, lying in the gutter. Bloom on the other hand, sinks into shameful reveries that are probably unconscious--"I rererepugnosed in rerererepugnant . . ." (*U* 15.3057)--but ends up rising from them to stand over Stephen in the pride of a paternal position (*U* 15.4945).

If Stephen and Bloom both encounter shame in "Circe," one reason is that this huge middle episode of *Ulysses* stages the underlying structure of the modern capitalist world; and this vision of a world of prostitution reveals that the real currency of society, its actual legal tender, is shame. All exchanges of masculinity and power, including the use of money, operate in the interface between shame and pride, the place where power interpellates us, calling men toward pride and away from shame--yet sending reverse signals on another level. This is why the place of shame is where the action is.

[13] p. 7.

[14] Donald L. Nathanson, *Shame and Pride: Affect, Sex, and the Birth of the Self* (New York: W. W. Norton, 1992), pp. 188-89.

Robert Stoller found through extensive research that thoughts of shame were even central to masculine sexual arousal: "[A]ll of us . . . each time we contemplate a sexual event, think about those moments in our childhood lives when we have been traumatized by shame."[15] In the first half of "Circe," Bloom moves toward the realm of shame as he moves toward that of lust, and this is one reason why images of humiliation keep occurring to him. Wurmser says that the power sphere around a person includes an inner limit covering an intimate area that one cannot bear to expose, and shame threatens to violate this boundary.[16] For both Bloom and Stephen, it is women who are designated as the violators of this inner limit, if only because male violation cannot be countenanced, so that when Bloom, for example, contemplates an embarrassing situation (peeing in a bucket), he thinks, "Lucky no woman" (*U* 15.594).

This seems to be an area in which women have power, but like many conventional powers of women, it depends on the allocation of shame. One reason it is dangerous for a woman to see a man's weakness is that women are repositories for male shame. The traditional sexual paradigm in which the man is supposed to be victor and the woman, vanquished, means that the shame through which both have to get release is projected onto her in many ways, such as through stereotypes of weakness and lust.

In Bloom's case, however, he acknowledges his shame by projecting a series of aggressive women, such as Molly in Turkish costume, the three society ladies--Mrs. Yelverton Barry, Mrs. Bellingham, and Mrs. Mervyn

[15] Stoller paraphrased by Nathanson in *Shame and Pride*, p. 285.

[16] Wurmser, p. 62.

Talboys--and Bella Cohen. These vixens are all masculine fantasies, though some of their assertions may correspond to female possibilities.[17]

What these fantasy women suggest to Bloom, at the same time that they keep him from perceiving it, is his own need to attack himself, his enjoyment of shame--which is the deepest level of shame, abjection. On this level, there is no self to defend against invasion. The coherence of his subjectivity disintegrates insofar as he realizes his responsibility for these violent fantasies against himself. Part of himself has to resist, to deny his attraction to what debases him. His self-division expresses society's opposition to his freedom, an opposition that he has been conditioned to internalize.

When Bella turns into Bello, his ultimate threat is that Bloom *wants* the abuse offered, that he can be enclosed in the negative stereotype of the woman. Bello insists that Bloom should beg for torture: "Pray for it as you never prayed before" (*U* 15.2941), and his description of the violence done to Bloom is intended to be strangely, disturbingly exciting to Bloom and to the reader.

Joyce here brings to the surface a deep inner level of ideological apparatus relating to masculinity in a semi-colonial position. There is no more powerful, crucial function of the colonizing state than to make people desire to punish themselves. A state that does not use religion or ideology to make people ashamed enough to desire pain would have no chance of surviving because it could not

[17] For example, when Bella tells Bloom that now he'll find out what it feels like to be treated the way men treat women, she touches on feminist insight: "As they are now so will you be, wigged, singed, perfumesprayed . . . .You will be laced with cruel force into vicelike corsets" (*U* 15.2972-75). Women are processed by men in a way that disguises and trammels them so as to reconstruct their sensory features.

motivate people to work hard, not to mention to fight to protect its territory. The paradigm of manhood operates to make its partakers seek punishment to avoid the greater shame of losing the coherence of gender/identity.

But even in a noncolonial realm, men develop as men by taking on difficulties. The male code is designed to conceal the extent to which it centers on self-torture and self-humiliation. The suffering of women is more often imposed on them from outside, while men may tend to choose to embrace hardship actively. Athletic activity, for example, depends on accepting pain, confronting fear, and learning from mistakes. There are some natural athletes, but most men push themselves to enhance their masculine images.

An even more paradigmatic scene in which men are obliged to enjoy suffering if they want to succeed is labor. Unlike athletics, work is usually defined negatively as a hardship to be gone through. Yet if one wants to excel in one's work, one must get great pleasure from it. In fact, the athletic enjoyment of pain is a preparation for the more serious competition of work, playing for keeps. Manhood continues to be defined by one's ability to seek suffering in such activities and in the most extreme one of all, war. The sharpest edge of shame that drives these activities is that if one makes oneself suffer so and then fails, it must be because one wants to suffer; and to be good at something is usually to recognize one's failures continually.

Therefore we should not partition Bloom off into the category of "pervert": we should see his need to punish himself as the machinery of manhood. Since his fantasies in "Circe" are not remembered, they do not seem to be conscious; but rather, they are representations of processes that go on beneath consciousness in his sensitive masculine mind.[18]   Bloom   has   conscious feelings of shame and guilt at being in Nighttown, but his fantasies enact his subjection as a subject of hierarchical language more radically than any shame he could be conscious of. Wurmser says that the shame we undergo consciously generally serves to conceal a deeper level of shame.[19] For example, one may embarrass oneself by being shy because one fears to expose a more terrible inner shame by communicating.

This deeper level of shame at its terrible root corresponds to Julia Kristeva's idea of abjection. Kristeva speaks of the abject as a return to an archaic, pre-objectal mode of relationship from before the child became a subject by separating from the mother.[20] In abjection, identity, order, and meaning collapse. Kristeva defines the abject as a deep level in everyone's construction that must be held down by the prohibition and law that maintain form and identity.[21] Judith Butler adds that one desperately avoids this breakdown of identity and gender because it threatens the subject's existence, but that such disruption should be used "as a critical resource in the struggle to rearticulate the very terms of symbolic legitimacy and intelligibility"--that is, to reconstitute oneself through the approach to abjection.[22] Bloom could not redefine himself as ready to

[18] The first to point this out was Hugh Kenner in *Ulysses* (London: George Allen & Unwin, 1980), p. 120.

[19] Wurmser, pp. 50, 56.

[20] *Powers of Horror: An Essay on Abjection*, trans. Leon S. Roudiez (New York: Columbia University Press., 1982), p. 10.

[21] Kristeva, p. 16.

[22] *Bodies That Matter: On the Discursive Limits of "Sex"* (New York: Routledge, 1993), p. 3.

accept some measure of Stephen's intensity if the older man did not on some level attack himself to release his homosexual potential.

Bloom differs from the stereotypical male in being able to use the sensitivity that most men deny, and this difference may be related to his being Jewish. He can make shame a vehicle for regeneration because he is an outsider. He accepts his lack of a proper identity, as when he writes, "I . . . AM.. A" on the sand and then thinks, "No room. Let it go" (*U* 13.1258-65). Bloom's ability to find freedom in humiliation is structurally parallel to Abdul R. JanMohamed's idea of negating the negation, or turning oppression against oppression.[23] Having lived in a group defined as shameful by the dominant culture, Bloom gains knowledge and strength from his shame.

When Bella encounters Bloom, he imagines her fan as recognizing that he is shamefully deficient. The fan invades Bloom's boundary not only by claiming to know his inside feelings, but by asking him a question men typically ask women to seduce them: Haven't we met before? The gesture of the fan says, "Have you forgotten me?" (*U* 15.2764). Since they have not met, the fan is claiming something in Bloom's mind that he does not remember. Here Bloom's ability to distinguish breaks down and he says, "Nes. Yo" (*U* 15.2766). As his boundaries disintegrate, the fan speaks with an extreme breakdown of syntax that anticipates *Finnegans Wake*: "Is me her was you dreamed before? Was then she him you us since knew? Am all them and the same now me?" (*U* 15.2768-69). That Bloom hears such nonsense is a sign of the power he projects on Bella: the power of the Other to speak for the

---

[23] "Negating the Negation: The Construction of Richard Wright" in *Richard Wright: Critical Perspectives Past and Present*, ed. Henry Louis Gates, Jr., and K. A. Appiah (New York: Amistad, 1993), pp. 285-301.

Real by disintegrating language and identity, decomposing the discrete boundary of the signifying unit. While the disordering of these lines allows an excess of interpretations, the main theme of the lines may be the breakdown of identity, including the following suggestions: "I'm the one you dreamed of, the one you knew. This one you dreamed of was really a male ('Was then she him'). I'm you, and we're all me." The ability to pass out of oneself in passion is here linked to and perhaps based on the ability to pass out of one's stereotypical gender role.

It may be useful to put this in a wide perspective by pointing out that it has usually been recognized in the West that a man who is smitten with passion plays a feminine role. Passion is the passive opposite of action and was most often represented as being shot with an arrow. Yet Joyce's shameful interior exposure of lust goes far beyond conventions to undermine the genders by reversal, and to suggest a hidden power of woman that has to be represented as male. One main thrust here is the insertion of Bella's identity into Bloom, a pattern found in man's traditional relation to woman and in the sadist's relation to the masochist. Having the frontiers of his male rational construct dissolved, Bloom gives himself a new form in a shameful, passive position as he replies, "Powerful being" (*U* 2772).

Kristeva says, "Abjection appears as a rite of defilement and pollution in . . . societies with a dominant or surviving matrilinear character."[24] It seems relevant that both Bloom and Bella are Jewish, and that while Judaism is highly patriarchal, it is in fact matrilinear, for one is a Jew if one's mother was. Moreover, such archaic, matriarchal rites of defilement would seem to be represented by the figure of

[24] p. 17.

Circe in the *Odyssey*, who magically debases men. Samuel Butler, in *The Authoress of the "Odyssey"* (1902), which Joyce appreciated, sees Circe as a feminist figure. Butler points out that she had no male servants, implying that she lived in a community of women.[25] And he says that Circe is as great a prophet as Tiresias, the greatest ancient male (nominally) prophet: "[A] writer who was less desirous of making out that women know as much as men would not have made Circe know quite so much."[26] Joyce may have seen Circe--not just Bella, but the spirit of Nighttown, with its most vital aspect represented by Zoe-- as an image of the power of women to reshape men. This would be supported by both Butlers, for Judith sees gender identity as something that is unstable or even shapable because it is performed.[27]

As he heads for the brothel, Stephen says of the prostitute he seeks (and does not find), "*[A]d deam qui laetificat iuventutem meam*" (*U* 15.122). This substitutes the female *deam* for the male *deum* of the liturgy: "To the goddess who made glad my young days." Both Stephen and Bloom are headed for versions of the goddess in Nighttown, but both goddesses are corrupted. The central version of Bloom's goddess/goal, Bella, is loaded with fetishes, such as fan, cigar, and whip, all of which tempt Bloom. He gets one of his most intense fantasy sensations from the cigar in his ear (*U* 15.2936)! Here masculine and feminine attributes have become marking signifiers.

Stephen's version of the goddess, his mother, is

[25] *The Authoress of the "Odyssey": Where and When She Wrote, Who She Was, the Use She Made of the "Iliad," and How the Poem Grew under Her Hands* (Chicago, University of Chicago Press, 1967), p. 107.

[26] p. 149.

[27] Butler, pp. 16-22.

missing her nose, her eyes, and her teeth (*U* 15.4159-61), and Stephen is absolutely horrified at the thought that she might touch him because her touch represents paternal authority: she says, "Beware God's hand!" (*U* 15.4219). While Bloom gains strength from his contact with the degraded version of the maternal principle, Stephen seems more in touch with political reality: he realizes that the idea of the goddess of desire is always already allied with patriarchy and capitalism.

The force Bella uses to reduce Bloom to submission has to be seen as made up of social codes, for the idea of dominance has always been built on class structure, as is indicated by the aristocratic status not only of Bloom's three imaginary lady friends but of the Marquis de Sade. I have pointed out elsewhere that Bella/Bello bears images of capitalism, such as the "Stock Exchange cigar" that has such an effect on Bloom (*U* 15.2897) or Bello's references to rich friends and financial deals.[28] Enda Duffy covers this aspect of "Circe" well in *The Subaltern Ulysses*.[29]

As Bloom looks into Bella's eyes and sees her change into Bello, Bloom mumbles, "Awaiting your further orders we remain, gentlemen, ..." (*U* 15.2833). Before this, he had taken the role of tying her shoes, which was related to a job he had once considered as a "shoefitter in Manfield's" (*U* 15.2813). The language of business that he slips into as Bella changes has to be seen as a language of humiliation, for his marathon of shame in "Circe" bristles with references to all

[28] "Social Significances of Bloom's Psychology in 'Circe'" in *Joyce and Paris, 1902 . . . 1920-1940 . . . 1975: Papers from the Fifth International James Joyce Symposium*, ed. Jacques Aubert and Maria Jolas (Paris: Éditions du CNRS, 1979), p. 22.

[29] (Minneapolis: University of Minnesota Press, 1994), pp. 155-58. Duffy sees Bella as "late capitalist Brittannia" (p.156).

aspects of the social machinery that oppresses him. In the following sentence, for example, Bello uses British idioms, for Gifford and Seidman point out that "Kentucky cocktails" is an English term for cocktails,[30] and "old son" also sounds English: I'll bet Kentucky cocktails all around I shame it out of you, old son"(U 15.2867-68). What Bello will shame out of Bloom is unclear, something like the truth that Bloom is not a man. In any case, Bello claims he will win the contest by shaming Bloom. This model of exchange is basic to patriarchal intercourse on all levels in that one party takes manhood from the other by imposing shame on "her."

A major part of Bloom's work, arguably the main part, consists of shaming himself. In "Aeolus," when we see him at work, the journalists he deals with treat him with condescension. In "Aeolus," on the page after the section called "WE SEE THE CANVASSER AT WORK," Bloom stands in front of Joseph Nannetti's desk hoping that the foreman will explain more about the high terms he has set Bloom. Nannetti scratches himself in Bloom's presence and does other work while Bloom waits (U 7.162), so Bloom recalls here how he was snubbed earlier by John Henry Menton (U 7.171-73).

Bloom is also obliged in this episode to pursue the editor Myles Crawford to ask for an ad for his client Alexander Keyes. When Bloom says, "What will I tell him Mr Crawford?" Crawford says, "Will you tell him he can kiss my arse?" (7.978-79, 981). This touchy reply is the occasion for Bloom's outstanding opportunity of the day to show his mettle as a canvasser. It is the trickiest and therefore most definitive point of Bloom's craft. And Bloom

---

[30] Don Gifford with Robert J. Seidman, *Ulysses Annotated: Notes for James Joyce's "Ulysses,"* revised ed. (Berkeley: University of California Press, 1988), p. 502.

passes the crucial test, doing his job well by continuing to supplicate Crawford until he gets a fuller answer: "He can kiss my royal Irish arse, Myles Crawford cried loudly over his shoulder. Any time he likes, tell him" (7.991-92). In response to this answer, which Crawford makes with his back to Bloom, "Mr Bloom stood weighing the point and about to smile" (*U* 7.993).

Bloom has a policy of putting up with abuse from people. When Menton earlier responded to Bloom's effort to be helpful by treating Bloom coldly in "Hades," Bloom thought, "Never mind. Be sorry later perhaps when it dawns on him. Get the pull on him that way" (*U* 6.1031). Bloom's ability to take humiliation is essential to maintaining his position, especially since he is a Jew dealing with Christians. Crawford may not be competent, but his position as editor seems to involve a great deal of self-assertion. It is better for Bloom to accommodate Crawford's derisive contempt, for if Bloom loses his temper, he will lose the business connection. While all such situations involve economic factors, such factors are usually shaped by impulses of self-assertion, which often take priority over any approach to pure economic interests. As Tomkins indicates, such pride always involves administering shame.

That Bloom is a Jew representing a Jewish client to Christians with powerful positions means that he is successful, for he is in contact with a higher echelon; yet this increases the shame he has to endure. He might try to advance himself by self-assertion like Crawford, but this would be hard for a Jew to accomplish. If being humiliated is the most difficult and crucial part of his job, then it is what he really does for a living, and he may represent the majority in this respect. Joyce recognizes an economy of shame in which embarrassment is the main role people play. In effect, this is by far the world's greatest industry-- the production of pride or status for a few through the expenditure of shame by   the many.

A worker is a repository for his boss's shame as a woman is a repository for a man's, a Jew for a Christian's, or a black person for a white's. The *Wake* uses the phrase "every Klitty of a scolderymeid" (*FW* 239.18) to refer to young women in a general way. A scolderymaid, as my student Siphokazi Koyana pointed out, is a maid whose principle duty is to be scolded, and Joyce recognized that this was an important role for many maids and women.

When Bloom seems to speak of himself collectively in "Awaiting your further orders we remain, gentlemen" (*U* 2833), it stirs Bello to a new level of brutality: "Hound of dishonour!" (*U* 15.2835). Mark Osteen points out that in "Circe" sadomasochism involves an implicit contract in which the two parties agree to play certain roles;[31] so the form of this sexual practice is the very form of business. Bloom's line--taking the tone of a petty clerk trying to sound respectable but ending up servile--is effective in a negative way. It disintegrates Bloom's identity by showing his effort to be respectable as a collapsing facade, a clown's breakaway jacket. So it succeeds in its aim of stimulating his shame more intensely. Joyce portrays the moment in which Bloom's sexual desire is swelling as one in which his well-being and the reality and the gender of the object he desires are insignificant compared to the ideological apparatus of power play that supports that desire. This shows how desire itself consists of the aftereffect of the exchange of pride and shame.

Bloom's quest for shame is a way of seizing the attack of society in order to exploit it. He turns his victimization by social forces into a demand of his own that

---

[31] *The Economy of "Ulysses": Making Both Ends Meet* (Syracuse, N.Y.: Syracuse University. Press, 1995), p. 330.

gives him his best chance to know himself. His
marriage is as much based on the drive toward shame as
are his job and his sexuality. His main action toward Molly
on Bloomsday is to give her away. Through his cultivation
of shame, Bloom participates in and disseminates the
Joycean project of self-regeneration announced by the ur-
Bloom Richard Rowan in *Exiles*: "To be forever a shameful
creature and to build up my soul again out of the ruins of
its shame."[32]

The choice of shame, shame's choice of self-
development through abjection, is the only action of Joyce's
protagonists: they either accept shame and grow or refuse
shame and are paralyzed. But this choice is highlighted
against an ordinary world in which people consciously
strive to reject shame. Indeed, one cannot consciously *choose*
shame, for it engages its shamefulness by being denied. The
appropriation of shame that leads to psychosexual progress
is accomplished as unconsciously as the fantasies of
debasement that lead Bloom to be ready to help Stephen at
the end of "Circe."

In the conscious world, shame is allocated to the
loser, who feels it keenly, by the winner who thus avoids
feeling it. Those who succeed best in this world are
shameless people like Donald Trump. Whatever else
workers or women may do, their indispensable function is
usually to be susceptible to shaming. Although there are
many other factors involved in exchanges between people,
pride and shame tend to control most conditions. In
business terms: pride and shame constitute the bottom line.
In "Circe," Joyce insists on revealing the actual forces
involved in social interchange.

Temple University, Philadelphia

[32] James Joyce, *Exiles* (New York: Viking, 1961), p. 70.

THE HAUNTED INKBOTTLE: SHEM'S SHIT-SCRIPT AND ANAL EROTICISM IN FINNEGANS WAKE

MICHAEL HEUMANN

Abstract. This essay examines the relationship between art, creation, excrement, and authorship as they pertain to the "Haunted Inkbottle" section of *Finnegans Wake* (FW 182.30-186.10). In this passage, the narrator, Shaun, repeatedly links his brother, Shem, to excrement and foulness; in so doing, he seeks to position himself (as author and authority) outside his brother's debasement. Shem's forced exile in the "haunted inkbottle," however, offers him a space where he is free to wallow in the very filth for which Shaun denounces him. By examining aberrant or "perverse" pleasures, including excrement and homosexuality, Joyce raises several unique questions concerning the nature of language, the role of the artist, and the sublimation and desublimation of the body's functions and desires.

"Can excrement or a child or a louse be a work of art? If not, why not?" (*P* 214). This question, which Stephen Dedalus asks towards the end of *A Portrait of the Artist as a Young Man*, conflates the notions of artistic and excremental production. According to Stephen, the value of an art work is revealed to the artist as a realization of "the *whatness* of the thing," which "is felt by the artist when the esthetic image is first conceived in his imagination" (*P* 213). Unlike art, however, the production of excrement is an act whose value is commonly sublimated or entirely erased. By positing a relationship between "art" and "shit," Stephen offers an interpretation of art that blurs the boundaries between the public act of making art and the private act of defecation. The end result of Stephen's question is yet another question: Is art shit, or shit art?

Although defecation and urination are common

themes throughout Joyce's writings,[1] the specific connection between shit and art is most evident in the "Haunted Inkbottle" section of *Finnegans Wake* (*FW* 182.30-186.10). While Joyce's final novel is accurately portrayed as a "middenpile" of dead words, old wars, and bodily waste, the many figures, leitmotifs, recurrent stories, and numerous themes that litter the pages attempt to bring a certain narrative order to this "wit's waste" (*FW* 185.7-8). In particular, this tension between order and chaos is evident in book I, chapter 7, where the narrator, Shaun, repeatedly links his brother, Shem, to excrement and foulness; in so doing, he seeks to position himself (as author and authority) outside his brother's debasement. This separation is magnified when, according to Shaun, Shem seeks refuge from an angry mob within the "house O'Shea or O'Shame." Although it functions as a prison, for Shem cannot leave without incurring the wrath of the mob and his brother, the "haunted inkbottle" in fact offers Shem a space where he is free to wallow in the very filth for which Shaun denounces him. This passage's dissection of aberrant or "perverse" pleasures, including excrement and homosexuality, posits several unique questions concerning the nature of language, the role of the artist, and the sublimation and desublimation of the body's functions and desires.

To create a link between excrement and the role of the artist, it is important to understand how shit and art relate to a subject's psychological, social, and sexual

---

[1] Besides the "haunted Inkbottle" section, other specific references to excrement or waste in Joyce's writings include Bloom's defecation in the "Calypso" chapter of *Ulysses*, Stephen's snot and defecation in "Proteus," Molly's urination and menstruation in "Penelope," and the Buckley and the Russian General passage in *Finnegans Wake* (II.3). This list does not, of course, include the many incidental references to foulness, dung, decay, stench, rot, and filth that litter Joyce's writings.

development. In his overview of infantile sexuality, Sigmund Freud points out several "characteristics of infantile sexual life," including "the facts that it is essentially autoerotic (i.e., that it finds its object in the infant's own body) and that its individual component instincts are upon the whole disconnected and independent of one another in their search for pleasure.[2] Unlike the "normal sexual life of the adult," where, according to Freud, the reproductive organs determine the "pursuit of pleasure,"[3] the sexuality of an infant is polymorphous: he or she searches for pleasure in any way and through any part of the body that is available. In each of the three stages of infantile sexuality -- that is, the oral, anal, and genital stages -- the "normal" child's object of desire shifts, first to the mother's breast, then to the child's own anus, until finally desire is fixed upon the genitalia of the opposite sex. During the anal stage, the child recognizes "the opposition between two currents, which run through all sexual life," but which "cannot yet... be described as 'masculine' and 'feminine,' but only as 'active' and 'passive.'[4] Freud's use of the terms "masculine" and "feminine" suggests the social definitions of gender, as well as the "active" and "passive" roles occupied by men and women, respectively, in a patriarchal society. However, the implication of his claim is that, within the anal stage, the object of pleasure is not the penis or the vagina, but rather the somatic musculature and erotogenic mucous membrane of the anus. As Freud notes,

> Children who are making use of the susceptibility to erotogenic

[2] Sigmund Freud, *Three Essays on the Theory of Sexuality*, trans. James Strachey (New York: Basic Books, 1962), p. 63.

[3] Freud, p. 64.

[4] Freud, p.52.

stimulation of the anal   zone betray themselves by holding back their stool till its accumulation brings about violent muscular contractions and, as it passes through the anus, is able to produce powerful stimulation of the mucous membrane. In so doing it must no doubt cause not only painful but also highly pleasurable sensations.[5]

The pleasurable sensations produced from the "anal zone" are, according to Freud, transitory, and they are "sublimated" once the subject reaches the "genital" stage, which usually occurs around the time of puberty and which establishes "the primacy of the genitals" and the goal of reproduction as the objects of one's sexual life. However, in order to accept the genitals as the goal of sexual development, Freud must distinguish genital pleasure from other types of pleasure. In the third of his *Three Essays on the Theory of Sexuality*, Freud calls the pleasures associated with infantile sexuality (the mouth, the anus) "fore-pleasures," which produce "sexual excitement" but not sexual satisfaction. The pleasure of genital orgasm, on the other hand, "is the highest in intensity" because "it is brought about entirely by discharge: it is wholly a pleasure of satisfaction and with it the tension of the libido is for the time being extinguished.[6] According to Freud's definition of pleasure, then, only sexual excitation that produces a climax (and, as a result, releases sexual tension) can be constituted as pleasure. If end-pleasure is "wholly a pleasure of satisfaction," then fore-pleasure, which is the "excitation of the erotogenic zones,[7] exists outside Freud's definition of pleasure. As Leo Bersani argues, "[T]he distinction between

[5] Freud, p.65.

[6] Freud, p.76.

[7] Freud, p. 74.

fore- and end-pleasure really amounts to *two distinct ontologies of sexuality itself*[8] meaning that the activities associated with the sexual excitation of the anus produce a kind of pleasure that cannot be accounted for within Freud's definition of sexual development.

Freud's theories on infantile sexuality are based upon the premise that the anus is a transitional space that the child must pass through (and hence "exit") in order to achieve a "normal" sexual identity. As a result, the excitations produced from the anus must be sublimated so that the aim of normal sexuality might be reached. Freud points out that, for those who properly sublimate anal desires, excrement becomes a site of "disgust, shame, and mortality, for it marks the aspect of the subject which must be subsumed in order for sexual codes to make sense.[9] The act of "shitting," then, desublimates anal desire and resituates it within normal sexuality; the threat which excrement poses must be reacted to with disgust if it is to be properly resublimated, recontained, and redisplaced outside normal sexuality. In *Homosexual Desire*, Guy Hocquenghem suggests that this process of sublimation does not so much erase anal desire as conceal "the old sexual longings of the infantile component instincts which have now become unserviceable.[10] In Freud's system, he says, "control of the anus is the precondition of taking responsibility for property. The ability to 'hold back' or to evacuate the feces is the necessary moment of the constitution of the self. Whereas in Freud's system subjectivity is not produced except through a displacement

[8] Leo Bersani, *The Freudian Body: Psychoanalysis and Art* (New York: Columbia University Press, 1986), p.33.

[9] Freud, p.44

[10] Trans. Daniella Dangoor (London: Allison and Busby, 1978), p.66.

of anal desires, Hocquenghem's Marxist and homosexual critique emphasizes the link between production and anality, and hence it offers a challenge to Freud's Oedipal structure by marking the anus as constituent of the self.[11]

Hocquenghem's reading of anal desire reconfigures the anus within a private space outside of Freud's normal sexuality. This private space suggests Bersani's separation of fore-pleasure and end-pleasure, positioning anal desire as a private sexuality that is separate from Freud's public and heterosexual sexuality. Because "your excrement is yours and yours alone,[12] and is not to be circulated publicly, Hocquenghem argues that the desires produced through the anus are necessarily disarmed of their significance within a patriarchal system that prioritizes the phallus. As Judith Butler notes, "To 'be' the Phallus is to be the 'signifier' of the desire of the Other and *to appear* as this signifier. In other words, it is to be the object, the Other of a (heterosexualized) masculine desire, but also to represent or reflect that desire.[13] Although Butler's critique examines the notion of the phallus in relation to a Lacanian/Freudian conception of "Being," she notes that the desire for the phallus in a patriarchal culture, where heterosexual

---

[11] This critique is not without its problems. The reinscription of the anus as the site of formation of the self locates meaning within a constructed notion of identity. This construction is, therefore, still associated with the very binary structures that Hocquenghem's Marxist rereading of Freud is seeking to undo. Nevertheless, Hocquenghem's historical situation at the early stages of the gay/lesbian movement necessitated a more radical stance than is generally approved of in the "queer" environment of the 1990s.

[12] Hocquenghem, p. 83.

[13] Judith Butler, *Gender Trouble: Feminism and the Subversion of Identity* (New York: Routledge, 1990), p, 44.

masculine desire determines meaning, is founded upon the role of language as its ability "to appear" to represent desire. This appearance of signification requires that one ignore the forms of desire which exist outside it. As such, anal desire can be read as a hole in the Oedipal narrative, which must be sublimated and reorganized through the penis if the fiction of the phallus is to be maintained.

According to Freud, sublimation of anal desire often finds an outlet in artistic expression.[14] Nevertheless, in each case, the product's relationship to that self is read differently, so that while feces are determined only from an apparent level (that is, as waste product), a novel's meaning emerges on an immanent level, where its physical appearance is secondary to its literary or artistic significance. A novel (unlike excrement) is not so much the words on the pages but the meaning that one extracts from those words. Hence, if a novel's meaning is determined in and through excremental production, the result is the recognition of art as the same kind of waste product that constitutes shit. As Vincent Cheng notes in regard to Stephen's creative impotence in *A Portrait of the Artist as a Young Man*: "If . . . we are what we eat . . . we are also perhaps what we crap -- which is one of Stephen's fears and may lie at the source of his artistic blockage.[15] Cheng is referring to the many images of scum, defecation, and debris that litter Joyce's depiction of Dublin. Stephen's repulsion for his country is made visible to him through

[14] Freud, p. 60.

[15] Vincent J. Cheng, "'Godinpotty': James Joyce and the Language of Excrement" in *The Languages of Joyce*, ed. R. M. Bolletieri Bosinelli, C.M. Vaglio, and C. van Boheemen (Amsterdam/Philadelphia: John Benjamins, 1992), p. 85.

this filth, to the point that it   becomes a catalyst for his exile from Ireland. Hence, in this case, both the refuse that constitutes the act of defecation and the labors of artistic creation are intertwined, for Stephen's own inability to produce art, to express himself, is directly linked to his recognition that the excrement around him threatens his own artistic endeavors.

To a degree, Stephen's anxiety is similar to the anxiety suffered by many first-time readers of *Finnegans Wake*, who, after reading a few pages, give up in disgust because they cannot understand what the many allusions, puns, and obscure references *mean*. Although *Finnegans Wake* does possess a narrative structure (the book is evenly divided into four sections and seventeen chapters), the exact definition of this structure is a continual problem for many critics. As a result, a great deal of critical attention has focused upon either figuring out the "plot" of the story or excavating the text's myriad influences and motifs. Other interpretations of the work are necessarily subsumed under this foundational one, so that the effect becomes a negation of the text itself in favor of a synopsis. A reading of this sort is consistent with Freud's analysis of sublimation, for it suggests a need to erase what does not fit within the parameters of a particular ideology. It suggests, in other words, that *Finnegans Wake* occupies what, in Jennifer Bloomer's words, is a space "unspeakable and unapproachable because it . . . is a vessel of -- what else? -- excrement, a violation of the ideal. In persistent avoidance . . . of shit, shit becomes the focus, the center.[16]

To make sense of *Finnegans Wake*, one must translate the text into a cohesive and discernible story, thus eliding

---

[16] *Architecture and Text: The (S)crypts of Joyce and Piranesi* (New Haven: Yale University Press, 1993), pp. 100-101.

the excessive language which many critics read as innocuous. Harry Levin, for instance, notes that "while not differing greatly in kind from the books we are accustomed to reading, it [*Finnegans Wake*] happens to have been written in a rather *queer* language, and must therefore undergo the process of translation to which all foreign books -- including the Scandinavian -- are regularly subjected.[17] To Levin, the ability to make sense of *Finnegans Wake* depends upon a translation -- a rewriting -- of the excessive language which obscures the text's meaning. In other words, the multiplicitous words deny the artistic significance which a novel is supposed to produce. Levin's anxiety over the text is magnified by his use of the term "queer," which has been linked with homosexuality since the 1920s. By using "queer" in this context, Levin connects his own inability to make sense of what the text says with the very anxiety over production which anal sublimation (specifically aligned with homosexuality) reveals. Levin, in short, associates the language of *Finnegans Wake* with shit -- that is, with matter that has no meaning until a critic or a narrator *translates* its significance into recognizable language. Levin admits as much when he notes, in a different work, "The latent fantasy of homosexuality and incest, however close to the surface, should be kept on a subliminal Freudian level or sublimated to the plane of primitive myth.[18] By sublimating the theme of homosexuality within the language of the text, Levin articulates the very anxiety which anal desire produces when critics attempt to transform *Finnegans Wake* into a

[17] Harry Levin, *James Joyce: The Critical Heritage*, ed. Robert Deming (New York: Barnes and Noble, 1970), Vol 2, pp. 695-96. Emphasis added.

[18] Harry Levin, *James Joyce: A Critical Introduction* (New York: New Directions, 1941), p. 159.

literary object. This anxiety   is nowhere better expressed than in the "Haunted Inkbottle" section in I.7. It is here where all the forces -- shit, narrative, language, anxiety, sublimation, and criticism -- coalesce and provide both a comment upon the act of creation and an acting out of the very anxiety at work in artistic expression.

Finnegans Wake (so the standard reading goes) takes place during a single night above a small pub in the Chapelizod section of Dublin. Humphrey Chimpden Earwicker (HCE), who owns the pub, is sleeping beside his wife, Anna Livia Plurabelle (ALP). The couple has three children -- a daughter, Issy, and twin boys, Shem and Shaun. While HCE and ALP remain more or less stable figures (except for their names), the brothers' identities shift as the text does, so that at one point the two are polar opposites, at another they are indistinguishable, and at still another their identities are difficult to determine in any way. The primary narrator of I.7 is Shaun, in his guise as the antithesis of Shem. This is expressly understood through the continual barrage of insults levied at Shem, ridiculing his filth, depravity, arrogance, stubbornness, stupidity, and obsessiveness. Shem is the base, the abject, the scoundrel; however, he is also the artist, the shaman, the other. Shaun accuses Shem of every crime imaginable.[19] then leads an angry mob which chases Shem into a house and locks him in. Shem is enclosed in a space, "O'Shame," that is positioned at "no number Brimstone Walk" and the word "SHUT sepiascraped on the doorplate" (*FW* 182.30-33). The absence of an address, the shame attached to the space, and the word "SHUT" (which suggests shit) "sepiascraped on the doorplate" ("sepiascraped" conflates

[19] This is, of course, Shaun's version of the story. Within the narrative, these generalities are broken down so that Shaun's obsession with his brother reveals many of his own fixations.

both "sepia," the excremental ink of a cuttlefish, and "crap") suggest that Shaun, the author of this passage, has written his brother into a space associated with repressed desires and shameful acts. In other words, Shem is inprisoned in an unmarked anus.

Shem's new environs are described in intricate, excremental detail. The catalogue of objects lining "The warped flooring of the lair and soundconducting walls thereof, to say nothing of the uprights and imposts" (*FW* 183.08-09), constructs a "lair" containing numerous excremental objects, including "fluefoul smut," "undeleted glete," "seedy ejaculations" (with its alignment of sexual potency with unreproductive waste), and an inordinate number of linguistic or literary terms, such as "ahems and ahahs," "telltale stories," and "once current puns" (*FW* 183.08-184.02). Whereas Shaun's tone is one of horror and condescension, Shem's interest is (not surprisingly) the reverse -- he enjoys reveling in waste products (including verbal waste such as noises, grunts, and puns), for it allows him to be "self exiled in upon his ego" (*FW* 184.06-07). Shem's house, tied both to a physical space and to the creation of art, is presented here as an excremental fantasy, which allows the construction of identity to transpire in and through this enclosed space. The catalogue "ex-presses" Shem's own desires to "write the book of himsel" by constructing his space of desire as the space through which the abject can be configured within language, rather than being sublimated, deferred, and displaced outside it.

Although the division between Shem and Shaun appears to be clearly marked, with Shaun outside and Shem inside the inkbottle, Shaun's description of Shem's environment problematizes this separation and suggests a very mixed fear and fascination regarding his brother's depravity. While discussing Shem's eating habits, for instance, Shaun notes that his meal includes within it "his cantraps of fermented words, abracadabra calubra culorum, . . . in what was meant for a closet" (*FW* 184.26-33). Although this section (which is interrupted by a parenthetical listing of egg recipes, which I will discuss shortly) appears to reassert Shaun's attack on Shem, the wording of the passage is curious. The Latin term "*culorum*," for instance, is defined "of the posteriors," while "*colubra*" means "snake"[20] thus, it can be inferred that the "culorum," or phallic snake, penetrates a posterior comprised of "fermented words,[21] which are configured (via "cantrap" or "cantrip," which is "a spell for necromancy") as magical symbols, which will reveal particular "truths" once they are "abracadabraed" out of the "closet."[22] While the figure of the "closet" can certainly be read as a metaphor for the anus and for anal desire, Shaun's revulsion against his brother suggests both an inability and an unwillingness consciously to make such a connection, for the "closeting" of Shem's desires implicates Shaun's own narrative within a defecatory space which he adamantly rejects. There is, in other words, a clear anxiety at work in the language of this passage, to the point that the narrator is neither willing nor able to position himself as wholly exterior to the forces he is working against.

The ambivalence in this passage is nowhere better demonstrated than the catalogue of egg recipes: "his oewfs à la Madame Gabrielle de l'Eglise . . . his soufflosion of oogs

---

[20] Roland McHugh, *Annotations to "Finnegans Wake"* (Baltimore: Johns Hopkins University Press, 1991), p. 184.

[21] Note that "fermented words" suggests *Finnegans Wake*.

[22] This statement elides other possible readings of this section, including alchemic, Orientalist, Marxist, and so on. Nevertheless, in order to make my point as clear as possible, I feel that it is necessary to limit my subject to issues relating directly to the anus and excremental desire.

with somekat on toyast à la   Mère Puard" (*FW* 184.26-31). Because of the relationship between eggs and reproduction, this list suggests a connection between genital sexuality and the aim of reproduction. However, configured as these concepts are, between "abracadabra" and a "closet," the eggs seem more closely aligned with the productive forces outside the reproductive organs than with the creation of new life. That eggs are positioned here, however, presents the very process of creation (in this case, artistic) as occurring inside, not outside, a space identified with excremental desire. Shaun's eggs reveal the bifurcation of his position within the text as one which seeks to configure Shem within an anal space while simultaneously seeking to position Shaun as far away from this space as possible. By seeking to write Shem into an anus, Shaun exposes his own narration of the events as a function of the desires he is trying to refute.

Shem is constructed by Shaun as the artist, the writer. However, because Shaun's reference to eggs positions his own artistic narrative as the matter that is performatively reproduced within a space of anal penetration and artistic production, he must not allow himself to be implicated within the system that produces Shem's "mystery of himsel.[23] The remainder of the paragraph dramatically departs from the excessive conflation of eggs, writing, and excrement, detailing the boycott against Shem "of all muttonsuet candles and romeruled stationery for any purpose" (*FW* 185.04-05). Deprived of materials to create "himsel," Shem is exiled from the realm of public discourse, since to write without paper or ink separates Shem's private scratchings from

---

[23] Note that the word used in this case is as much a "self" as it is a "cell," which further highlights his desire to separate himself from his brother.

Shaun's public discourse. By doing this, Shaun negates the very connection which implicates him within the private inkbottle. Despite the lack of public access, Shem retaliates through implosion: "he winged away on a wildgoup's chase across the kathartic ocean and made synthetic ink and sensitive paper for his own end out of his wit's waste" (*FW* 185.05-08). Shem, denied materials with which to write, seeks to express his self with the only materials he has available: his own body. Through an array of "goups," "ends," and "waste," he "kathartic"-ally expurgates the very fluids, forces, and excrements from his body and turns them into text. In short, as Jennifer Levine points out, "the production of language and of human excrement" literally merge in this section, to the point that "Shem is creating ink -- and ultimately words --out of his own piss and crap.[24] What this implies, first and foremost, is the very conflation of art and shit which Freud's notion of sublimation seeks to defer. At the same time, however, Shem clearly wishes to break down the walls which separate him, not simply from Shaun or those who surround him (who forced him into this cell), but from the narrative that erected the walls in the first place.[25]

In this section of *Finnegans Wake*, what is at stake is not simply the creation of ink and paper, but Shem's desire to self-subvert a system of signification that denies him access to representation. Shem's strategy is to align his body with his art, so that one cannot be defined without the

[24] Jennifer Schiffer Levine, "Originality and Repetition in *Finnegans Wake* and *Ulysses*,"*PMLA* 94(1979): 106-20.

[25] Book I is generally associated with the figure of Shem but narrated by Shaun. Book II, on the other hand, deals principally with Shaun and is narrated by Shem. Although this is a highly reductive way of looking at the issue of narrative voices in *Finnegans Wake*, it is at least possible to read the novel with this framework in mind.

other; through this, he links   art with the materials of production, in direct opposition to Shaun's attempt to separate art from "base" matters. The converging point for both strategies is the many references to alchemy, which is defined as "the transmutation of the so-called base metals into gold by means of an ill-defined something called the Philosopher's Stone.[26] As Barbara DiBernard explains, the alchemic tradition plays a large role in *Finnegans Wake*, to the point that the work can be read as "Joyce's alchemetical Philosopher's Stone," because the stone is both "the lowest substance and yet the most valuable, the most common and yet the hardest to be found.[27] Because the notion of "base metals" used in the alchemic process includes not only lead but eggs and shit, alchemy works in this passage as a narratological tool used by Shaun, the narrator, to justify and contextualize Shem's writing. In this case, Shaun replaces Shem's excrement with the "ill-defined something called the Philosopher's Stone" -- organic matter that retains the mystery and sublime nature of art, which Shaun then uses to distinguish his own writings from those of his brother. Throughout the passage, there are references to many of the signs, symbols, metaphors, and elements associated with alchemy, including "athanor," which is a "digesting furnace used by alchemists," various stages of micturition and embrocation, and the numerous egg references I have already mentioned. Shaun's narrative configures excrement as both base and high, as a space of revulsion and as a space which, when properly transformed, will reveal the truth that Shaun's language

[26] Stanley Redgrove, *Alchemy: Ancient and Modern* (London: William Riden and Son, 1922), p.1.

[27] Barbara DiBernard, *Alchemy and 'Finnegnans Wake"* (Albany: SUNY Press, 1980), p. 13.

wants to control but which   Shem's shit-script attempts to refute. This process reaches its apex when Shaun interprets Shem's transformation of excrement into ink:

> *Primum opifex, altus prosator, ad terram viviparam et cunctipotentem sine ullo pudore nec venia, suscepto pluviali atque discinctis perizomatis, natibus nudis uti nati fuissent, sese adpropinquans, flens et gemens, in manum suam evacuavit* (highly prosy, crap in his hand, sorry!), *postea, animale nigro exoneratus, classicum pulsans, stercus proprium, quod appellavit deiectiones suas, in vas olim honorabile tristitiae posuit, eodem sub invocatione fratrorum geminorum Medardi et Godardi laete ac melliflue minxit, psalmum qui incipit: Lingua mea calamus scribae velociter scribentis: magna voce cantitans* (did a piss, says he was dejected, asks to be exonerated), *demum ex stercore turpi cum divi Orionis iucunditate mixto, cocto, frigorique exposito, encaustrum sibi fecit indelibile* (faked O'Ryan's, the indelible ink).(*FW* 185.14-26)

According to McHugh, the passage translates thus:

> First the artist, the eminent writer, without any shame or apology, pulled up his raincoat and undid his trousers and then drew himself close to the life-giving and all-powerful earth, with his buttocks bare as they were born.   Weeping and groaning he relieved himself into his own hands (highly prosy, crap in his hand, sorry!).   Then, unburdened of the black beast, and sounding a trumpet, he put his own dung which he called his "down-castings" into an urn once used as an honoured mark of mourning. With an invocation to the twin brethren Medard and Godard he then passed water into it happily and mellifluously, while chanting in a loud voice the psalm which begins "My tongue is the pen of a scribe writing swiftly" (did a piss, says he was dejected, asks to be exonerated).   Finally, from the foul dung mixed, as I have said, with the "sweetness of Orion" and baked and then exposed to the cold, he made himself an indelible ink (faked O'Ryan's, the indelible ink)[28]

[28]   McHugh, p.185

Perhaps the most obvious   alchemic connection in this passage is the use of Latin for the acting out of this excremental scene.[29] Latin was, in Joyce's time, the official language of the Roman Catholic Church; it is also the language of the philosopher's stone (at least, in the European context in which Joyce was writing). As Bloomer suggests, to use Latin in this passage suggests that the words in this passage transcend their material form and represent that "for which the other side is unknown or unspeakable. It is what language cannot describe.[30] The unknown here is an immaterial essence that transforms shit into gold. Latin, as the material that makes this transformation possible, becomes the means through which Shaun's narrative elides the anal associations which his words imply. Rather than shit revealing anal desire, shit is transfigured into a realm beyond matter and beyond words.

On one level, Shaun employs Latin in order to elide the threat which his brother's excrement poses to his own position within the text. The English asides interspersed within the paragraph help break down any unified dis-association between Shem and Shaun. Phrases such as "crap in his hand, sorry!" and "did a piss" refute the divine aura of the Latin prose; likewise, they undermine Shaun's textual authority by revealing his own anal sublimation. Shaun cannot simultaneously escape a connection between himself and his brother and act as the narrator of Shem's obscenities. However, it is uncertain if, in this Latin/English passage, Shaun is the exclusive narrator. Throughout *Finnegans Wake*, the presence of multiple narrators is

[29] See Robert Boyle, S.J., "Miracle in Black Ink: A Glance at Joyce's Use of His Eucharistic Image," *JJQ* 10, 1 (1972): 46-70.

[30] Bloomer, p. 98.

commonplace. Although most of I.7 is narrated by Shaun, the English asides suggest the presence of another narrator. If this is the case, it is entirely possible that Shem, or a version of Shaun that incorporates an aspect of Shem (ShemShaun), is providing commentary for Shaun's Latin prose. While this alters how the passage is read, the positioning of English slang within the Latin paragraph merely reasserts the subversion which Shem's shit-script already demonstrates, by resublimating anal pleasure even as Shaun attempts to conceal it.

As the Latin concludes and the "piss" and "crap" are made into ink, Shem, "pious Eneas" (both Aeneas and anus), takes the material "at hand" and "produce[s] . . . from his unheavenly body a no uncertain quantity of obscene matter" (*FW* 185.29-30). Because there is no paper, however, Shem is forced to improvise:

> the first till last alshemist wrote over every square inch of the only foolscap available, his own body, till by its corrosive sublimation one continuous present tense integument slowly unfolded all marryvoising moodmoulded cyclewheeling history (thereby, he said, reflecting from his own individual person life unlivable, transaccidentated through the slow fires of consciousness into a dividual chaos, perilous, potent, common to allflesh, human only, mortal). (*FW* 185.34-186.06)

This section is often cited by critics as Joyce's self-referential description of *Finnegans Wake*, with Joyce in the Shem role, writing all "cyclewheeling history" down on his own "foolscap." Following this reading, Shem's body aligns the "continuous present tense integument" of the body as text with Vico's "cyclewheeling history," to create in himself a universal formula through which all can be made known. In this way, the body-text becomes not so much an act of excremental writing as a writing "transaccidentated" from the base matter of shit into gold, or from communion wafer into the body of Jesus, or from words into divine truths. As Robert Boyle argues, "[U]nder the accidents of this human ink, the artist makes himself available to his race by plunging the individual artist into the dividual human chaos, substantiated in the verbal chaosmos of *Finnegans Wake*.[31] By positioning language in and through excrement, Shem's body and Joyce's pen construct a "carnivalesque corpus" where, according to Cheng, "word and turd" play in and through each other to construct a meaning that overrides their differences and unifies them in a transcendent world beyond matter and language.[32]

To read *Finnegans Wake* as a self-referential text, where Joyce is the author and the novel itself is the "cyclewheeling history" referenced in this passage, is to recognize in alchemy and the Eucharist the power to transform matter into supra-matter, and to turn shit into gold. However, the use of the word "sublimation" problematizes this reading. The word has two relevant uses: in alchemy, it marks one of the later, crucial stages in the conversion of "base matter" into gold; in psychoanalysis, as I have already shown, it refers to the significant act of denying the base desires associated with infantile sexuality, in order to transform oneself into a normal sexual subject. In this section, sublimation suggests both the alchemic desire to transform Shem's shit-script into a divine truth as well as the psychological desire to conceal Shem's excrement-soaked body and reposition Shaun as exterior to the anal space of the haunted inkbottle. Just as this transformation from low to high is established, however, it is immediately exposed, or desublimated, by the parenthetical aside: "(thereby, he said, reflecting from his

[31] Boyle, p. 53.

[32] Cheng, p. 98.

own individual person life   unlivable, transaccidentated through the slow fires of consciousness into a dividual chaos, perilous, potent, common to allflesh, human only, mortal)" (*FW* 186.02-06). This brief section seems connected to Vico's "cyclewheeling history," in which history begins as a mass of "individuals" living "unlivable" lives, which are then transformed by "dividuals," who subsequently create a society, worship a god, and bury the dead. At the center of this reference to Viconian history, however, is not the "unifying universalism" associated with God and transcendence, but rather the "chaos" of an accidental (or "transaccidentated") world, created by "human[s] only, mortal." Just as Shem's linking of shit and writing desublimates Shaun's anal desires, so too does this passage desublimate Shaun's desire to read the shit-script as a transcendental truth. In other words, when truth is mortal, art is merely shit.

The preceding pages have configured Shem within an anal canal of creative production, wherein his own excrement serves as his locus of meaning, while his body acts as the slate upon which this meaning is determined. This process has problematized both Shaun's attack on his brother and Shaun's own identity by conflating Shaun's writing with Shem's shit-script.[33]   Nevertheless, what follows the parenthetical remarks demonstrates the "chaosmos," or the void, at the center of Shaun's outlook: "but with each word that would not pass away the squidself which he had squirtscreened from the crystalline world waned chagreenold and doriangrayer in its dudhud" (*FW* 186.06-08). The reference to squids and their "inklike screen" (which they use to ward off enemies) suggests, among other

---

[33] I am assuming that the two figures, Shem and Shaun, are distinguishable here -- although this is not necessarily the case.

things, Lacan's notion that   the screen acts as a veil that covers or obscures one from seeing an object "as it really is.[34] Within Shem's text, then, is a meaning that he cannot understand, a protective device set up by Shem to obscure Shaun's omnipotent vision of the events.   Further, this anxiety is encapsulated in a body "waned chagreenold and doriangrayer in its dudhud." While this suggests that the truth of Shem's writing is nothing other than a dull gray blur, a closer examination offers two curious novelistic references: Oscar Wilde's *The Picture of Dorian Gray* and Balzac's *Le Peau de Chagrin* (the inspiration for Wilde's novel). Wilde -- an Irishman, raised as a Protestant, who suffered a fall through the public persecution of his crime of homosexuality -- is continually referenced in *Finnegans Wake*, primarily in connection to HCE's numerous trials and public shames. In this section, Wilde seems linked to Shem, the artist, who is both persecuted by a hoary mob and sealed into a homosexual space -- a space which, as Hocquenghem notes, "is always connected with the anus.[35] James Atherton reads this passage as a mocking indignation of Wilde, noting that "[i]t seems as if Joyce, who wrote wittily of sexual misconduct, could not forgive people who were actually guilty of it.[36] I would argue, however, that within the context of this passage, to reference Wilde is not to poke fun at him but to reveal the sexual anxiety at work in the separation of Shem and Shaun.   Although the haunted inkbottle serves to isolate

[34] Jacques Lacan, "The Line of Light," in *Four Fundamental Concepts of Psycho-Analysis*, trans. Alan Sheridan (New York: Norton, 1981), p. 91.

[35] Hocquenghem, p. 89.

[36] James S. Atherton, *The Books at the Wake: A Study of the Literary Allusions in James Joyce's "Finnegans Wake"* (Carbondale: Southern Illinois University Press, 1959), p. 95.

Shem's abject desires, the link made between the
anus, writing, and sexual desire is given a physical presence
through the reference to Oscar Wilde, who was not only
convicted of sodomy, but who was also well known as an
author. By reinforcing the connection between artistic
production and anal desire, art's very power to transcend
its "base" materials in favor of a higher end is revealed as an
illusion, in the same way that Dorian Gray's portrait
conceals the link between Dorian's aesthetic desires and his
temporal alterations. At this moment in the text, it is
Shaun's own fear of homosexuality which is desublimated;
by revealing his own anus and his own shit, Shem unmasks
Shaun's textual body as one produced in and through
anality.

Shaun's reaction to this moment is both babble and
Babel: This exists that isits after having been said we know.
And dabal take dabnal! And the dal dabal dab aldanabal!"
While many readings could be taken from these lines, one
of the most significant is Vico's notion that human society
began when certain men first heard thunder and, then
sought to replicate its sound in their own voices. To Vico,
the first word was "pa! Here, however, the words are "dal,"
"dapal," and "danapal."[37] According to McHugh, these
words come from the Santali language of India, Nepal, and
Bangladesh; in this language, "dal" means "strike," "dapal"
means "strike each other," and "danapal" means "covering.[38]
Together, the words suggest both fighting and hiding. The
fighting references seem to reaffirm oppositional positions
such as good and bad, left and right, and Shem and Shaun.

[37] Giambattista Vico, *The New Science of Giambattista Vico*, trans Thomas
Goddard Bergin and Max Harold Fisch (Ithaca: Cornell University Press,
1948), p. 150.

[38] Mc Hugh, p. 186.

Although the reference to "covering" could suggest the act of concealing the anal anxiety produced by Shaun's shit-script and the Wilde reference, it could also be a reference to Shaun's own attempt to escape from the fears brought on by his association with his brother. In any event, the result of this outburst is a re-separation of Shem and Shaun into opposite and oppositional figures. The next lines return to a moment prior to the inkbottle -- to an account of Shem's "last public misappearance, circling the square" (*FW* 186.12).

The end of this section (which is arbitrary because the chapter does not end here, merely my analysis) reveals the very point at which the production of desire breaks down. When Shaun recognizes his own desires smeared across his brother's body, language stops making sense. In this suddenly "crystalline world," where all can be seen yet nothing understood, the inkbottle is suddenly opened -- like a window, a sleeper's eyes, or the singing asshole in John Water's Pink Flamingo -- and all that was not supposed to be visible becomes all too visible.[39] The eyes must shut, sense must become nonsense, and sounds must become noise, for the anus is on display, and with this exposure comes the implication that homosexuality, anal penetration, and excremental desires are all within the very public realm which the inkbottle is supposed to repress. In short, the "house O'Shame" becomes not Shem's internment but Shaun's recognition that he himself is implicated within that internment. Just as the remainder of *Finnegans Wake* positions the anxiety over creation (sexual, social, and artistic) as the means through which desire fluctuates, this section works to localize transgressive desires not outside the self but constructed within the very flow of desires that

[39] *Pink Flamingos*, 95 min. Fine Line Cinema/Dreamland, 1972.

are channeled through the   self. The anus in *Finnegans Wake* is, finally, the textual equivalent of white noise: neither object nor subject, it invades the figure's (and the reader's) psyches, tearing meaning into shreds, and turning everything into crap.

University of California, Riverside

POSTCOLONIAL MASCULINITY AND GENDER TRAUMA

CHRISTINE VAN BOHEEMEN-SAAF

Abstract. This essay argues that the history of the concept of "gender" needs revision in the light of its postcolonial derivation in Joyce, and its susequent theoretical articulation by Derrida and Cixous, who were raised in Algeria. Instead of facilitating identity, gender in the Irish colonial context provides cultural contradiction: Joyce's cultural marginality was understood as gendered feminine by nineteenth-century writers; in addition the Irish cultural tradition features the collectivity of the nation as feminine. This double and contradictory feminization brings with it a paradoxical relation to manhood. The *Bildung* of Stephen Dedalus produces gender trauma instead of stable masculinity.

That there is an important connection between Joyce's oeuvre and gender studies needs no argument. A substantial body of feminist criticism and gay studies testifies to the centrality as well as the ongoing provocation of Joyce's textuality. In this essay, I will suggest that the growing awareness of Joyce's colonial childhood and postcolonial textuality demands a revision of that gender debate, taking into account Joyce's subaltern position and gendered marginality, not overlooking the Irish cultural tradition which features the collective as feminine. Caught in a paradoxical relation to manhood, Joyce's protagonists suffer from the traumatic effects of the moment of genderization.

To begin with the advent of the concept of "gender."[1] It was Alice A. Jardine's *Gynesis: Configurations of Woman and Modernity* that brilliantly demonstrated that a number of the discourses of modernity labelled poststructuralist typically projected their difference from Western essentialism in and as their assumption of stylized femininity.[2] Thus structuralism itself became associated with transgressive femininity. From Jacques Derrida and Hélène Cixous (to select only the two examples most closely related to Joyce) we learned to see sexual difference as discursively mediated rather than as rooted in essentialist identities.[3] Sexual difference began to be seen as a style of expression, rather than as the reflection of true ontological identity.

Joyce scholarship profited considerably from this "linguistic turn," because it allowed feminist criticism to expand from the discussion of Joyce's representation of women, and to focus on the gender aspects of his textuality and style. Thus gender studies of Joyce branched out into

[1] Elaine Showalter, *Speaking of Gender* (New York & London: Routledge, 1989), p. 3, usefully reminds us that the term "sexual difference" relates to a poststructuralist and psychoanalytic perspective hinging on the assumption of discursive subjectivity, whereas "gender" indicates the belief that subjectivity is constructed "through social ascription or cultural practice."

[2] Alice Jardine, *Gynesis: Configurations of Woman and Modernity* (Ithaca: Cornell University Press, 1985).

[3] "Although there is no truth in itself of the sexual difference in itself, or either man or woman in itself, all of ontology nonetheless, with its inspection, appropriation, identification and verification of identity, has resulted in concealing, even as it presupposes it, this undecidability." Jacques Derrida, *Spurs: Nietzsche's Styles*. Trans. Barbara Harlow (Chicago: University of Chicago Press, 1979), pp. 104-05.

an inquiry into the function of gender in modernism. Joyce could be discussed as a feminist author. A recent example is Christine Froula's persuasively written *Modernism's Body: Sex, Culture, and Joyce*, which claims Joyce's self-portrayal of "masculinity as a symptom of the cultural law of gender."[4] Froula argues that Joyce unveils the authority of the mother which patriarchal culture suppresses, and that he stages the symptomatic effects of such a denial of female power. In this piece, I shall take Froula's argument as pre-text to my own, because I think that her perspective on Joyce-- however convincing in itself--stands to gain from historical contextualization. In her suppression of history and cultural difference, Froula turns Joyce's unusual treatment of gender, in Froula's text his "symptom," into a universal indictment of patriarchal culture, whereas I see it as the expression of a specifically Irish cultural contradiction. Joyce's portrayal of masculinity and his literary authority cannot be divorced from its specific cultural context, as I hope to show; similarly, we cannot identify Joyce with the modernist movement and ignore his Irish provenance. The interesting challenge is to articulate the relationship between Irishness and modernity.

Before I begin my argument, I must return to the history of the concept of gender itself. In retrospect, what strikes me is the extent to which Joyce was already implicated in the rise of poststructuralist writing that led to the establishment of gender as the dominant concept in our discourse about the difference between men and women. It was Cixous, mother of an "*écriture féminine*" modelled on Joyce (on whom she had published a dissertation in 1968),

[4] Christine Froula, *Modernism's Body: Sex, Culture, and Joyce* (New York: Columbia University Press, 1996), p.xiii.

who in turn introduced Derrida to Joyce when they met in the U.S.. That Derrida let himself be profoundly influenced by Joyce needs no further argument.[5] If we also take into account Jacques Lacan's preoccupation with Joyce around 1976 and the prominence of Joyce as figurehead of a "revolution of the word" in *Tel Quel*, it does not seem an overstatement to claim that Joyce's writings provided poststructuralist thought with its model object and material example of a revolutionary discursivity.[6] Joyce's textuality provided the cradle which rocked the new-born notion of discursive subjectivity and "gender." Although it may have been linguistics or philosophy which provided the intellectual grounding of the "linguistic turn," Joyce's writing offered an example of a subjectivity triumphantly conscious of its own rootedness in language, and transcendently transgressive of sexual and other forms of identity. What does that imply with respect to gender criticism of Joyce? Have we been engaged in the tautological pursuit of applying to Joyce's oeuvre insights deriving from Joyce's textuality in the first place? What is the relationship between colonial history and the rise of poststructuralism?

Postcolonial Manhood and Masculinity

Rather than addressing those queries immediately, I propose something else: I argue that the changing

[5] See Christine van Boheemen-Saaf, "Purloined Joyce," in *Re:Joyce/ Text, Culture, Politics*, eds. John Brannigan, Geoff Ward, and Julian Wolfreys (London: Macmillan, 1998), pp. 246-58.

[6] For detailed documentation see Geert Lernout, *The French Joyce* (Ann Arbor, Michigan: University of Michigan Press, 1990).

perspective opened up by postcolonial criticism demands that we reconsider the nature of Joyce's stylistic and textual deviance. Instead of understanding it primarily as the expression of a revolutionary subjectivity, a personal style (however heroic or politically correct), or the product of a decontextualized (post)modernist aesthetic, I move we understand Joyce's peculiar textuality, as well as its supposed femininity or feminism, as the product of the contradictory gender situation of Irish subaltern subjectivity. As we shall see, such a shift has important consequences with regard to our understanding of the construction of gendered subjectivity. Rather than a subjectivity predicated discursively, sustained by the fact that language allows the subject to see himself/herself as in command, in Joyce we find a subjectivity fixated on the moment of genderization because the contradictory nature of the Irish colonial symbolic precludes the primary imaginative identification necessary for predication to become possible at all. The masculine subject-in-language can never accede to the relation of basic security and faith in the power of language to inhabit language and name his world, to say: "I am this"; or: "You are that."[7] Joyce's portrayal of the intellectual and emotional insecurity of Stephen Dedalus provides an illustration: the shakiness of his sense of self, as shown in his attempts to make sense of his world through a definition of the meaning of words; his impulsive wanderings; the moments of depersonalization that annihilate his sense of who and where he is. Whereas

[7] This piece was completed before the publication of *Joyce, Derrida, Lacan and the Trauma of History* (Cambridge, Cambridge University Press, 1999). My argument partly follows the book, but has a different focus and conclusion.

Portrait shows us Stephen's social, linguistic, and emotional insecurity, *Ulysses* adds Stephen's intellectual incertitude in "Proteus" and his desperately botched attempts to make sense in "Scylla and Charybdis." Stephen lacks the basic attachment to the "symbolic order" that founds secure subjectivity.

Part of the explanation for this insecurity may be the peculiar alienated or self-conscious situation of the masculine colonial subject who always, simultaneously, sees himself from two perspectives. In addition to our ordinary self-awareness, there is the long view from the perspective of the normative colonizing other. In order to understand his own position in the scheme of things, the subaltern learns to see things from the point of view of the surveying gaze. This double perspective diminishes the sense of selfhood, not in the least because the self is always already measured against a standard that is designed to mark the superiority of the colonizer. Self-possession, or "true self-consciousness" as W.E.B. Du Bois spoke of it in his denunciation of the effects of racial prejudice, is the prerogative of the hegemony which need not query the centrality of its own authority and example. Du Bois added:

> It is a peculiar sensation, this double-consciousness, this sense of always looking at one's self through the eyes of others, of measuring one's soul by the tape of a world that looks on in amused contempt and pity. One ever feels his twoness,-- an American, a Negro; two souls, two thoughts, two unreconciled strivings; two warring ideals in one dark body, whose dogged strength alone keeps it from being torn asunder.[8]

---

[8] W.E.B. Du Bois, *The Souls of Black Folk* (New York: NAL Penguin, 1982), p. 45.

Du Bois defines the history of the American Negro as the history of the struggle to "attain self-conscious manhood, to merge his double self into a better and truer self." Although the history of slavery and its aftermath is not directly comparable to the history of Irish oppression, Du Bois's expression of the experience of being marginalized alerts us to the self-conscious condition of Irish masculinity during Joyce's youth. Manhood, never fully attained, was the painfully elusive norm to which the colonized male continuously aspired while always falling short of that mark. Consequently, a preoccupation with manhood dominated his split consciousness.

Du Bois's use of the term "manhood" is significant, but may need translation to be applicable to an Irish context. In *Manhood in America: A Cultural History*, Michael Kimmel suggests that at the end of the nineteenth century a shift took place from the signifier "manhood" to "masculinity." "Manhood" had been the traditional term reserved for the maturity and psychological qualities associated with the adult male; and it was used in semantic opposition to "boyhood."[9] It would seem that Du Bois uses "manhood" in this sense: the emancipation from "boyhood." By the end of the century, however, a new term, "masculinity" was gaining currency as a term applied to a set of behavioral traits and attitudes associated with males and contrasted to "femininity." Instead of age or maturity, the distinctive marker becomes gender difference. Moreover, unlike manhood, masculinity required and still requires constant demonstration and reaffirmation. With regard to the Irish situation, it seems to me that the term "masculinity" as defined by Kimmel is more appropriate

[9] (New York and London: The Free Press, 1996), pp. 119-20.

than the term "manhood."[10]   The Irish male was always already feminized. In addition to his marginal positioning as provincial and poor, the nineteenth century added the attribution of a certain "femininity." In the writings of Matthew Arnold or Ernest Renan, the Celtic race was characterized as especially graced with feminine qualities. This gendered positioning over against the, by implication, "masculine" Anglo-Saxon may have spurred a perpetual drive to emphatically assert one's non-femininization. Around the turn of the century, the Irish male was under constant pressure to prove his masculinity. It is this explicit genderization of racial and cultural difference that may be one of the factors contributing to the insecurity of Irish manhood as we see it portrayed in Joyce's work.

Portraying Postcolonial Masculinity
The Early Work

Both *Portrait* and *Dubliners* may be read as studies in failing masculinity. The young protagonist of "The Sisters" finds that his identification with the male role model entails a mysterious and unnamable contamination with lack and paralysis. The young boys in "An Encounter," who try to live out the liberating myth of masculinity as delineated in the Western, are confronted with an example of what their desire for open spaces produces in an Irish context: repetition compulsion, perversion, and frustration. "Araby" provides a painful illustration of a boy's initiation into the

---

[10] Note, however, that Patrick Pearse, in "The Coming Revolution," voices his call not to shrink from bloodshed as a call to "manhood." Seamus Deane, ed., *The Field Day Anthology of Irish Writing*, Vol. 2 (Derry: Field Day Publications, 1991), p. 558.

self-consciousness of subaltern existence, always aware of the futility of the aspiration to self-sufficiency in the face of the colonizing gaze.[11] "Eveline," "A Little Cloud," and "Counterparts" show how colonialism intensifies patriarchal relations. Men disenfranchized in the public realm become more tyrannical at home. "After the Race," "Two Gallants," "Ivy Day in the Committee Room," and "Grace" depict failed, failing, or collusive strategies of masculine self-affirmation. At first sight, "A Painful Case" might seem the exception. James Duffy's overly phallic "masculinity" as projected in his self-sufficiency, his intellectualism, and his scorn for female weakness, would seem unquestionable. But are his display of autonomy and his avoidance of the disorder of adultery and his fear of sympathy not a defensive reaction formation against acknowledging his own excentric position vis-à-vis the centrality of power? Is his preoccupation with self-sufficient manliness not the very symptom of his insecurity on that subject? Is his disdain of Mrs Sinico's need not also a strategy to avoid acknowledging his own desire, hence his own insufficiency? As Edward Said suggested, "Joyce's work is a recapitulation of those political and racial separations, exclusions, prohibitions instituted ethnocentrically by the ascendant European culture throughout the nineteenth century."[12] The intense self-consciousness and the preoccupation with masculinity of Joyce's masculine characters in *Dubliners* and *Portrait* might be viewed as testifying to their subaltern position.

[11] Garry M. Leonard's *Reading "Dubliners" Again: A Lacanian Perspective* (New York: Syracuse University Press, 1993) provides incisive readings to which this postcolonial perspective is indebted.

[12] *The World, the Text, the Critic* (London: Faber, 1984), p. 48.

Although "The Dead" is often read as a story about masculinity under attack from femininity, it is perhaps not sufficiently recognized that this story may also be understood as an allegory of subaltern self-consciousness in process. The female voices of Lily, Miss Ivors, and Gretta Conroy with their connotations of independence, youth, and/or authentic Irishness, may also be understood as the "inner voice" in the protagonist's ongoing self-conscious dialectic of self and soul, engaged in the activity of keeping Gabriel's masculine self-possession afloat. It is precisely Gabriel's orientation to the east that makes him vulnerable. It betrays the suppressed consciousness of his own provincialism, which he patronizingly projects on his environment. When feminine support stops performing its required function and punctures his defensive illusion of masculine independence:

> [a] shameful consciousness of his own person assailed him. He saw himself as a ludicrous figure, acting as a pennyboy for his aunts, a nervous well-meaning sentimentalist, orating to vulgarians and idealising his own clownish lusts, the pitiable fellow he had caught a glimpse of in the mirror.(D195)

Like the little boy in "Araby" overwhelmed by a sense of his own insignificance in the face of an indifferent hegemony, Gabriel's failing support system leaves him with a sense of alienation from himself, a split- or double-consciousness. In the mirror he perceives himself not as a person of flesh and blood but as a piece of masculine clothing, an object, a "well-filled shirt-front." The distance between his present lack of self and the desired unquestioned self-identity is indicated by his estranged reaction to seeing his own "face whose expression always puzzled him when he saw it in a mirror" (D194). Gabriel Conroy's depersonalization and evaporating masculinity mark the end of *Dubliners* and illuminate what is at stake in Joyce's narrative.

But not only Joyce's protagonists labor under the necessity to demonstrate their non-femininization. Surveying the panorama of Joyce's Dublin one notices the proliferation of pieces of clothing, masculine attributes, and objects that denote masculinity and/or social status. Walking sticks, umbrellas, ashplants, trousers, hats in all shapes and varieties, as well as writing utensils feature prominently in Joyce's text -- more prominently than in any other modernist writer (or so it would seem). We may attribute this peculiarity to Joyce's fascination with fetishism and with commodity culture; we may also see it as another feature of his mimetic genius. The props of masculinity take on added prominence and significance in a society in which status and identity labor under the necessity of constant reassertion.[13] The plethora of cultural signs of gender and power in Joyce's narratives may be a psychologically apt rendering of the feel of the contemporary Irish scene.

Masculinity in *Ulysses* and *Finnegans Wake*

In Joyce's later works, his masculine protagonists are eerily deprived of self-identity, even if that may not be apparent at first sight. Instead of existing autonomously, they function in contrasting opposition to a rival antagonist. Thus Bloom's meek "character" as the cuckolded husband is paired inversely with the swaggering Don Juanism of

---

[13] See Benjamin Harder, "Stephen's Prop: Aspects of the Ashplant in *Portrait* and *Ulysses*," and Mark Osteen, "A High Grade Ha: The 'Politicoecomedy' of Headwear in *Ulysses*," in *Joycean Cultures/Culturing Joyces*, pp. 241-53 and pp. 253-84.

Blazes Boylan who seduces Bloom's wife Molly. Bloom's exaggerated femininity, which in "Circe" leads to his degradation and humiliation as well as the proclamation of the "new womanly man" (*U* 15.1798-99), is mirrored inversely in the machismo and masculine display of overly well-dressed toff Boylan, the great stud. Similarly, Stephen Dedalus functions as the put-upon, feminized antagonist to blusterously masculine and socially popular Buck Mulligan who usurps Stephen's home and the recognition due to his talent. In *Exiles* a similar pairing binds Richard Rowan to Robert Hand, both men of letters and rivals for Richard's wife Bertha. Instead of "being" either true men or dismally effeminate wimps, Joyce's protagonists derive their "character" from contrasting opposition. The text often emphasizes this by letting their names begin with a shared initial letter. These figures exist as masculine "equals of opposites, evolved by a onesame power of nature . . . and polarised for reunion by the symphysis of their antipathies" (*FW* 92.8-11). Instead of self-identity and individuality they possess a mediated character which cannot be viewed in isolation from its opposite--just as colonial identity is always already mediated, both for the colonized subject and the colonizer. It is as if Joyce stages within his narrative the structural mimeticism that (unconsciously) determines masculinity in a situation of racial, class, or colonial oppression.

In *Finnegans Wake* this structural construction of masculine "character" takes on parodic intensity and blatancy. Shem and Shaun, penman and postman, seem to reverse into each other like Yeats's gyres. This peculiarity of Joycean masculinity seems significant to me as a strategy of character construction denoting that true self-identity or true masculinity is a fictional illusion. Joyce never shows us self-sufficient masculinity. If masculinity is ever offered to the reader in full exercise of its natural function, as in the case of Boylan's penetration of Molly, the text does not present this scene directly, in a witnessing description focalized by the author. Here too, the assumption of ontological rootedness is vitiated. The scene is presented as always already mediated and viewed by the antagonist's perspective. Thus Boylan's penetration of Molly comes to the reader as "seen" by Bloom. Boylan's full genital masculinity may tell us more about Bloom's consciousness and the processes of desire than about Boylan's individuality and identity.

Joyce's strategy of mediation also has a peculiar effect on the reader, who is asked to keep those self-projected contraries in dialectical tension. We must always take into account that Shem, the dirty alchemist whose masturbatory "act of writing" transforms bodily waste into indelible ink, is thus ventriloquized or narrated through his opposite, the pompously common-sensical materialist Shaun (a bourgeois Don Juan obsessed with money and success whose pretense to learning and truth kills the spirit of the letter.) Shaun, in turn, is perceived through the discourse of Shem as the source of bad, pedestrian prose and exploitatively self-interested sociability. The text oscillates from one interpenetrating perspective to the other without settling on a definitive image. It leaves the reader no secure point within the text from which to derive a stable point of view. Thus the literary text is the *material location* of the intersubjective experience of transference, in which patient and analyst undergo the unsettling effect of mirroring: the self-image is projected in the mirror of the other where it seems to belong as long as one's own projective activity is not recognized and understood. Joyce not only presents us with protagonists insecure about their masculinity; his polarized construction of masculine character visits the affliction of insecurity upon the reader who is similarly "emasculated."

The Gender of Irishness

However, self-consciousness and insecurity are not specifically Irish cultural conditions, nor is overcompensation. On the contrary, they appear to be a constant feature of social, racial, or cultural marginality worldwide. What makes the gender situation of the Irish male more precarious than that of the male in other marginal cultures is his peculiarly ambivalent, gendered relationship to the collectivity of the nation. Patrick Pearse, who voiced his call to bloodshed and revolution in terms of a choice between "manhood" or "slavery," also expressed his identification with Gaelic Ireland (always featured as a woman and as a mother) in the poems he wrote as a literary testament in the year before the Easter Rising:

> I am Ireland: I am older than the Old Woman of Beare.
> Great my Glory; I that bore Cuchulain the valiant.
> Great my shame: My own children that sold their mother.
> I am Ireland:
> I am lonelier than the Old Woman of Beare."[14]

The son of Ireland is always already identified with the collectivity of the nation which is understood as female and maternal. In the participation mystique inherited from traditional Irish culture, which experienced a representational tie between the single individual and the collective, the narrative of the individual is, at once, understood as the allegory of the nation.

[14] *Field Day Anthology.* Vol 2, p. 558.

Although the allegory of the nation changes shape and connotation over the centuries, her femininity remains unquestioned. Whether Hibernia or Erin, whether appearing in political cartoons, paintings or engravings, historical or fictional narratives, songs, or even Yeats's play *Cathleen ni Houlihan* (1902), the collectivity of Irishness tended to be figured as a woman. Although her specific characteristics may differ, until the eighteenth century, this female figure tended to be endowed with extraordinary power. I note the ancient mother goddess "mother Dana"(*U* 9.376) invoked by Stephen Dedalus. She may have had many other incarnations. I mention the Morrígan, the ancient demonic queen symbolized as the bird on Cuchulain's shoulder; Medhbh, the guiltlessly adulterous warrior queen who features in the *Táin Bó Cáuilnge*; Gráinne Mael and Shan Van Vocht (the trickster-figure who changes from old hag into young girl), who also symbolize Ireland; and great-bladdered Emer, whose urinary power was legendary. Especially important is the older Celtic goddess, the "Sovereignty," whose union with the king symbolized not only the prosperous tie of the soil with the extension of the reign but especially the spiritual and juridical dominion of the king. Disasters and epidemics were taken as signs of an improper union between the king and the Sovereignty -- just as the plague in Oedipus's Thebes was related to his incestuous union with the mother.[15] As we come closer to the present century, the magical power of this female figure makes way for qualities like grace, purity, and endurance.

[15] See Maria Tymoczko, *The Irish "Ulysses"* (Berkeley: University of California Press, 1994); and Rosalind Clark, *The Great Queens: Irish Goddesses from the Morrígan to Cathleen ní Houlihan* (Gerrards Cross: Colin Smythe, 1991).

The eighteenth-century *aisling* typically depicts Ireland in a dream vision as a beautiful damsel in distress (James Clarence Mangan's well-known "Dark Rosaleen" is a reworking of an older folk song).

I suggest we see Irish masculinity in its contradictory historical context and tradition that placed the Irish male in a double relationship to the feminine. As an individual male, his masculinity is in oppositional contrast to the femininity of the female of the species; but as an Irishman he is feminized in contrast to the English. Simultaneously, he partakes in the collective projection of the self-identity of the cultural heritage as female and feminine (Mother Ireland, Mother Church, mother tongue).[16] Not only is this situation complex and contradictory; it is also rife with cultural ambivalence. Irish mythology and the Irish tradition featured women of extraordinary power and infinite resource. The figure of the "Sovereignty" whose favor confirms kinghood has the power to confer the phallic power that we now consider the patriarchal prerogative and the principle of the "symbolic order." Indeed, the ancient Irish model queries western patriarchy which founds origin on the masculine principle. The binary division of gender difference as western culture has institutionalized it is undercut and scrambled in a different heritage in which women have phallic qualities and power. In short, the Irish male may have been faced with a double problem. First, he is feminized by his cultural and racial marginality (which requires the emphatic display of masculinity to balance the threat of inferiority). Let us call

---

[16] See Richard Kearney, "Myth and Motherland," *Ireland's Field Day*, ed. Seamus Deane et al. (Notre Dame: University of Notre Dame Press, 1986), pp. 74-78.

this an "emasculating" feminization. In addition, his identification with the collectivity of the nation represented as a female figure (often credited with extraordinary powers) offered an empowering feminization. How can one balance and reconcile the threat of emasculation with the empowering lure of national identification? The latter's charge of femininity not only counters the English stereotype; given the colonial context it also reinforces it.

Joyce's protagonists suffer from the contradictory doubleness of gender inscription in various ways. Stephen's inability to find an artistic or social identity derives from his gender trouble. Instead of feeling empowered, he struggles against his identification with the collectivity of the nation. Owing to an acute social sensitivity and snobbery which have taken due note of the fact that Catholic Irishness takes the feminine position in the social hierarchy, he construes the feminization entailed in the identification with the collective as a threat to his manhood. As the "old sow that eats her farrow" (*P*203) the femininity of the nation offers no possibility for identity construction. Instead of sustaining him, its implied femininity is seen as a double threat which is lurking to annihilate him, as it has sacrificed so many others in Stephen's view. In Stephen's universe, masculine example fails to offer a counterweight to the double inscription of femininity. The improvidence and the job shifting of his own father are proverbial; the lure of the priesthood is attenuated by the threatening feminizing association with "*les jupes*" (*P*155). If there are figures with masculine authority in *Portrait*, they tend to be literary and non-Irish. The figures of Byron and of the Count of Monte Cristo offer identification with revenge, while that of Daedalus, the "great artificer," holds the prospect of escape from the labyrinth of contradiction. In contrast to these imaginary or literary figures, the historical Parnell functions in the text as the concrete icon of the loss of masculine self-sufficiency.

In this context, Stephen's intense mourning of his recently deceased mother in *Ulysses* seems more than an attempt to cope with personal loss. He appears engaged in a struggle to extricate himself from the primal mire of the threat of double feminization in the Irish colonial situation. Fighting his identification with the maternal archetype, he confronts a spectre which threatens to drag him with her into extinction. Called a "Ghoul! Chewer of corpses! No, mother! Let me be and let me live" (*U* 1. 278), Joyce presents the appearance of this orientalized vampiric spirit on one of the first pages of the text. Stephen's preoccupation with her is so intense that he hallucinates her presence. The bowl shape of the landscape prospect before him turns into the deathbed basin into which she spit up her innards, "[h]er hoarse loud breath rattling in horror" (*U* 1.275). May Dedalus is presented in the full horror of physical decay, bile trickling from her mouth, spitting up her rotting liver. She returns from the grave in "Circe" and *"raises her blackened withered right arm slowly towards Stephen's breast with outstretched finger"* (*U* 15.4217-18). *"A green crab with malignant red eyes sticks deep its grinning claws in Stephen's heart"* (*U* 15.4220-21). Stephen "traverses" this apocalyptic fantasy (the color green relates the mother to the nation) by means of the acceptance of absolute annihilation:

> *Nothung!*
> (*He lifts his ashplant high with both hands and smashes the chandelier. Time's livid final flame leaps and, in the following darkness, ruin of all space, shattered glass and toppling masonry* (U 15.4242-46).

This moment, also a turningpoint in the relationship

between "son" Stephen and "father" Bloom, seems to suggest that the threat of identification with the mother (and mother country) is only to be laid to rest by the desperately accepted risk of an "Absolute Nothingness."

It is not only the son-figure in the novel who encounters the spectral effect of this maternal imago. Bloom is likewise unable to separate himself from an identification with the feminine. He is visited with apocalyptic sensations of ultimate extinction:

> A cloud began to cover the sun slowly, wholly. Grey Far.
> No, not like that. A barren land, bare waste. Vulcanic lake, the dead sea: no fish, weedless, sunk deep in the earth. No wind could lift those waves, grey metal, poisonous foggy waters. Brimstone they called it raining down . . . . A dead sea in a dead land, grey and old. Old now. It bore the oldest, the first race . . . . The oldest people. Wandered far away over all the earth, captivity to captivity, multiplying, dying, being born everywhere. It lay there now. Now it could bear no more. Dead: an old woman's: the grey sunken cunt of the world.
> Desolation.
> Grey horror seared his flesh (*U* 4. 218-30).

As we know, Bloom's antidote to this spectre of material entropy and death is the memory of the physical warmth of foreign-born Molly's flesh and the reassurance of ordinary sensual perception: "To smell the gentle smoke of tea, fume of the pan, sizzling butter. Be near her ample bedwarmed flesh. Yes, yes" (*U* 4.237-40). Bloom's uxoriousness functions as a defense against the maternal imago, but it is also a strategy of accommodation. His dependency on Molly does not basically change the precariousness of a masculinity unable to find a strong and stable gender identification. The "Circe" chapter in Ulysses, which plays out the gamut of gender inversion, illustrates the point.

Neither Stephen nor Bloom can extricate himself from the contagion of femininity. In the context of 1904 Dublin, unself-conscious masculinity is presented as a precarious and elusive ideal in the face of the overwhelming threat of feminization.

Gender Trauma

It seems to me that *A Portrait of the Artist* is Joyce's sustained inquiry into the possibility of subaltern masculinity, and that the elusiveness of its ending marks the impossibility of its achievement, whereas the opening passage of the text situates the Irish masculine subject as caught in a traumatizing gender dilemma. This passage in Joyce has been read as illustrating Lacan's theory of the symbolic cut and its conjunction of gender division.[17] Let us consider it once more and note that the scene stages a cultural contradiction hinging on the inscription of gender identity.

The story begins with the projection of language or the symbolic as a fairy tale which glosses ugly Irish reality as pastoral bliss.

> Once upon a time and a very good time it was there was a moocow coming down along the road and this moocow that was coming down along the road met a nicens little boy named baby tuckoo" (*P* 7).

Earnestly endeavoring to identify with his own preinscribed indentity in this scenario provided by the

[17] See Hélène Cixous, "Devant le pome," *James Joyce: Cahiers de l'herne* (Paris: L'herne, 1985), pp. 193-203. Christine Froula, in *Modernism's Body*, sees Joyce as a split subject articulating the pathological effects of the patriarchal denial of the pre-linguistic identification with the mother.

father--of a maternal animal (Ireland) encountering a "nice" child -- the little boy thinks of himself from the beginning in an alienated masculine third person ("*He* was baby tuckoo"; "*His* father told him that story";"*his* father looked at him through a glass" [italics added]). To place himself in the verbal picture conjured up by the father (a representative of masculine authority who looks through a glass), the child, assuming the split between "I" and "he" and seeing himself from the father's position, is seduced to an alienating identification with the gender role of the father.

But as we read on, we note that this split in the self does not provide the authority and masculinity supposedly attending masculine gender in patriarchal cultures. The father's language, hence the symbolic, is here already placed as falsely glossy and unstable -- a fairy tale. This instability increases in the song "*O, the wild rose blossoms/ On the little green place*" which the father, it seems, offers the child as "his" song. This rendition, however, practises a revision of the original words in Thompson's "Lily Dale," which speak of "*the little green grave.*"[18] Adoption of the father's language means joining in a repressive falsification of the Irish actuality of oppression and division and the denial of its heritage of death. When Stephen accepts the song as his ("He sang that song. That was his song") his lisping of it as "the green wothe botheth" in turn substitutes "green" for "wild." The wild rose turns Irish green, a fantasy creation, and Stephen unwittingly redoubles the "fairy" element of the father's tale. The symbolic as handed down by the father (note that it is already feminized as "fairytale" and "song") does not provide the stability of a God term or an "In the beginning." Intertextuality, revision

18 *Notes for Joyce*, ed. Don Gifford (New York: Dutton, 1967), p. 86.

or rewriting, and the inability to denote and found truth are inscribed at the point of origin. In fact, the passage itself rhetorically enacts that groundlessness, displacing it upon the reader. It locates the reader in mediated speech from the first word ("Once upon a time and a very good time it was."); nevertheless, it drops the line "*O, the wild rose blossoms*" as if it were Stephen's, immediately contradicting that suggestion in its lisped copy. From the first, the reader, like the little boy, is deprived of a sure footing in Joyce's symbolic, never able to ground language in a specific human agent or referential reality. In the Irish situation masculinity is always already feminized, and the "symbolic order" is deprived of stability and truth.

The conceptual deadlock of that instability in the Irish symbolic is in turn actualized as the conflicting social reality Stephen enters. With language, he also, immediately, encounters conflicting claims and different forms of appeal and modes of being preinscribed in his culture. Whereas the father "frames" him in a fairy tale, the mute mother aims to capture him with music that invites to a dance. Culture provides two forms of symbolic address: structured language (narrative, song) primarily but not exclusively associated with the father (later the mother and aunt Dante will utter the rhyming threat to Stephen's eyesight), and music, the rhythmic periodicity of sound, pitch, and melody which enlists Stephen's body, related primarily to the mother who tends it. Neither of these modes of appeal provides a sense of stability. Each is already partial and incomplete and complementary to the other. In contrast to earlier readings then I do not find here a classic Lacanian allocation of the symbolic and speech to the father and the relegation of the mother to the prelinguistic. The symbolic, "language" itself, is split into two modes of expression that rival to engage the child.

Neither the claim of the father nor the music and rhythm of the muted mother offers a point of identification for a seemingly stable subjectivity predicated upon a lacanian split.   Truth and the promise of a solid positioning of the subject are lacking in the father's word, while the mother's materialization of language as rhythm and sound--although more physical and perhaps more primary--can never ground the self in language.   Indeed, Joyce's splitting redoubling of language in this scene violates Kristeva's or Lacan's temporalization of the moment of entry into language as that in which the bond with the mother is superseded and broken by the symbolic. Here the mother *shares* the split symbolic with the father, and its splitting seems to set up a series of dissociative redoublings which the text itself must try to overcome.

The Irish father's language cannot constitute truth, and is always engaged in debate with a female countervoice.   This situation is emblematized when Stephen's father cannot prevent the quarrel at the Christmas dinner, provoked by one of the women at the table who invokes the transcendent authority of the Church to condemn Parnell's masculine lack of sexual constancy. The passage concludes:

> --Poor Parnell! he cried loudly. My dead king!
> He sobbed loudly and bitterly.
> Stephen, raising his terrorstricken face, saw that his
> father's eyes were full of tears (*P* 39).

Stephen is traumatically confronted with the failure of the masculine principle. Moreover, in Joyce's works the figure of the mother is not seen as muted in the conventional sense of "silenced." She is the repository of a wordless language (a language of flowers), a public secret, a riddle, a hidden letter, or a "word known to all men," which she may transmit to her son. Moreover, she usurps masculine authority when she utters the command that Stephen must apologize.

After situating this constitutive conceptual knot which generates splitting and redoubling, the "prelude" to *Portrait* introduces a series of successively more complex forms of splitting. The two symbolic colors (maroon for Michael Davitt and green for Parnell) of aunt Dante's brushes introduce the treacherous divisiveness of Irish politics ("Irrland's [Errorland's] split little pea" [*FW* 171.6]). This split, in turn, brings into the text the breach between Protestants (Eileen's family) and Catholics (his own). The passage concludes its buildup of repetitive splitting with the threat of violence to the boy: "[T]he eagles will come and pull out his eyes" (*P* 8). This threat is not motivated in the tale but follows upon Stephen's naive wish to marry Eileen. What did Stephen do to deserve such violence? In wanting to marry Eileen, he conforms to the paternal example and answers the mother's invitation to the dance of sexuality. Yet, in styling himself masculine, the child incurs inexplicable wrath. It is as if Joyce dramatizes that it is the split reality of Irish history itself that makes clear gender identity impossible and creates a traumatic conceptual deadlock or double bind for the child.

Representation and Gender Trauma

Thus Stephen Dedalus, who shows the same psychological reaction in each chapter, each new situation, not only "has" a complex. He also "is" a complex, in that the text that inscribes this portrait constantly hovers on the brink of the dissolution of the self and practises strategies of containment to hold contradictory claims in one focus, while never escaping the imprisonment in the contradiction in its reenactment of that traumatic moment of its constitution as conflictually gendered Irish subjectivity. The later chapters of A *Portrait* rehearse this primal scene of the anxiety of selfhood at ever more sophisticated levels, but always repeating its invariable paradoxical scenario, as Hugh Kenner was the first to point out.[19]

Such repetition is not only compulsive. It may also be a sustained attempt to overcome the contradiction in the symbolic. It does present a problem to the literary critic, however. What is the semiotic status of such a "symptomatic" text? How do we define the structure and meaning of A *Portrait*? Is the repetition *in* the text the repetition *of* the text? How do we know that Joyce gives us a "portrait" of Stephen Dedalus (an "identificative paper," to use the words from the early "epiphany").[20] Can we be sure that this is not just the "acting out" of Stephen Dedalus's or even Joyce's own "curve of an emotion"? How do we distinguish between representation and performance? How can we tell "portrait" from "auto-graph" (in the sense of "inscription" of the "self"). Which criterion allows us to separate art from pathology?

As will be clear, it seems to me that the distinction between those modes of presentation is undercut in Joyce's text. Instead of a circumscribed image, Joyce provides a spacing without end, a patterning of representation

[20] "The *Portrait* in Perspective," in William M. Chace, ed *Joyce: A Collection of Critical Essays* (Englewood Cliffs, N.J.: Prentice Hall, 1974), pp. 33-50.

[20] James Joyce, *Poems and Shorter Writings*, ed. Richard Ellmann, A. Walton Litz, and John Whittier-Ferguson (London: Faber and Faber, 1991), p. 211.

through rhythm and repetition that establishes at once a break and a connection between the temporal and the spatial, the same and the different, the text and the world -- what Derrida named *"différance"* and Les Murray spoke of as "time broaden[ing] into space."[21] Resisting the reduction to either partition, just as it avoids exclusive gender identification, Joyce's text, practising a form of *archi-écriture*, moves dialectically between oppositions, inscribing the spacing that articulates all signifying. It repeats, ad infinitum, the traumatic moment of its original constitution as the precariously gendered subject-in-language, because that subject is never constituted definitively. Through this pattern of repetition venturing into the future, it breaks through circumscribing frames: the end of the individual work, the boundary between text and life, realism and postmodernism, writing as physical act and as representation.

The paradox of the prelude to *Portrait* also sets up an internal dialectic within Joyce's oeuvre which becomes a continual self-address. Instead of the communication of a prior sense, Joyce's writings enact the discovery of modes of coping with the tension between the opposite poles. Each work presents a new and different way of repeating the same. The forward movement within writing itself becomes a rhythmic dance that will eventually lead to the pure performativity of *Finnegans Wake* which inscribes the rhythms and acoustic patterns of narrative rather than its content. The forward movement of Stephen Dedalus's wanderings through Dublin finds its analogue in Joyce's

[21] Bill Ashcroft, Gareth Griffiths, and Helen Tiffin, *The Empire Writes Back: Theory and Practice in Post-Colonial Literatures* (New York and London: Routledge, 1989), p. 34.

"forward flight" in the process of confrontation with the alienation within identification and signification itself. Rearing his "disunited kingdom on the vacuum of [his] own most intensely doubtful soul" (*FW* 188.16-17), Joyce repeats that initial moment that brought a sense of contradiction, and he inscribes the impossibility of stable gender identification into representation itself.

I suggest we return to the prelude of *A Portrait* as the impossible record of the moment of trauma that establishes Stephen's at once tenuous and overcathected linguistic subjectivity. It is the moment of inscription of the division within the trait, infinitely repeating a failed predication instigating the faultline in the mirror of the self. Stephen's first confrontation with threatened annihilation is here:

--O, Stephen will apologise.
Dante said:
--O, if not, the eagles will come and pull out his eyes.

Pull out his eyes,
Apologise,
Apologise,
Pull out his eyes.

Apologise,
Pull out his eyes,
Pull out his eyes,
Apologise."

* * *   (*P* 8)

The "emasculating" threat to Stephen's physical integrity, subsequent to an event excluded from the story, sends language into a spinning turmoil. In its chiasmic pattern of crossing over and redoubling it instigates infinite repetition--only to be framed by three stars or dots, carefully drawn by Joyce in the manuscript. The experience is rendered as overwhelming, annihilating, hence unconcluded and inconclusive; the young child is confronted with anxiety so massive that there is no response possible. He lacks language, words of his own to ward off the experience or work it through. No gesture or act, except trying to hide underneath the table, can let him escape. But underneath the table the voice still booms; now resounding in his own consciousness, his own memory. Perhaps it is not by accident that in *Finnegans Wake* thunder marks the commencement of life as "auradrama."[22] The archetype of the paternal is there incarnated as "Earwicker" (ear whacker?) or "Persse O'Reilly" (French *"perce-oreille"*["earwig"] is literally "ear-piercer"), an incestuously penetrating violator of his children's orifices. Though it is the mother (seconded by the aunt, Dante) who speaks in *A Portrait*, I suggest we do not understand this allocation to one gender as exclusive. Important is not the attribution to a single cause; we must note that cultural inscription is felt as piercingly invasive and annihilating: a "thunner in the eire" (*FW* 565.17). Acculturation entails a colonization of the self by ideology; this colonization is symbolized by the eagles of the Roman empire, the emblems of colonial-religious imperialism. I hardly need point out that "ear" rendered as "eire" extends the application of the trauma of the invasion of the subject to that of the nation.

The sole strategy of survival for the child deprived of personal speech (and by extension the colonial subject invaded by the hegemonic language) is therefore, paradoxically, to cling to language, to speech, even if in his

---

[22] John Bishop, *Joyce's Book of the Dark: Finnegans Wake* (Madison: University of Wisconsin Press, 1986), p. 300.

state of shattered anxiety the only words available are the ones sounding the trauma, and to transform those words into poetic art: pattern and rhyme. Moreover, through such repetition, language may be given an additional, punning dimension. That dimension, as Homi Bhabha argues, is the liminal linguistic space from which change or resistance may be negotiated.[23] This scene in *A Portrait*, a reworking of Joyce's first epiphany, suggests a moment of wounding acculturation which constitutes masculinity as a wound (note Joyce's identification with martyrs like St. Stephen and with Christ). It also locks the subject in a perpetual struggle to escape its trauma, while binding the self to its pain and contradiction as its originating inscription.

"Symptom" or Postcolonial Authority

The following question now arises: If Stephen Dedalus cannot transcend the conflicting inscription of Irish culture, what about his author? Is all Joyce's work an attempt to cope with the trauma of cultural inscription? Is Joyce's writing steadily engaged in trying to overcome the deadlock of Irish genderization? Should we see the increasing repetitiveness of Joyce's oeuvre as a symptom of repetition compulsion instigated by the unconscious desire to transcend the gender dilemma and the insecurity of self-identity? If that is so, what about Joyce's humor, his conscious craftsmanship, his playfulness, his deliberate construction of puzzles for the reader? Although one cannot deny that Joyce was compulsive about his writing, he seems far too deliberate a craftsman for us to label his

---

[23] See *Nation and Narration* (London and New York: Routledge, 1990).

work with the single epithet "symptomatic."[24]

Let us try to see how Joyce, as author, attempted to cope with the complexity of Irish genderization. In addition to the strategy of infinite repetition and rewriting begun in *Portrait* (which Joyce eventually turns into the splitting of language and meaning, as in the pun, to negotiate a postcolonial authority), Joyce resorted to other strategies of authorization. In fact, a number of different answers come to mind. First of all, as I already indicated, Joyce deliberately exploits the fact of cultural contradiction. He gives his masculine protagonists shape by means of a conflictual structure of inverse mirroring which guarantees the forward movement of his text because it can never arrive at resolution. Thus, increasingly, he turned the lack of masculine self-determination into the motor of his narratives. The irresolvability of the gender conflict engineers the openendedness or, in the case of *Ulysses*, the ambivalence of Joyce's endings.

What should also be noted is that Joyce's textual strategy exploits the participation mystique of the Irish male. His female protagonists tend to be powerful and phallic. In *Ulysses*, the figure of Molly Bloom, larger than life, re-creates the mythic stature of ancient Irish feminity. Molly decides and chooses; her will is the still point of the turning world for uxorious Leopold Bloom, but also for the reader. Molly's monologue recapitulates the story and is given the pride of place which assigns her the last word. Perhaps this assignation of mythic stature to Molly relates

---

[24] Note that Lacan spoke of Joyce as "le sinthome" in his later writings as in "Le sinthome: Bouts-de-réel," *Le séminaire de Jacques Lacan*. Text established by J. A. Miller, *Ornicar* 9 (1982): 32-40. As I said, Christine Froula points to Joyce as the "symptom" of western patriarchy.

to another feature of Joyce's stories. The men in Joyce's universe tend to wait passively for the women to turn to them to single them out or to initiate sexual contact; Joyce himself even claimed that his wife had made him a "man."[25] I remember my initial surprise when first reading Hélène Cixous's dissertation, which expresses her exasperation at Leopold Bloom's lack of masculine forcefulness.[26] Her evaluation of Bloom contrasted so strongly with the praise of his gentle humanity which seemed standard in Anglo-American criticism. Now I see that she pointed to a psychosexual peculiarity that may relate to the contradiction of Irish acculturation. Perhaps Stephen's passive desire that an "unsubstantial image" so "constantly beheld" by his soul will, "without any overt act of his" (*P* 65), come to encounter him and "transfigure" his insufficiency is to be understood as similarly motivated. Stephen is proudly passive in his encounter with the prostitute; and he is passively delighted that the "ciborium had come to him" (*P* 146). Stephen's attitude, in turn, reminds me of "The Dead." Gabriel's frustration at Gretta's absentmindedness is lifted when she suddenly turns to him: "Just when he was wishing for it she had come to him of her own accord" (*D* 217). A woman's favor has the power to transfigure the man; but, in order to warrant its magical effectiveness, the other must extend this favor freely without prior invitation to do so. Not surprisingly, men in Joyce's fiction tend to be managed by women and

[25] For a discussion of Joyce's uxoriousness I refer to Brenda Maddox's *Nora: The Real Life of Molly Bloom* (Boston: Houghton Mifflin, 1988).

[26] Hélène Cixous, *L'Exil de James Joyce; ou l'Art du remplacement* (Paris: Grasset, 1968).

manoeuvered by women's designs, from Bob Doran in "The Boardinghouse" to Jarl van Hoother's encounter with the Prankquean in *Finnegans Wake*.

Joyce the Penman

Most important is, it seems to me, not the representation of gender trauma on the screen of Joyce's fiction, but our understanding of its effect on Joyce's textuality and authorial stance. Let us return to the figure of Molly Bloom: However "original," "obscene" and revolutionary Joyce may have conceived his allegory of an impure woman, paradoxically, Joyce, while defying contemporary figurations of Irish womanhood as pure, remains within an Irish gender tradition -- albeit the older, Celtic one.[27] Molly's flow of urine may derive from the example of the great-bladdered Emer; her open sexuality from the phallic woman Medhbh, who also wields her tongue as if it were a weapon; and Molly's metamorphic function in the text of *Ulysses* from the shape-shifting figure of Shan Van Vocht, who embodies the concept of metempsychosis and transforms herself from an old woman into a young girl. Moreover, like the sovereignty, Molly eludes possession by one man.[28] Thus Joyce's myth of sexuality as the source of

[27] Molly's sexiness should be seen against the backdrop of the myth of purity of "true" Irish womanhood dominant around the turn of the century as a countermyth. See Tymoczko.

[28] See Robert Welch, *Changing States: Transformations in Modern Irish Writing* (London and New York: Routledge, 1993), pp. 272-82, who emphasizes the mobility of the Sovereignty, and the men she finds acceptable as king. Bonnie Kime Scott's *Joyce and Feminism* (Bloomington: Indiana University Press, 1984) points out mythical contexts for Molly. She refers to Janet Grayson,"'Do You Kiss Your Mother?': Stephen Dedalus'

autonomous consciousness remains expressed in images provided by Irish culture. It does not escape its nets. He repeats the Irish gesture of the participation of the image of the masculine individual in the female figure of the nation, one representing the other. In resorting to attributes of figures from ancient rather than nineteenth-century myths and history, he places himself as different from and in reaction to the prevailing representation of the nation, but not as "other" or "outsider." Paradoxically, he becomes the father of its cultural memory. In short, instead of hiding behind the skirts of the pure, maternal image of contemporary tradition, Joyce, always the son of Mother Ireland, hides behind the skirts of the sexy phallic mother. It is from the safety of this position that he wages war upon the King's English and usurps the tradition of the English novel.[29] Instead of being "symptomatic" of the gender system of western culture, Joyce's authorial strategy, in contrast to that of Stephen Dedalus who experienced the maternal imago as a threat, may be understood as being a way of making empowering use, however ambivalently, of the resource of maternal identification offered by his cultural tradition.

Finally, it seems to me that we must consider the possibility that, in devising his own strategy of attaining

Sovereignty of Ireland," *JJQ* 19 (1982): 119-26, for an application of the idea of the female Sovereignty to Joyce.

[29] On the relation of modernist textuality to the fetish of writing and the skirts of the phallic mother, see Marcia Ian, *Remembering the Phallic Mother: Psychoanalysis, Modernism, and the Fetish* (Ithaca: Cornell University Press, 1993). Ian pays little attention to Joyce. Also see my *The Novel as Family Romance: Language, Gender, and Authority from Fielding to Joyce* (Ithaca: Cornell University Press, 1987).

writerly authority, Joyce, like his characters, may have resorted to a strictly conventional method of asserting his masculinity by means of a (hypostatized) prop. If the men walking Dublin's streets sport an umbrella or a walking stick, and a hat to mark their gender and class, Joyce, who was extraordinarily sensitive to dress, depicted his alter ego artist figure as marked by his constant possession of an ashplant. It is this ashplant that shatters the chandelier in "Circe" -- an intervention with Wagnerian overtones which gains Stephen a measure of credit for his masculinity.[30] Stephen also handles language as if it were a masculine weapon: he speaks of his "dagger-definitions." I propose that Joyce's sexualized "pen" functioned as his masculine prop or prosthesis, just as the ashplant functioned for Stephen.

The autobiographical sketch *Giacomo Joyce* records a midlife crisis between late 1911 and mid-1914, when Joyce was beginning *Ulysses*. *Giacomo Joyce* ends its dream of renewal through a dip in the adulterous fountain of youth with renunciation: "It will never be. You know that well. What then? Write it, damn you, write it!"[31] At first sight this phrase in *Giacomo Joyce* suggests sublimation, turning experience into art, drive into secondary process. But Joyce's words are not "write it down" in the sense of make a record of it, turn it into a story; he speaks of *"writing"* it, where writing, a pure materialization, takes the place of experience and substitutes for it without the *Aufhebung* of

[30] On Stephen's ashplant as a masculine prop, see Harden, *Joycean Cultures*, p. 241 ff.

[31] James Joyce, *Giacomo Joyce*, ed. Richard Ellmann (London: Faber, 1968), p. 16.

sublimation. We may even interpret the words to mean that the activity of writing, the forward movement of the hand holding the pen over the page, comes to replace the activity of sexual intercourse. Here, as often, it is Joyce's rewriting in *Finnegans Wake* that offers confirmation. Note how Joyce re-inscribes the phrase from *Giacomo Joyce* in *Finnegans Wake*, playing on the "feminine O": "wrote it, wrote it all, wrote it all down, and there you are, full stop. O, undoubtedly yes, and very potably so" (*FW* 118.13-15). Assuming the feminine "O," and referring to the fetishized full stop that separates the masculine "Ithaca" chapter from the feminine "Penelope" in *Ulysses*, the speaker, suspiciously close in tone to Molly Bloom, commends himself for the writing of the conclusion to *Ulysses* and speaks of the achievement as "potably so." In addition to the dictionary meaning "drinkable" (the success of the novel provided ample drinking opportunity), the word seems to contain an allusion to "potency." Thus writing may impersonate and identify with the feminine, but doing so gains masculine social and authorial credit. Other references to "Penelope" in *Finnegans Wake* confirm this reading.

Most obviously appropriate as an image of prosthetic masculinity in *Finnegans Wake* is Shem the Penman. He writes "himself" using the pen as if it were an extension of the body. Featuring a "simulchronic flush in his pann (a ghinee a ghirk he ghets there!)," with this masturbatory pen/masculine organ he:

> scrabbled and scratched and scriobbled and skrevened nameless shamelessness about everybody ever he met . . . while all over up and down the four margins of this rancid Shem stuff the evilsmeller . . . used to stipple endlessly inartistic portraits of himself" (*FW* 182.12-19).

It is as if narcissistic Shem were primarily engaged in

materializing his own identity as a writer. The penman wants to be an "author" according to the words in the text. Shem's proclaimed ("ser Autore, q.e.d." [*FW* 182.21]) is immediately followed by an illustration of what authorship would entail. He would be transfigured into his opposite: an icon of masculine attractiveness:

> a heartbreakingly handsome young paolo with love lyrics for the goyls in his eyols . . . cutting a great dash in a brandnew two guinea dress suit and a burled hogsford . . . anna loavely long pair of inky Italian moostarshes glistering with boric vaseline and frangipani" (*FW* 182.22-28).

In other words, achieved authority confirms masculinity; and the pen is the instrument to achieve it. Thus the pen is Joyce's prosthesis of masculine authority.

By the time he was writing this passage for *Finnegans Wake*, Joyce had already proved himself as an author by the success of *Ulysses*. The necessary demonstration of authority ("ser Autore, q.e.d.") had been given. As an internationally famous author, Joyce's authorial stature was founded so unassailably that he could risk foisting the oddity of *Work in Progress* upon the world without loss of masculinity. The appearance of his photograph on the cover of *Time* magazine to mark the publication of *Finnegans Wake* shows that Joyce had become an icon of modernity -- even if relatively few people had read *Ulysses*. His authority rested not on direct reader response but on a reputation founded on authoritative critical opinion. Ironically aware of this, in his writing, Joyce could now begin to stage and parody its own ambivalent relation to masculinity and authority, just as "Circe" had travestied the conventions of the gender system of western culture. Joyce could even boast, as above and elsewhere in *Finnegans Wake*, that it was the impersonation of the feminine, the writing of

"Penelope," that earned him his international fame. The paradox thus evolved that as a great Modernist author his masculine status was so secure that such a confession could only enhance his reputation.

In retrospect, it seems to me that Joyce's reputation was created in a manner resembling the way masculinity is constructed in the genre of the Western. The Western, which became popular around the time when the term "masculinity" began to replace "manhood," is the masculine genre par excellence. However, since the hero's masculinity is not a natural given and must be defined in one way or another, the genre of the Western does not just depict masculinity; it stages the process of its construction.[32] The outsider, the tenderfoot, or the newcomer must prove his mettle in order to become a hero. The plot of the Western presents a process of transfiguration. That transfiguration is dependent upon an object that symbolizes masculine power. The indispensable instrument for the showdown is the gun. In wielding this masculine prop more accurately or faster than his competitors, the hero proves his true grit. Just so, young Joyce, a provincial outsider escaping from the contradictions of his culture, entered the international literary stage to demonstrate his talent and authority by means of his competitive activity with the pen. The gun belongs to the hero. It is the extension of his identity. Just so the pen is the extension of the author. It is the hero's superior command over that little piece of metal that proves his heroism--just as it is the author's superior style that ousts his competitors.

However, in itself the performance at the showdown

---

[32] See Peter Verstraten, *Screening Cowboys: Reading Masculinities in Westerns* (Amsterdam University Dissertation, 1999).

is not enough. The hero must be viewed as superior by others and be recognized as such. He only becomes a hero in the eyes of the participants or the gaze of the crowd. A showdown without audience or viewers does not provide social identity or reputation. The masculinity of the hero not resides not in the hero himself but in those who cherish it as his reputation. Just so, writerly authority is not just a matter of producing brilliant books. Reputation and authority are only constituted by public recognition; and, as Joyce understood extremely well, they are especially the products of wide mention in literary circles, newspapers, and other media. Contemporary literary hypes show that notoriety sometimes does not even require any literary talent at all.[33]

The construction of masculinity in the Western harbors a paradox. The Western constructs the plot in such a way that the hero eventually becomes what he already is in principle. Although initially taken for a coward or an innocent fool, there is always something in the future hero's look that suggests his true grit to the right beholder. It is his success in the gunfight that brings about the retrospective recognition of the hero's true identity. The Western needs this metaleptic feature to suggest that heroic masculinity, even though it needs public recognition to establish itself as

---

[33] In addition, in the Western, masculinity gains shape against a background of wide open space. The hero has the unique ability to mediate between civilization and wildness. Joyce's decision to go into exile is often placed in the context of Ovid's myth of the escape from the labyrinth. Perhaps we ought not to underestimate to what extent Joyce himself, not only the boys in "An Encounter," was influenced by the myth of transfiguring masculinity as foisted upon the world in the contemporary genre of the Western. The decision to go abroad may also have been founded on the mythic allure of a nomadic lifestyle.

such, is nevertheless an inborn and essential quality.[34] Like all essences, it will come out. A similar metaleptic paradox governs Joyce's achieved masculine authority. One of the most curious aspects of Joyce's life and career is the way in which his "genius" -- established and confirmed, as I argue, by the reception of *Ulysses* -- was understood to be already augured in his youth. "Genius" (different from just talent, and a quality generally reserved for the male of the species, as the masculine gender of this noun also suggests) functions in the plot of masculine authority as the hero's true grit functions in the Western. It is a quality that only comes into existence after public recognition; but thereupon it is projected back upon the protagonist's earlier history and proclaimed as the essence of his identity. Not only Joyce's doting family, but Joyce himself believed in his predestined fame. With regard to the genre of the Western, we may not find it too difficult to acknowledge the tautology of a structure that stages and constructs the "being" of masculinity as the metaleptic projection of qualities subsequent upon their public recognition. With regard to artistic authority we may experience more difficulty. The myth of genius may be even more hardy than that of masculinity. Our resistance to conceiving of genius as a social attribute dependent for its coming-into-being on good fortune and the willingness of the public/reader to recognize it, as well as on exceptional talent remains strong. We hesitate to give up the myth of a unique, innate quality which will realize itself against all odds. Such revisions of our cherished illusions force us to look in the mirror as Gabriel Conroy did, and to put down our vanity.

[34] See Verstraten, *Reading Masculinity*.

Historicizing Gender

I began this paper with a query about the provenance of the concept of gender and its historical relationship to the work of Joyce. After my discussion, the following claim will need no further argument, I hope. If Hélène Cixous took Joyce as a model of revolutionary writing on which to mold her own *écriture féminine* as a style of writing transgressing the limitation of essentialist identities, her tribute may be based on a miscognition. What she took as affirmative, transgressive, and revolutionary[35] may also be understood as Joyce's attempt to attain authority in the face of the contradictory inscription of gender in Ireland around the turn of the century. Instead of taking on a "feminine" style, Joyce may have been engaged in the act of demonstrating his writerly masculinity -- exploiting his ambiguous relationship to gender. The so-called flowing style of "Penelope" and *Finnegans Wake* may not testify to an achieved transgression of sexual identity, but, on the contrary, to the Irish male's sustained participation in the authority of the collectivity of the nation always figured as female. Its final affirmative and redoubled "yes" -- also object of Derrida's commentary -- may also betray the redoubling echo of subaltern self-consciousness. Remember that Bloom's defense against the encroachment of the spectre of death linked to the maternal imago also concludes with "Yes, yes": "Be near her ample bedwarmed flesh. Yes, yes." The repetition of affirmation first enters

[35] In *The Newly Born Woman*, trans. Betsy Wing (Minneapolis: University of Minnesota Press, 1986), p. 85, Hélène Cixous specifically refers to Molly's affirmative "yes."

the text in defense of threatened masculinity. In other words, Joyce's style ought not to be viewed from a universalizing perspective as if it were the product of a French or German turn-of-the-century author.

The point of my argument is to suggest that the construction of the subject-in-language as projected by French poststructuralism is due for contextualization. If the construction of gender as found in Joyce's text is culture-specific and relates to the insecurity about masculinity of the colonized male and to specifically Irish cultural conditions, we may need to think again about its role as model for an *écriture féminine* or poststructuralist textuality. Both theories have globalizing tendencies although they argue for anti-essentialism. Indeed, one of the surprising aspects of the French reception of Joyce is its repression of Joyce's cultural situation. This becomes even odder when we remember that both Cixous and Derrida came from Algeria!! [Even Althusser had an Algerian connection]. Should we explain their fascination with Joyce as their (unconscious?) recognition of a similar struggle in their placement over against a hegemonic culture and language? However this may be, it seems to me that the history of the concept of "gender" needs further study, especially in the light of postcolonial studies.

University of Amsterdam.

CONTRIBUTORS

Christine van Boheemen-Saaf, Chair of English Literature at the University of Amsterdam, has published widely on Joyce and many other prose writers, poststructuralist theory and gender theory. Her most recent book is *Joyce, Derrida, Lacan and the Trauma of History: Reading, Narrative, Poststructuralism* (Cambridge 1999).

Sheldon Brivic, Professor of English at Temple University in Philadelphia, Pennsylvania, has written four books on Joyce, the latest of which is *Joyce's Waking Women: An Introduction to "Finnegans Wake."* He is now completing a book called *The Racial Interface of the Modern American Novel* after which he expects to write another book on Joyce.

Richard Brown is Senior Lecturer in the School of English at the University of Leeds in England. His *James Joyce and Sexuality* was published by Cambridge University Press in 1985 and *James Joyce: A Postculturalist Perspective* by Macmillan in 1991. He is currently completing a study of Joyce's reltaionship to English literature.

Elizabeth Brunazzi holds a Ph.D. in Comparative Literature from Princeton University. Her articles in the field of Joyce Studies have appeared in *Lettres Modernes, The Languages of Joyce,* and the *James Joyce Quarterly*. She is coeditor of a collection of essays, *Culture and Daily Life in Occupied France,* which will appear as the fall 1999 issue of the interdisciplinary journal *Contemporary French Civilization.*

Michael Heumann received his Ph.D.in English from the University of California, Riverside. His dissertation, "Ghost in the Machine: Sound and Technology in Twentieth-Century Literature," includes two chapters analyzing the role of technology in *Finnegans Wake*. He is currently a Lecturer at the University of California, Riverside.

Colleen Lamos is Associate Professor of English at Rice University. She is the author of *Deviant Modernism: Sexual and Textual Errancy in T. S. Eliot, James Joyce, and Marcel Proust* (Cambridge 1998, and of numerous articles on modernism and queer theory. She is working on a book entitled "'I'm Not a Lesbian, I Just Loved Thelma': Lesbian Denials in Modern Literature."

Karen Lawrence is Professor of English and Comparative Literature and Dean of Humanities at the University of California, Irvine. A former president of the International James Joyce Foundation, she is the author of *The Odyssey of Style in "Ulysses"* (Princeton) and editor of the recently published *Transcultural Joyce* (Cambridge). Other books include *Penelope Voyages: Women and Travel in the British Literary Tradition* (Cornell) and *Decolonizing Tradition: New Views of Twentieth-Century "British" Literary Canons* (Illinois). She is writing a book on the relation between fiction and theory in the works of Christine Brooke-Rose.

Paul Lin is a graduate student in the Department of English and Comparative Literature at the University of California, Irvine. He is currently working on a project that, very broadly, reconsiders the process of subjectivation within an Irish colonial context.

Vicki Mahaffey is the author of *States of Desire: Wilde, Yeats, Joyce and the Irish Experiment* (Oxford, 1998) and *Reauthorizing Joyce* (Cambridge, 1988; Florida 1995). She is currently working on an introduction to Modernism and a book on feminist fairy tales. She is a professor of English at the University of Pennsylvania.

Margot Norris is Professor of English and Comparative Literature at the University of California at Irvine, where she teaches modern literature. She is the author of *The Decentered Universe of "Finnegans Wake"* (Johns Hopkins University Press, 1976), *Beasts of the Modern Imagination: Darwin, Nietzsche, Kafka, Ernst, and Lawrence* (Johns Hopkins University Press, 1985), and *Joyce's Web: The Social Unraveling of Modernism* (University of Texas Press, 1992). She has recently completed a book on mass warfare called **Writing War in the Twentieth Century** and continues to work on a book on Joyce's *Dubliners*.

Tracey Teets Schwarze has lectured at the University of Nevada, Las Vegas, and at Auburn University. Her articles on Joyce and the nineteenth century have appeared in *Twentieth Century Literature* and *Joyce Studies Annual*. She is currently finishing a book that is tentatively titled "Joyce and the Victorians: Changing the Subject."